1962

Word Wealth Junior

by Ward S. Miller

A classroom textbook for the junior high school years that introduces an approach to efficient study of vocabulary, word building, and spelling. Although organized basically to integrate all aspects of word study, its flexible construction permits teachers and students to concentrate on particular areas when most pertinent.

As you examine WORD WEALTH JUNIOR, please note especially:

★ **Five Kinds of Approach**

Vocabulary study (41 units in all); **Spelling** study (thirteen units); **Word Elements** study (eight units); **Word-Building** study (seven units); and **Foreign-Word** study (six units).

★ **Road Signs**

In each vocabulary unit, words are indicated according to use in the sentence: nouns (**n**); verbs (**v**); adjectives (**aj**); adverbs (**av**).

★ **Words in Different Languages**

Ten everyday words in different languages (pp. 230-231) showing similarities, and, in some cases, derivation of our own English words.

★ **Sources of English Words**

A chart (p. 233) showing the way words migrate from one language to another in the Indo-European family of languages.

★ **Final Unit Tests**

At the end of each Part (pp. 103, 213, and 346), a set of Final Unit Tests gives specific attention to the material in each unit studied.

★ **Teacher's Manual**

A valuable teaching instrument, the manual helps the teacher to: (1) adapt the use of WORD WEALTH JUNIOR to the individual differences among students, (2) plan for different approaches to word study in a class situation, (3) extend the material of the text through additional notes, queries, and exercises. A set of Division Tests for each Part of WORD WEALTH JUNIOR is found in the manual.

HOLT, RINEHART AND WINSTON, INC.

Word
Wealth
Junior

A VOCABULARY BOOK AND SPELLER

Word
Wealth
Junior

By **WARD S. MILLER**

HOLT, RINEHART AND WINSTON, INC.   NEW YORK

WARD S. MILLER was formerly teacher of English and adviser of publications, John Marshall High School, Rochester, New York. He is now Associate Professor of English, University of Redlands, Redlands, California. He is the author of WORD WEALTH.

Illustrated by Johannes Troyer

64C10

PREFACE

WORD WEALTH JUNIOR is far more than merely a vocabulary builder. The basic material for understanding word usage which it presents is augmented by other approaches to word study that give the book added attractiveness and effectiveness as a speller. The whole is a carefully integrated series of 75 units that are varied, challenging, and efficient.

1. Base-Word Clusters. Forty-one of the 75 units in the book are the vocabulary-building type. These units offer 12 or 15 base words, each with from two to five variant forms or synonyms, thus comprising a cluster of related words. In this way the base words may add as many as two or three thousand words to a student's vocabulary. These words are carefully selected from the crucial area between the words that most elementary school graduates know and those which relatively few recognize meaningfully.

The units are set up so that a student has several experiences with each base word. He sees it defined and studies two or three illustrative sentences. He then copies it, with correct spelling, in the *First Practice Set* and provides a definition. Next, in doing the *Quests* (mostly from the *Teacher's Manual*), he may write a sentence containing the word or he may look up its origin. In the *Second Practice Set*, he fits the right base word into each blank or he may turn to the final test, which provides a definition for each blank and asks the student to supply the word. A *Division Test* in the *Teacher's Manual* covers each Part in sections of two or three units each.

2. Word Elements. Eight of the units in this book present familiar *prefixes* and *roots* instead of base words. There are more than two hundred of these elements, arranged in pairs having similar meanings, one being from Latin, the other, Greek in most cases. Learning these elements gives a student the key to meaningful recognition of several thousand words he will meet in school, home, business, professions, technical areas, and otherwise.

The importance of knowing these two hundred word elements can hardly be overemphasized. Not only do they increase a student's recognition vocabulary by multiplication rather than by mere addition, but they also teach him how words are built, fostering fluency and flexibility in the use of familiar words, and improving his spelling skill.

3. Word Building. Seven of the units, mostly in Part Two, are devoted specifically to word building. These units introduce a student to variant forms of familiar words and thus increase his fluency, flexibility, and insight. They broaden his vocabulary, they teach suffixes informally, and they are at the same time important as spelling exercises, even though they are not so labeled.

4. Formal Spelling Units. Thirteen units, nine of them in Part One, are primarily and specifically spelling units. These units, in conjunction with the seven word-building units and the eight root-and-prefix units, comprise a total of 28 that together cover as much ground as does a separate spelling book. They do so subtly and scientifically by grouping words around principles or problems and by tying spelling to pronunciation effectively.

5. Foreign-Word Units. The six foreign-word units in Part Three offer a practical introduction to groups of French, German, Spanish, Italian, Scandinavian, and Oriental words which have considerable use in English. Thus they provide an elementary insight into the pronunciation and spelling patterns of the respective languages. The first unit in Part Three, with its chart showing how words have migrated from one language to another in the Indo-European family of languages, is a feature that was especially popular with teachers who used the first edition of WORD WEALTH JUNIOR.

Thus, with its five kinds of units intermingled for variety, this book is more than ever a unified whole that progresses logically toward better spelling, toward a more flexible command of everyday words, and toward a greatly enlarged recognition vocabulary. The units may be used by types if a teacher wishes to cover spelling, roots and prefixes, or general vocabulary intensively, but the book is designed to achieve all these purposes simultaneously.

Detailed instructions for the most effective use of each kind of unit and for making use of the ample provisions for individual differences may be found in the *Teacher's Manual*. The manual is well stocked with keys, problems, extra practice sets, and explanatory material.

WARD S. MILLER

ACKNOWLEDGMENTS

It is now twelve years since WORD WEALTH JUNIOR made its debut, one third of it devoted to new kinds of units designed to teach spelling in conjunction with vocabulary building. These special units in word-building and pronunciation had been tested by certain classes in the Rochester, New York, Public Schools and in schools in three other systems: in Ashtabula, Ohio, where the author formerly taught; in Corning, New York; and in Keego Harbor, Michigan. In addition, valuable suggestions were offered by Mrs. Clyde Roberts of McKinley High School, Washington, D. C., and Miss Ruth M. Stauffer, head of the Department of English, Divisions 1-9, in the Public Schools of the District of Columbia.

The writer wishes to thank all of these pioneer participants again. He wishes also to thank several teachers and supervisors in the public schools of Long Beach, California, who generously shared their experience with WORD WEALTH JUNIOR and made suggestions which have proved helpful in revising the book for greater usefulness: Miss Marilouise Kreidler, Supervisor of High School Education; Mrs. Nell O'Brien, Co-Supervisor; Mr. John K. Rice, Stanford Junior High School; and Mr. Robert F. Miles, at Hoover Junior High School. In addition, many valuable comments and suggestions were made by Miss Eleanor L. McGehan, of the Noah Webster School, Hartford, Connecticut; Mrs. Iris Nordberg, Chairman of the English Department, El Camino High School, Sacramento, California; and Dr. Bernard Weiss, Supervisor of Language Education, Detroit Public Schools.

The author wishes also to thank Mr. Richard Cox of Colton High School, Colton, California, who did much of the supplementary research involved in this revision. He furthermore wishes to thank those who did clerical and secretarial work on this revision, especially Mrs. Stanton Olson, and Miss Katherine T. Miller.

TABLE OF CONTENTS

PART TWO

UNIT

PART THREE

PART **I**

ROAD SIGNS

You will find one of four symbols beside each illustrative sentence in the regular units, thus:

v to mark a **verb** form of the base word or a verb form of a synonym

av to mark an **adverb** form of the base word or an adverb form of a synonym

n to mark a **noun** form of the base word or a noun form of a synonym

aj to mark an **adjective** form of the base word or an adjective form of a synonym

In the spelling units many of the most troublesome words are marked with a red star, thus: *

1

UNIT ONE

PRONOUNCING PAIRS

How would you pronounce *lan,* if there were such a word? Without thinking, you would probably speak it so as to rhyme with *can, ban, man,* and *tan.* It would sound like *lan* in *land.*

If you add an *e* to *lan,* you have the familiar word *lane.* Adding an *e* to *can, ban,* and *man* makes *cane, bane* (harm), and *mane* (long neck hair), which rhyme with *lane.* One could list many examples of the way the pronunciation (as well as the meaning) changes when *e* is added to a group of letters, such as those above.

Group I		Group II	
1. can	cane	1. pal	pale
2. Dan	Dane	2. pet	Pete
3. man	mane	3. bit	bite
4. pan	pane	4. sit	site
5. plan	plane	5. not	note
6. wan (*pale*)	wane	6. rot	rote (*repetition*)

3

How does the addition of a final *e* to a word or a syllable change the original vowel sound? State this change as a general spelling rule.

	Group III			Group IV	
1.	hast	haste	1.	bath	bathe (*th* as in *this*)
2.	past	paste	2.	breath	breathe
3.	pin	pine	3.	cloth(s)	clothe(s)
4.	prim (*stiff*)	prime	4.	lath	lathe
5.	con (*to study*)	cone	5.	loath	loathe
6.	human	humane (*kind*)	6.	sheath	sheathe
7.	mat	mate	7.	wreath	wreathe

Devise a rule that helps you spell the words in Group IV.

SENTENCES FOR PRACTICE

Write the following from dictation:

1. Please don't waste the paste.
2. He put his clothes on backward.
3. My pal looks pale this morning.
4. Uncle Ben is *loath* to make haste.
5. The cloth was wrapped in a bathing suit.
6. Do you learn rhymes by *rote*?
7. Does a pinprick make you whine?
8. A *lathe* is not used to make lath.
9. Motes (tiny particles) dance in the *wan* sunshine.
10. A *prim* lady carried a cute paper cutter in a *sheath*.
11. Low-hanging branches chafe the horse's *mane*.
12. The engine breathes like a human being.
13. The old lady *loathes* cats but is very *humane* to them.
14. The warrior refused to *sheathe* his sword.
15. She broke the seal on the envelope in haste.

Copy the italicized words in the sentences above and beside each write its meaning.

(The next special spelling unit is Unit No. 4, p. 13.)

UNIT TWO

"ONE-CYLINDER" WORDS

QUERIES

Answer each question with the most suitable word from the list at the right:

Words

First Six

1. cleave
2. glean
3. hoard
4. oust
5. quell
6. raze

1. Which one implies dampness?

2. Which suggests pain?

3. Which one does a miser do?

4. Which one suggests travel?

5. Which one will remove an old building?

6. Which one implies competition?

7. Which one sometimes prevents an auto accident?

Second Six

1. roam
2. seep
3. surge
4. swerve
5. vie
6. wince

"ONE-CYLINDER" WORDS—First Six

1. **CLEAVE** . . . . to cling, divide
   - v Cleave to the companions you trust.
   - n The meat man cuts up chickens with a cleaver.
   - n There was a cleavage (splitting apart) between the father and his sons.

     A **cleft** in the rock is a crevice or fissure.
     What animals have split or "cloven" hoofs? Why does ***cloven-hoofed*** mean *devilish?*

2. **GLEAN** . . . . . to gather or collect in small quantities, particularly grain
   - v Hannah gleaned her knowledge of planes from her brother's conversation.
   - n Ruth became a gleaner in the fields of Boaz after she returned with Naomi.

3. **HOARD** . . . . to save or accumulate more than necessary
   - v It is a crime to hoard food when neighbors are starving.
   - n Billy had a large hoard of empty rifle cartridges.

4. **OUST** . . . . to drive out, expel
   - v A Goonville dentist tried to oust the mayor.
   - v Society will ostracize (exclude, shut out) a person for bad manners.

5. **QUELL** . . . . to put down, overcome, subdue
   - v Police were able to quell the riot quickly.
   - v Sally tried hard to quell her fear of snakes.

6. **RAZE** . . . . . to destroy, tear down, level to the ground
   - v A tornado razed most of the houses on Myrtle Street.
   - v Wreckers will raze the old theater on Third Avenue next week.

"ONE-CYLINDER" WORDS—Second Six

1. **ROAM** . . . . to wander

   v When knighthood was in flower, minstrels liked to roam from castle to castle.

   n Tourists are roamers with money.

2. **SEEP** . . . . to soak through, ooze

   v Water will seep into the basement.

   n Seepage makes the cellar damp.

3. **SURGE** . . . . to push or rise

   v The waves surge up on the shore.

   n The upsurge in traffic deaths has been halted in several cities.

4. **SWERVE** . . . . . to change course or direction suddenly

   v A train cannot swerve to avoid an accident.

   aj Lincoln was a man of unswerving devotion to his country.

   v Watch the temperature drop when the wind veers from west to north.

   v The pilot did not deviate from his flight plan.

5. **VIE** . . . . to contend, strive in rivalry

   v Debaters vie with each other to win an argument.

   v The two basketball centers were vying with each other for points.

6. **WINCE** . . . . . to shrink, draw away (as from a blow)

   v Watch Jerry wince when I pretend to hit him.

   v Joan of Arc did not flinch from the fire.

   av She faced death unflinchingly.

   Wince is used of mild or merely threatened pain. ***Flinch*** applies to pain that is more certain and more severe.

FIRST PRACTICE SET

Write the meaning of the italicized word in each sentence:

1. He told the soldiers to *quell* the revolt and *raze* the temple.
2. The rains which *seep* into the ground in early spring cause rivers to *surge* over their banks.
3. Do you *wince* when a flash of lightning seems very close?
4. Babies naturally *cleave* to their parents, but when they get older they will begin to *roam.*
5. No one can *oust* the Indians from their reservation.
6. The two boys *vie* with each other over the candy they *hoard.*
7. The tornado began to *swerve* toward the village, where it destroyed the theater so completely that police could *glean* only a few details about who had been inside.

SECOND PRACTICE SET

What word fits best into each blank?

1. The British tried to __?__ the American colonists.
2. A nervous person will __?__ at a loud noise.
3. Modern spies __?__ much of their knowledge in small bits.
4. Puppies __?__ with each other playfully.
5. Oil will __?__ through the carton.
6. Why didn't the car __?__ before it hit the truck?
7. Fear made his tongue __?__ to the roof of his mouth.
8. __?__ the dog from the kitchen.
9. It was necessary to __?__ his home to build the highway.
10. A __?__ of reserve energy made him able to reach the goal.
11. During the war it was illegal to __?__ gasoline.
12. Wild animals __?__ about freely in the forests and the jungle.

A STORM

Write one or two paragraphs about a thunderstorm, flood, tornado, or hurricane you have seen or read about. Use as many of the words in this unit as you can.

UNIT THREE

HOT AND HATEFUL

Read aloud the words in the column at the right two or three times, then answer the questions about them. (See Part One, Unit 1, Group IV, for pronunciation of those which end in *th* or *the*.)

Words

First Six

1. Which word gives up territory?

  1. cede

  2. chafe

2. Which two most definitely involve heat?

  3. cringe

  4. loathe

3. Which one expresses hatred or dislike?

  5. probe

  6. secrete

4. Which one hides something?

Second Six

  1. seethe

5. Which word searches out something?

  2. sheathe

  3. singe

6. Which one expresses intense pain?

  4. swathe

  5. wane

  6. writhe

9

HOT AND HATEFUL—First Six

1. **CEDE** (pronounced like SEED) . . . . . to yield, grant

   v In 1867 Russia ceded Alaska to the United States.
   v Joe concedes (admits) his lack of musical talent.

2. **CHAFE** (rhymes with SAFE) . to rub, wear away, fret, produce heat

   v A stiff collar chafes one's neck.
   v Why chafe over handicaps you can't remove?
   n Chaff is light stuff like wheat shucks.

3. **CRINGE** (rhymes with FRINGE) . . . to shrink, crouch, cower

   v Jimmie cringes when he sees the nurse's needle.
   aj The man's cringing attitude at the scene of the murder showed a sense of guilt.

4. **LOATHE** . . . . to hate, dislike, detest

   v Some children loathe spinach.
   n Sandra cannot hide her loathing for snakes.
   aj Leprosy is a loathsome disease.
   aj Frank was loath (reluctant) to give up his seat to the elderly man.

5. **PROBE** . . . . to pierce, search out

   v The surgeon had to probe the wound for fragments of metal.
   n Judge Johnson placed the boy on probation (release subject to good behavior) for two years.

   Cf. **probably,** which means true, subject to searching out. **Probity** is honesty, integrity, uprightness.

6. **SECRETE** . . . . to hide

   v Dick tried to secrete himself in a closet.
   aj Grace is very ·secretive (inclined to have secrets) about what is in her diary.

HOT AND HATEFUL—Second Six

1. **SEETHE** . . . . . . to boil, erupt, suffer great agitation

   v The grease in the frying pan began to seethe.
   aj The basement soon became a seething mass of flames.
   aj Seething with anger, the man rushed from the room.

2. **SHEATHE** . . . . . put in a case or protective covering

   v "Sheathe your swords!" the King commanded.
   v After the sleet storm every twig was sheathed in ice.
   n The hunting knife is kept in its sheath (case).

3. **SINGE (rhymes with CRINGE)** . . . to scorch, burn slightly

   v The flames will singe your hair if you get too close to the stove.
   v Mother used to singe the chicken over a gas flame to burn off the hairs.

   Note the difference in spelling between **singeing** a roast and **singing** a solo. The *e* after the *g* in **singeing** keeps it soft, giving it a *j* sound.

4. **SWATHE** . . . . to wrap or envelop

   v The heiress likes to swathe herself in furs.
   v The burned man's arm was swathed in bandages.
   n The tornado cut a swath (path) only a few hundred yards wide through the town.

5. **WANE** . . . . to decrease, die down

   v "The long day wanes; the slow moon climbs."
   v Her fondness for the flowers will wane when she finds that they cause hay fever.

6. **WRITHE** . . . . . . to twist or turn, especially in pain

   v The injured snake began to writhe in agony.
   aj Writhing with hate, the men left the building.

FIRST PRACTICE SET

Copy the italicized words and beside each one write its meaning in the sentence.

1. The people would *loathe* anyone who would *cringe* before the enemy.
2. Mexicans would *chafe* at the suggestion that they *cede* any more territory.
3. The aluminum foil is there to *sheathe* the film from light, not to *secrete* it.
4. Did the fireman *singe* his hands trying to quell the *seething* flames?
5. Hold the man so he cannot *writhe* while we *swathe* his chest in bandages.
6. The *probe* of the group's activities made its influence *wane* noticeably.

SECOND PRACTICE SET

Place in each blank the word that best fits. Use each word only once.

1. Do you __?__ cockroaches? Do they make you __?__?
2. Do you ever __?__ with a toothache? Or __?__ with impatience to leave on a trip?
3. The Louisiana Purchase was a vast tract which France agreed to __?__ to the United States.
4. A squirrel likes to __?__ his hoard of nuts.
5. Each nut has a heavy shell to __?__ it.
6. An active volcano will __?__ anyone who gets too close.
7. Adults __?__ too much over little annoyances.
8. A detective's job is to __?__ murder mysteries.
9. Hugh's interest in bugs began to __?__.
10. She likes to __?__ her salads in lettuce leaves.

UNIT FOUR

HOPING AND HOPPING

Are you in the habit of *shining* your shoes or "shinning" them? You would be amused by anybody who said "shinning" for "shining." Yet some students make this kind of mistake in their writing *without realizing that the way you pronounce* shining *tells you how to spell it.*

What is the difference between *shining* and *shinning?* *Shining* is the *-ing* form of *shine,* which has a LONG *i,* pronounced "eye," followed by a single consonant and a final *e.* "Shinning" is the form of *shin* (to climb, say, a rope), which has a short *i* (see *pine-pin, bite-bit, wane-wan,* and other such pairs in Part One, Unit 1). The long *"i"* of shine leads you to expect that it will be followed by a single *n* in the *-ing* form. But *shin,* with its short *i* will have *nn* in the *-ing* form.

This principle works out with amazing regularity in *-ing* and other forms. Thus the *-ing* form of *chin* is *chinning.* The *-ing* form of *pin* is *pinning,* but the *-ing* form of *pine* is *pining.* Simple, isn't it? *The way you pronounce a word tells you how to spell its -ing and other forms.*

Here are some familiar pairs which show the contrast clearly because each member of the pair differs from the other

13

only in that one has a long vowel with an *e* at the end, and the other a short vowel and no *e* at the end.

You *pine*, you are *pining* for a week in camp.
You *pin*, you are *pinning* a map on the wall.

You *hope*, you are *hoping* for good weather at camp.
You *hop*, you are *hopping* across the room.

You *plane*, you are *planing* a knotty pine board.
You *plan*, you are *planning* an all-day hike.

Birds *mate*, they are *mating* in the spring of each year.
There's a *mat*, there is *matting* upon the porch floor.

FIRST PRACTICE SET

Complete the following word pairs.

1.	whine	__?__ing	11.	*begin	__?__
2.	sin	__?__ing	12.	grip	__?__
3.	tube	__?__	13.	gripe	__?__
4.	__?__	dining	14.	write	__?__
5.	win	__?__	15.	__?__	uniting
6.	can	__?__	16.	slap	__?__
7.	__?__	caning	17.	bite	__?__
8.	__?__	gaping	18.	spare	__?__
9.	tape	__?__	19.	rot	__?__
10.	__?__	tapping	20.	__?__	cutting

PAST TENSE FORMS

The rule of the long-vowel-single-consonant and short-vowel-double-consonant applies to past tense forms also, thus:

You pine, you are pining, you *pined* for camp life.
You pin, you are pinning, you *pinned* a map on the wall.

You hope, you are hoping, you *hoped* for good weather.
You hop, you are hopping, you *hopped* across the room.

You file, you are filing, you *filed* your fingernails.
You fill, you are filling, you *filled* your gas tank.

SECOND PRACTICE SET

On a separate sheet of paper write the word which goes in each blank, spelling it correctly:

1. You plan, you are __?__, you __?__ a long hike.
2. You __?__, you are planing, you __?__ a pine board.
3. You sin, you are __?__, you __?__ yesterday.
4. You __?__, you are dining, you __?__ today.
5. You __?__, you are * __?__, you began to eat spinach.
6. You write, you are __?__, you have * __?__ a letter.
7. You __?__, you are tapping, you __?__ on the door.
8. Birds mate, they are __?__, they __?__ last spring.
9. You rip, you are __?__, you __?__ your sleeve.
10. You __?__, you are __?__, you tipped the waiter.

Write the *-ing* form and the past or *-ed* form of the following words: *bite, combine, * complete, commit, dim, line, occur, omit, submit, worship.*[1]

THE LONG AND SHORT OF IT

You may have noticed that in words which end in *e* with *one* consonant in front of the *e*, the vowel in front of the consonant is usually long. There are thousands of examples, some being short words, some very long. Here are a few:

late[2]	slide	complete	arrive	accuse
slate	divide	delete	compose	abuse
slope	inside	(eliminate)	compute	amuse
grope	reside	devote	(calculate)	confuse
spoke	(live)	denote	expose	peruse
yoke	contrive	remote	refute	(read)
(collar)	beside	explode	repose (rest)	refuse

---

[1] *Worship, kidnap* and *travel* no longer require the double consonant.

[2] Note that the long-short principle automatically gives you the spelling of *later* (after the time mentioned) and * *latter* (opposite of *former*).

When there is no *e* at the end of a word the vowel in front of the final consonant is usually short. This fact is most clearly shown if a word is one from which the *e* has been dropped.

slat	slid	sublet	plod	rut
slop	rid	cannot	shot	glut ·

The spelling principle illustrated here and by the pairs of words in the first part of the unit may be summarized thus:

(1) Most words that end with a single consonant have a short vowel in front of the consonant.

(2) This consonant is nearly always doubled when you add a syllable such as *-er, -ing, -ed, -y,* or *-ie.*

sit	sitter	fit	fitter	——	flutter
gut	gutter	mad	madder	rat	ratty
hit	hitter	sad	sadder	——	ditty
lit	litter	glad	gladder	slip	slippery
but	butter	hat	hatter	wit	witty
rob	robber	fat	fatter	pet	petty
slip	slipper	——	sputter	Dot	Dottie

SENTENCES FOR PRACTICE

Write the following sentences from dictation.

1. The well-taped football players hoped they were winning.
2. There was a gaping hole in the dining room near the place where the map was pinned to the wall.
3. He has written a gripping story of his life from the beginning.
4. The winning paper was about a wagon that tipped over.
5. In combining the figures, he omitted the totals.
6. A baby sitter committed the bitter crime.
7. In writing the report, we omitted filling in his name.
8. Firemen, arriving later, found that the house had been gutted.
9. The titter that arose when Sam slipped made him angry.
10. The robber dropped the butter in the dining room.

(The next special spelling unit is Unit No. 7, p. 25.)

UNIT FIVE

BIG LITTLE WORDS

OFTEN

Which of the words at the right:

The Words
First Six
1. breach
2. crest
3. drone
4. gait
5. horde
6. lapse

1. Needs filling? __?__ and __?__

2. Comes in large numbers? __?__

3. Has to do with death? __?__

4. Requires a search? __?__

5. Suggests laziness? __?__

6. Plays the role of a victim? __?__

Second Six
1. prey
2. quest
3. niche
4. shroud
5. stud
6. truss

BIG LITTLE WORDS—Study Guide

First Six

1. BREACH . . . .   a break, opening, violation

    n The next attack made a breach in the city's defenses.
    n Loud talking is a breach of etiquette.

2. CREST . . . . . .   top, tuft or headpiece, coat-of-arms

    n The scouts climbed to the crest of the hill.
    n Sue likes to ride the crests of ocean waves at Laguna Beach.
    n The knight wore a plumed crest. His shield had the family crest emblazoned on it.

3. DRONE . . . .   male bee; lazy person, dull, steady sound

    n The worker bees kill all the drones.
    n A good squad has no place for drones.
    n The drone of motors could be heard all day.
    v The speaker droned on in a hollow, even voice for more than an hour.

    Drone is also a term for a pilotless plane, controlled from the ground.

4. GAIT . . . .   pace, manner of stepping

    n The horse's gait was lively and frolicsome.
    n The farmer's gait was heavy and even.

    Gaiters are a kind of footwear. See your dictionary.

5. HORDE . . . .   a crowd, mob, swarm

    n A horde of Gandhi's followers rushed into the streets.
    n Hordes of buffaloes once roamed the plains.

    Horde is a word of Turkish-Oriental origin which once meant a camp and came from a word meaning **to pitch** (camp). It has no connection with *hoard* (page 6), which is of Old English origin.

6. **LAPSE** . . . . a shortcoming, slip, oversight

    n A store clerk's lapse of memory caused the error.

    aj Do not let your insurance policy lapse (cease to be in effect because the premium has not been paid).

Second Six

1. **PREY** . . . . victim

    n Flies are often spiders' prey.

    v "Con" men prey upon persons who are too trusting.

2. **QUEST** . . . . a search or a seeking

    n Science offers a never-ending quest for new knowledge.

    n Theodore Roosevelt succeeded in his quest for health.

3. **NICHE** (rhymes with HITCH) . . . . a hollowed-out place
                                     (for a bust or statue)

    n That halfback deserves a niche in football's hall of fame.

    n The teacher made a niche for himself in the town's esteem.

4. **SHROUD** . . . a covering for a dead person, usually black;
                               winding sheet; to veil, or cover

    n The explorer's body was wrapped in a shroud.

    v The man's past life is shrouded in mystery.

5. **STUD** . . . . a small knob or projection

    n A diamond stud glittered on the actor's shirt.

    v Thousands of stars stud the sky on a clear night.

    Stud came from an Old English word meaning pillar or post; the upright supports of a house are known as studs.

6. **TRUSS** . . . . to support or brace

    n The crippled boy had to wear a shoulder truss.

    v The mowing machine was trussed up with wires.

    A **truss** is the framework which supports a roof or a bridge.

BRIEF EXCURSIONS

1. List words rhyming with *breach, crest, drone, gait, stud, truss.*
2. Change one letter of *prey* and get a word meaning *to talk to God.* Change another letter instead and get a word denoting *a pale, dull color.*
3. Change the second letter of *gait* and get *determination.* Change the first letter and get two familiar words. Change the first letter of *drone* and get *lying face downward.*
4. Change the first letter of *breach* and get *sermonize.* Change the fourth and fifth letters in *shroud* and get *sharp, clever.*

FIRST PRACTICE SET

Copy the italicized words and beside each write its meaning in the sentence.

1. A *horde* of invaders entered through a *breach* in the walls.
2. The *crest* of the Green Knight appeared above the saint's *niche.*
3. The umpire's *lapse* of memory led to a *quest* for his scalp.
4. Rivets *stud* the *truss* that supports the bridge.
5. Beneath the *shroud* lay the killer's fallen *prey.*
6. The man's *gait* marked him as a human *drone.*

SECOND PRACTICE SET

What word from the unit fits best in each blank?

1. Student leaders launched a __?__ to find out which __?__es of etiquette are most common.
2. The __?__ on his dress shirts carried the family __?__.
3. Because of his shambling __?__, the enemy spy quickly became the __?__ of our forces.
4. After a __?__ of thirty days, the statue was placed in its __?__ again.   •
5. __?__s of ghosts arrived, some still wearing their __?__s!
6. __?__s hummed about the hive beneath the __?__ which supported the beam.

UNIT SIX

DESCRIPTIVE WORDS

WHICH ONE?

From the words in the list at the right, choose
the one which best describes:

Roster

First Six

1. A bird that no longer exists. —?—

   1. bleak

2. A package undamaged in a wreck. —?—

   2. dormant
   3. extinct

3. Trees that are few and widely separated.
   —?—

   4. ghastly
   5. intact
   6. opaque

4. A bear wintering in a log. —?—

   Second Six

   1. prone

5. Wind blowing over frozen wastes. —?—

   2. sallow
   3. sparse

6. A brick wall blocking one's view. —?—

   4. terse
   5. vain
   6. void

21

DESCRIPTIVE WORDS—First Group

1. **BLEAK** . . . . barren, desolate, harsh

    aj Storms beat wildly on the bleak New England shores.

    aj The plane crashed above timberline on one of the bleakest slopes in the Rocky Mountains.

    n The bleakness of the barracks chilled him.

2. **DORMANT** . . . . sleeping or inactive

    aj Bears often lie dormant in logs during the winter.

    aj The plans for the new city hall remained dormant.
    Cf. **dormitory,** a hall which is literally a *sleeping* place.

    aj My teacher spent a quiescent summer (inactive in sense of resting) in a mountain cabin.

3. **EXTINCT** . . . . lifeless, dead, no longer existing

    aj Mt. Etna is an almost extinct volcano.

    aj The dodo, a bird which could not fly, is extinct.

    v Firemen exist to extinguish (put out of existence) unwanted fires.

    n Extinction (destruction) of pests such as the corn borer has proved difficult.

4. **GHASTLY** . . . . horrible, ghostlike, deathly

    aj Shooting his uncle instead of the burglar was a ghastly mistake.

    n The ghastliness of her appearance shocked everyone who saw her.

    aj The boy's parents looked aghast (horrified) at the wreckage of their car.

5. **INTACT** . . . . unharmed, undamaged

    av The field glasses came through the wreck intact.

    av The boy's moral character came through the war intact.

    Intact literally means *not touched.* Cf. *tact, tactual, contact.*

6. **OPAQUE** . . . . . not letting light through, dull, obscure

     aj Brick walls are opaque, but glass walls and frosted windows are usually translucent (letting light through).

     n It is the opaqueness of bones which makes it possible for x-rays to "see" them.

DESCRIPTIVE WORDS—Second Group

1. **PRONE** . . . . . inclined, stretched out flat (face down)

     aj Human beings are prone to make mistakes.

     aj The FBI agent was shooting from a prone position.

     n The man's proneness (inclination, tendency) to take bribes got him into prison.

2. **SALLOW** . . . . yellowish, sickly looking

     aj Helen looks sallow when she first gets up in the morning.

     n The man's sallowness was the result of several years in a prison camp.

3. **SPARSE** . . . . thinly distributed, scattered

     aj Greenland has a sparse population.

     av The interior of Australia is sparsely settled.

     n The sparseness (sparsity) of the crop made prices high.

4. **TERSE** . . . . brief, crisp, pithy

     aj A terse command brought the scouts to attention.

     av Newspaper headlines give the day's news tersely.

     n The ancient Spartans made terseness a virtue.

5. **VAIN** . . . . useless, empty, conceited

     aj Hugh made a vain effort to start the stalled car.

     aj Slight success makes a little man vain.

     n A year in the army reduced Hugh's vanity considerably.

6. VOID . . empty (in sense of space), of no value (any longer)

    aj A check becomes void if the amount is changed.

    v Failure to make the payments on time will void (make useless) the agreement.

    aj Her face was devoid (empty) of fear as she faced the judge.

FIRST PRACTICE SET

Copy the italicized words and beside each write its meaning in the sentence.

1. The germs remain *dormant* for years without becoming *extinct.*
2. "The ship is *intact,*" was the captain's *terse* comment after the storm subsided.
3. Her face was *sallow* and *devoid* of color.
4. Uncle Ned's hair is *sparse,* and his efforts to restore it are *vain.*
5. When someone dies, Mother is *prone* to think a *ghastly* crime has been committed.
6. The pirate's face was *bleak* and his thinking *opaque.*

SECOND PRACTICE SET

Which word in this unit applies to each of the following?

1. Northern Siberia? __?__
2. The language of a telegram? __?__
3. Space between stars? __?__
4. Iris bulbs during the winter? __?__
5. A sickly boy? __?__
6. A volcano that will never erupt again? __?__
7. A board over one's eyes? __?__
8. Population in Nevada? __?__
9. A girl on her stomach? __?__
10. Wanting to stay alive a thousand years? __?__
11. Death in the electric chair? __?__
12. A piano unharmed in a tornado? __?__

UNIT SEVEN

SPELL-A-LUDE

PLURALS IN -ES

Most nouns in English form the plural simply by adding an -*s*. Why do some require -*es*? Can you think of a reason? Study the following examples of plurals and try to discover how the plurals are alike:

Usual		Different	
chart	charts	class	classes
color	colors	dress	dresses
mother	mothers	glass	glasses
shadow	shadows	press	presses
tablet	tablets	moss	mosses
troop	troops	stress	stresses

The words in the second group are alike in that they end in *ss*. What happens if you add a third *s*? You get an ending that looks queer and one you just can't pronounce—not without a slight pause and a kind of gulp which is a vowel sound and

25

makes the third *s* an extra syllable. An *e* is the natural way to represent the gulp, and it is thus natural to use *-es* for the plural of nouns which already end in *-ss*. Again the way you pronounce a word helps you to spell it, just as it did in Units 1 and 4.

   Problem: Write the plural of *grass, tress, caress, distress, compress.* What would be the plural of *spless* if there were such a word?
   Several dozen verb forms also end in *-ss*, and the third person singular adds *-es* instead of the normal *s*. For example:

I confess. He confesses.	We impress. He impresses.
You express. She expresses.	They caress. She caresses.

Group II

   There is another group of words that form the plural in *-es* instead of the usual *s*. Can you guess why this time? Here are a few examples:

Usual		Different	
bucket	buckets	birch	birches
citizen	citizens	brush	brushes
color	colors	bush	bushes
bubble	bubbles	church	churches
desk	desks	coach	coaches
dream	dreams	dish	dishes
needle	needles	relish	relishes
reader	readers	search	searches
task	tasks	wish	wishes

You must have noticed that each word in the "Different" column ends in a double consonant. So do *task* and *desk* in the first column, however. What is the difference between *desk-desks* and *dish-dishes*. Is it the way you *pronounce* them?

Note that you can say "desks" readily enough, but try to say "dishs." No doubt you found it almost impossible to say it without including the vowel sound that has become -*es* on such words as these.

Problem: Write the plural of *perch, gulch, mulch, ridge, bridge, dredge.* What would be the plural of *gidge,* if there were such a word? of *credge? firch? gurch? pletch?* Can you give a reason?

Group III

The plurals of nouns which end in *o* are not so simple as those which have a double consonant at the end. A majority add -*es,* but quite a few add only -*s* in the usual way. Here are examples:

Add -*s*		Add -*es*	
altos	solos	cargoes	mottoes
banjos	sopranos	dominoes	Negroes
pianos	studios	echoes	potatoes
radios	twos	embargoes	tomatoes
rodeos	coos	heroes	vetoes
silos	zoos	mosquitoes	volcanoes

How can one remember which are which? Note that the words using -*os* are mostly musical terms. Two of the words are numbers spelled out, and three have a *double* vowel at the end (in the singular). *Thus, if the word is a musical term, a number word, or a word ending in a double vowel, it takes only an -s to form the plural.* Otherwise, -*es* must be added to form the plural.

When in doubt, a wise person will do the same thing professional writers often have to do: LOOK IT UP. In doing this you may discover that "volcanos" is permitted but not preferred and that "banjoes" is no longer wrong. "Zeroes" will get by. If you follow the rule stated above, however, you will rarely be wrong.

   Problem: Write the plural of *avocado, buffalo, cameo, desperado, domino, dynamo, Romeo, stiletto, torpedo.* From what language do the musical *-os* plurals come, for the most part? Do any of the other *-os* words come from the same language?

Group IV

   There is a fourth kind of plural ending in *-es.* Words like *baby,* which end in *y* with a consonant in front of the *y,* change the *y* to *i* and add *-es* thus:

Different

baby	babies	company	companies
colony	colonies	enemy	enemies
bunny	bunnies	library	libraries
country	countries	memory	memories

You have no doubt known this rule for a long time—and thanked the language makers of all the past ages that the rule is so simple.

   If there is a vowel before the *y,* you simply add *s.*

deploy	deploys	alley	alleys
boy	boys	alloy	alloys
day	days	essay	essays
array	arrays	guy	guys
gray	grays	turkey	turkeys
monkey	monkeys	valley	valleys

   Problem: Write the plural of *apology, army, battery, bay, colony, copy, duty, family, fancy, gallery, galley, grocery, inquiry, pony, quality, quantity, society, supply, testimony, theory, treaty, turnkey, way.*

   (The next special spelling unit is Unit No. 10, p. 37.)

UNIT EIGHT

STORY PERSONS

WHO'S WHO

1. Which one is a small and imaginary person?

2. Which one is poor because of bad luck or bad habits?

3. Which embraces poverty as a religious duty?

4. Which one travels, often for religious reasons?

5. Which one is a seafaring robber?

6. Which combines hiding and traveling?

Directory

First Six

1. buccaneer
2. cavalier
3. friar
4. ghoul
5. gnome
6. huckster

Second Six

1. pauper
2. phantom
3. pilgrim
4. pixie
5. stowaway
6. vagabond

STORY PERSONS—Directory, First Six

1. BUCCANEER (buk·ə·nïr') . . . . a pirate, freebooter

   n Captain Kidd was a bold buccaneer.
   n Buccaneering was a dangerous life.

2. CAVALIER (kav·ə·lïr') . . a knight, gallant gentleman or soldier

   n The cavalier who saved the king was his cousin.
   n During the English civil wars (1640–1645) the Cavaliers fought the Roundheads under Oliver Cromwell.
   aj The actor's cavalier (gay, careless) behavior made him popular at parties.

   Cavalier behavior may also be haughty or disdainful.

3. FRIAR . . . . member of male religious order

   n A friar found the children in the forest.

   Note: *Friars* went about preaching; *monks* lived in retirement in monasteries, praying, studying, working with their hands.

   n Monks lived simple lives of prayer, labor, and meditation.

4. GHOUL . . . . . . an evil creature; one who robs graves

   n Ghouls had been at work in the cemetery.
   aj There was a ghoulish leer on the man's face.

5. GNOME . . . . a dwarf

   n Gnomes were said to live underground and protect mines or treasures.
   aj A gnomelike (dwarfish) old man lived in a cabin on the mountain.

6. HUCKSTER . . . . a peddler or hawker

   n There was a huckster at the fair selling turtles.
   n The advertisers on radio and television are a modern kind of huckster.

STORY PERSONS—Second Group

1. **PAUPER** (pô′pər) . . . . a beggar, very poor person

   n Laziness and disease made the architect a pauper.
   v Wars pauperize thousands who live in the path of the armies.

   Mendicant is another term for a person who is a beggar.

2. **PHANTOM** . . . . a ghost, specter, false idea

   n A phantom could be seen each evening in the moonlight.
   aj Phantom figures appeared on the stage, laughing wildly.

3. **PILGRIM** . . . . a traveler or wayfarer

   n The young squire was a pilgrim on his way to visit the shrine at Canterbury.
   n The Boy Scout canoe trip is a kind of pilgrimage.

4. **PIXIE** . . . . a fairy or elf

   Pixies appeared on the lawn in the late afternoon.
   The pixie-faced girl is my cousin.

5. **STOWAWAY** . . . . a hidden or illegal passenger

   n The stowaway on our ship was arrested when we docked.
   n Secret documents get the safest possible stowage (storage).

   Stow comes from the Old English word *stow,* place.
   Stowaway is used chiefly of persons who steal rides in ships and airplanes.

6. **VAGABOND** . . . . a wanderer, vagrant

   n Autumn "calls and calls each vagabond by name." (Bliss Carman, *A Vagabond Song*)
   aj A vagabond (traveling-from-place-to-place) worker was killed by lightning.

   A *waif* is a homeless person or animal.
   A *hobo* is a tramp, a wanderer, and often a beggar.

QUESTIONS FOR STUDY

1. Why were the Pilgrim Fathers so named? Who were the pilgrims in "Pilgrims' Chorus" from *Tannhäuser?* Who was the pilgrim in *Pilgrim's Progress* by John Bunyan?
2. What is the relation between *migrant* and *immigrant? migrant* and *emigrant? migrant* and *migrate?*
3. Find more about friars and monks. What does *cloister* mean?
4. What do paupers, mendicants, and waifs have in common?
5. You often read in the newspaper, "He was arrested on a vagrancy charge." What is a vagrancy charge?

FIRST PRACTICE SET

What is the meaning of each italicized word?

1. The Magi were *pilgrims* seeking the Christ child.
2. The *huckster* had come to America as a *stowaway.*
3. While traveling disguised as a *vagabond,* the king met a *friar.*
4. The *buccaneer* gave seven gold pieces to a *pauper.*
5. A *pixie* does not like to be confused with a *gnome.*
6. The *phantom* who terrorized the city was called a *ghoul.*
7. The wounded *cavalier* hid in the attic of an inn.

SECOND PRACTICE SET

Which of the personalities in this unit would you find:

1. Riding on a spirited horse? ___?___
2. Commanding a ship? ___?___
3. Hidden in a plane? ___?___
4. Riding in a box car? ___?___
5. Traveling to a shrine? ___?___
6. Dancing in the woods? ___?___
7. Selling gadgets at a fair? ___?___
8. Appearing in a graveyard at midnight? ___?___
9. Preaching on the street? ___?___
10. Haunting a deserted castle? ___?___
11. Peeping out of a rabbit hole? ___?___
12. Begging in the street? ___?___

UNIT NINE

ACTIVE WORDS

DO IT

Which word would you use to tell about each of the following?

The Actors

First Six

1. bristle
2. cherish
3. contend
4. convulse
5. dedicate
6. foster

Second Six

1. recline
2. relish
3. subside
4. vary
5. venture
6. warrant

1. A dog angry or suspicious? It would —?—.

2. A new church ready for use? First you —?— it.

3. A person who is always the same? His habits do not —?—.

4. A violent storm? After a while it began to —?—.

5. A cheap trinket you lost in the woods? Its value did not —?— the effort to find it again.

33

ACTIVE WORDS—First Six

1. **BRISTLE** . . . . . . to stiffen (in anger), stick out bristles

    v Watch Dad bristle when Junior asks if he can use the car tonight.

    v The fort bristled with guns.

    Bristle comes from the Old English word **byrst,** meaning a short, coarse hair of a pig. Do you see the connection? Have you seen a dog's hair stand up?

2. **CHERISH** . . . . to treat with fondness

    v Chuck will cherish his new bicycle more than anything else he owns.

    v He likes to fondle (pet) his cocker spaniel.

3. **CONTEND** . . . . . . to strive, struggle, fight, argue

    v Sailing ships must contend with the wind and the waves.

    v The defending lawyer contends that the man was fifty miles away when the crime occurred.

    n There is ceaseless contention and rivalry between the two boys.

4. **CONVULSE** . . . . to shake, stir, upheave

    v Earthquakes convulse California at times.

    v The comedian can convulse the studio audience with laughter.

    n The victim of tetanus died in convulsions.

5. **DEDICATE** . . . . to devote to lofty ends

    v "But in a larger sense we cannot dedicate, we cannot consecrate, we cannot hallow this ground." (Lincoln, The *Gettysburg Address*)

    v Florence Nightingale dedicated her life to the relief of suffering.

    n The dedication of the new library took place in April.

6. FOSTER . . . . to encourage, nurture, sustain

    v This school fosters good sportsmanship.

    aj The boy's foster parents were quite wealthy.

        Foster parents are so called because they **support** and **nurture** a child as if they were his real parents.

ACTIVE WORDS—Second Six

1. RECLINE . . . . to lean back, lie down

    v It's fun to recline in the sun on the French Riviera.

    n Reclining at banquets was a Roman custom.

2. RELISH . . . . to enjoy (the taste or flavor of)

    v Teachers relish excuses the way cats relish baths.

    n The tray of relishes (tidbits for flavor) contained celery, olives, and carrot sticks.

    n Mary plays Monopoly with zest (hearty enjoyment).

    n Gordon, our bulldog, eats fish with great gusto (zest or relish).

3. SUBSIDE . . . . to cease, die down

    v It took an hour for the applause to subside.

    v The weather was cool after the winds had subsided.

    n Subsidence (downward settling) of the earth made Long Beach, Calif., famous as a "sinking city."

4. VARY . . . . to change, alter, differ

    v The value of a dollar will vary from year to year, but it usually decreases.

    v The temperature will vary as much as thirty degrees a day in some parts of the country.

    aj "Variable high cloudiness today," the weatherman said.

    n Mr. Cowbell and his wife were at variance about how to punish Martin.

5. **VENTURE** . . . to go (where risky), to dare to go, undertake

  v Do not venture near the fallen power line.
  n Operating a milk bar is a profitable business venture.
  aj Skin diving is a venturesome pastime.

6. **WARRANT** . . . . to justify, guarantee

  v Our car is too old to warrant the cost of repairs.
  n There is no warrant (justification) for thinking girls cannot play baseball well.
  n The policeman has a warrant for your arrest.

QUESTS

1. *Re-* in *recline* is a prefix and *-cline* is a root which comes from the Latin verb meaning *to lean*. List two other *-cline* words, using prefixes listed on page 195.
2. *Contend* consists of a prefix, *con-*, and a root, *-tend*. The root, *-tend*, comes from the Latin word *tendere* and means *strive* or *stretch*. Using the lists of prefixes on pages 195 and 275, list five other *-tend* words to go with *contend*.
3. *Cherish* and *relish* are words which came to us from Latin by way of Old French. List three similar action words ending in *-ish?*

PRACTICE SET

Copy the words in italics and write the meaning of each in the sentence.

1. Americans *cherish* their freedom and *relish* their sports.
2. Custom *fosters* antique styles of furniture which do not *vary*.
3. The tale will either *convulse* you with laughter or make you *bristle*.
4. The drivers *contend* in a race which may prove fatal to those who *venture* to enter it.
5. Her condition does not *warrant* waiting until the floods *subside*.
6. It would be rude to *recline* on the grass while we *dedicate* a war memorial.

UNIT TEN

PERILOUS PAIRS

The English language contains numerous pairs of similar words that bother all who are not wary.

Group I—All So

Read the following pairs of sentences aloud several times.

1. They were *also* sorry.　　They were all so sorry.
2. We were *almost* happy.　　We were all most happy.
3. You were *already* outside.　　You were all ready outside.
4. Scouts are *always* prepared.　　Scouts are prepared all ways.
5. Come, *although* you were not invited.　　Come all, though you were not invited.
6. We are *altogether* satisfied.　　We are all together satisfied.
7. . . . .　　Everything is all right.
8. He will be there *maybe*.　　He may be there.

Write sentences using each italicized word correctly.

Group II—Angles and Angels

What is the difference between an angle and an angel? The boy who wrote, "The streets make a sharp angel at that point," probably knew better. He was just careless.

Read the following pairs several times, noting the definitions and the differences. Exaggerate the pronunciation enough to show the differences.

1. angle—a figure formed   angel—heavenly being
   by lines that meet   caret—omission mark (∧)
2. carrot—a vegetable   carat—unit of jewel weight
                               seize—grasp
3. cease—stop   seminary—training school
4. cemetery—burial park   diary—daily record
5. dairy—home for cows   formally—done in accordance
6. formerly—in time past   with rules or forms
7. *loose—not tight   lose—suffer loss of
8. *quite—really   quiet—(*two syllables*) not noisy
9. route—path or road   rout—drive away (*an enemy*)
10. sphere—globe   spear—a sharp weapon

PROBLEMS

1. Write sentences using, first, the words in the first column, and then the words in the second column. You may wish to devise some sentences that show pa˙rs of words in contrast. Be sure that you spell each word correctly.
2. Write the following words in two columns. Be sure you can pronounce each and explain the differences in meaning; *adapt, adopt; advise, advice; carless, careless; celery, salary; decease, disease; duly, dully; facet, faucet; latter, later; liable, libel; profit, prophet; roomer, rumor; series, serious; suit, suite; trail, trial.*
3. Knowing the principle of spelling discussed on page 13 should help you spell the words *carless* and *careless* properly. What other pairs of words can you find in Group II which the principles you learned in Units 1 and 4 will help you spell correctly?

Group III—Homonyms

Homonyms are words spelled differently but pronounced alike. They are plentiful in English. Study the following:

1. coarse—rough, unrefined   course—path, route, or study
2. canvas—cloth   canvass—sell or solicit
3. compliment—a bit of praise   complement—something that completes
4. council—a group   counsel—advice or a lawyer
5. current—in motion   currant—red fruit
6. desert—dry land   dessert—tasty sweet dish
7. metal—cold, shiny stuff   mettle—courage
   medal—a decoration
8. principal—money, chief   principle—a rule, generality
9. *stationary—immovable   *stationery—writing paper
10. troop—group or collection   troupe—a group of actors, usually

QUESTS

1. Write sentences using each of the homonyms above correctly. Can you devise a single sentence for each pair?
2. Write a homonym for: *alter, birth, boarder, bough, capitol, dough, flour, foreword* (to a book), *hanger, kernel, might, meddle, morn, piece, scent, soul, stake, strait, through, throne, to, vain, vale, weakly, who's.*

SENTENCES FOR PRACTICE

Write the following sentences from dictation:

1. The advice about the suite of rooms came later.
2. An angel left an envelope in the cemetery.
3. The colonel's trial came in the latter part of August.
4. The detour made us lose the route past the seminary.
5. He will loose a series of libel suits.

6. The diary tells of a troupe of actors living in a dairy.
7. A carrot lay beside the hollow metal sphere.
8. The disease formerly made it dangerous to view the deceased.
9. The principal would not offer a coarse compliment.
10. His principal use for stationery is in offering counsel.
11. The gift made her almost happy.
12. The injured player was all right, and the coach was altogether satisfied.
13. I advise you to cease offering careless advice based on rumor.
14. The colonel won a medal for trying to seize the trail along the strait.
15. You must be all ready when the principal of the school reaches the hangar where the plane is kept.
16. She tried not to lose the box containing her envelopes, her stationery, and her veil.
17. The scent of the steak reached the dog and it took two of us to keep him quiet.
18. It is all right to adapt the metal container for use on the desert.
19. The diseased went to the hospital on the hill; the deceased were placed in the cemetery in the vale.
20. The boarder, whose salary is paid weekly, is a member of a dancing troupe.

(The next unit for spelling emphasis is Unit No. 12, p. 45.)

UNIT ELEVEN

SPARK PLUG WORDS

ACTIONS

In terms of the verbs at the right:

1. What does one do to water to make it pure? __?__

2. What does a guilty person sometimes do at the scene of the crime? __?__

3. What do bribes do? __?__

4. What is the first stage in stealing something? __?__

5. What does a father sometimes have to do about his son's actions? __?__

6. What is the best thing to do with worries? __?__

Spark Plug Words
First Group

1. banish
2. collapse
3. corrupt
4. covet
5. decline
6. detain

Second Group

1. dilute
2. filter
3. intrude
4. reprove
5. sever
6. supersede

41

SPARK PLUG WORDS—First Group

1. BANISH . . . . to drive or send away, expel

    v Laughter will banish sadness.
    n Roger Williams suffered banishment because of his religious beliefs.

2. COLLAPSE . . . . fall, break down, faint

    v Heavy snow made the roof collapse.
    n A Senator's angry blast brought the collapse of peace talks.
    aj A collapsible boat will fit into our car.

    Review *lapse* in Part One, Unit 5, and *relapse*, a falling back into the previous (bad) condition.

3. CORRUPT . . . . to debase, cause decay

    v "Evil communications corrupt good manners." (I Cor. 15:33)
    v Do the horror type of "comic" books corrupt their readers?
    n Graft and corruption were rife (prevalent) in the city's government.
    aj Lincoln was a man of incorruptible honesty.

4. COVET . . . . . . to crave (what belongs to another)

    v Gladys tried not to covet her sister's good fortune.
    aj Ted's covetous nature made him uneasy and dangerous.

5. DECLINE . . . . refuse, decrease, slant down

    v Grace had to decline the invitation to the party.
    v The value of the house will decline if we do not paint.
    n Would a sharp decline in prices bring a decline in wages also?

    Decline also means to describe the changes of a noun or adjective according to the *declension* to which it belongs. The term is used more in Latin than in English.

6. **DETAIN** . . . . . to hinder from going, hold back, delay

   v "Do not detain me!" the messenger shouted.
   n The state farm is a place of detention for boys who have committed crimes.

   Cf. **-tain** words (**-tain** = hold) in Part Three, Unit 14: **attain, contain, entertain, pertain, retain.**

SPARK PLUG WORDS—Second Group

1. **DILUTE** . . . . . to weaken, thin out, add liquid (water)

   v Dilute the syrup if it is too thick.
   v It is easy to dilute one's meaning by using too many words.
   n Dilution of the oil in a car may cause engine damage.

2. **FILTER** . . . . to strain (out impurities), purify, soak through

   v The cherry juice will be clearer if you filter it.
   v Only a little sunshine could filter through the smoky air.
   n The heating unit contains a filter to purify the air.
   n A plant for filtration of the city's water supply is needed now.
   v Enemy agents tried to infiltrate the factory that made jet bombers.
   Query: What is a **filterable** virus?

3. **INTRUDE** . . . . force (one's way) into, trespass

   v Jerry does not want anyone to intrude into his personal affairs.
   n Was the white man an intruder on the American continent?
   n Crashing a party is an intrusion.

4. **REPROVE** . . . . to scold, blame, rebuke

   v The officer had to reprove Joe for crossing the street.
   n "A reproof entereth more into a wise man than an hundred stripes into a fool." (Proverbs 17:10)

5. **SEVER** . . . . to cut (off), separate, discontinue

   v To fire a man is to sever his connection with the company.
   v The windshield glass severed both arteries in the girl's neck, and she quickly bled to death.
   n Severance of an Atlantic cable interrupted the messages from London.
   aj Severance pay is extra pay a person may get when he leaves a job.

6. **SUPERSEDE** . . . . . . to replace (with newer or better)

   v A new telephone directory will supersede the present one.
   v Will turbine engines supersede piston engines in automobiles?
   n Supersession of old models by new ones is a continuous process in industry.

PRACTICE SET

Copy the italicized words and beside each write its meaning in the sentence.

1. A wise king will *banish* a man who *covets* his job and is powerful enough to be dangerous.
2. Luxury did not *corrupt* Daniel or *dilute* his religious zeal.
3. An interruption did *intrude* into his schedule and thus *detain* him.
4. Uncle Ben's health had begun to *decline* several months before we saw him *collapse*.
5. If I *reprove* him, he may *sever* our friendship.
6. Your design for a plant to *filter* our water supply will *supersede* his design.

A RESEARCH PROBLEM

Choose ten words from this unit, no more than 1 from any category, and write down their origins. If you can, find some added information about the way in which the word has changed.

UNIT TWELVE

A SPELLING PROBLEM

Group 1

Quite a few words end in -*ar*. Those below are among the most common. Read them aloud several times. Exaggerate the -*ar* endings to fix them in mind. Write them and use them in sentences until you are sure you can spell them even when they are mixed up with other words.

beggar	circular	particular	scholar
burglar	collar	peculiar	similar
*calendar	familiar	poplar (*tree*)	singular
cedar	*grammar	popular	vinegar
cellar	liar (*teller of lies*)	regular	vulgar

QUESTS

1. What letter comes in front of the -*ar* ending most often? This observation will help you spell the words.
2. Which words contain a double letter? Which two words contain a *liar*?

45

3. The vowel in front of a *single* consonant in front of -*ar* is long in most cases. What are the exceptions?
4. Write the adverb or -*ly* form of eight of the words which have adverbial forms.
5. Add -*ity* to nine of the words which have an *ity* form, and write the words which result. Check in the dictionary any which you question.

Group II

Examine the following words ending in -*ary* in the same way you studied the words which end in -*ar*.

auxiliary	imaginary (-able)	secretary (-ial)
boundary	literary (-ature)	stationary (*fixed*)
customary (-ily)	military (-ist)	temporary (-ily)
diary (-ist)	primary (-ily)	(*not lasting long*)
dictionary	revolutionary (-ist)	voluntary (-ily)
elementary (-al)	salary	tributary
honorary (-able)	sanitary (-tion)	vocabulary

QUESTS

1. Write the form of each word as it is indicated in the parentheses.
2. Write sentences for each of ten of the words you have just listed.
3. What are verb forms of the words *boundary? honorary? imaginary? voluntary?*
4. Some words ending in -*ary* are nouns, some are adjectives, and a few can act as either part of speech. List as many as you can from Group II which can be both.
5. For each of the words that you listed in Quest number four, write two sentences, illustrating in one its use as a noun and in the other its use as an adjective.

Group III

Read the words, stressing the *-or* endings, and study the spelling of the following:

actor	elevator	janitor	radiator
author	emperor	labor	rumor
aviator	error	major	scissors
bachelor	favor	minor	senator
conductor	honor	mirror	tenor
director	horror	motor	terror
doctor	humor	odor	traitor
editor	flavor	pastor	vigor

QUESTS

1. What letter comes in front of the *-or* most often? Write sentences or a paragraph containing several of the words.
2. What do the spellings of *anterior, behavior, exterior, junior, inferior, interior, prior* (before), *senior,* and *superior* have in common? Pronounce them carefully, and make sure you can spell them.
3. Study the following familiar *-ory* words: *advisory, directory, dormitory, history, inventory, memory, territory, victory.* Write sentences containing them.

Group IV

Words ending in *-er* are regular and therefore more numerous. Most of the everyday agent words add *-er* to a base form: *doer, learner, speaker, shirker, worker.*

Relatively few common words end in *-ery.* They include:

celery	millinery	slippery
gallery	mystery	*stationery

Study these. From what language does each come? Write sentences containing them. Write the plural of *gallery* and *mystery.*

SENTENCES FOR PRACTICE

Write the following sentences from dictation:
1. The janitor found a beggar wearing no collar.
2. The scholar talked about a temporary boundary.
3. The Senator broke the actor's mirror.
4. His diary is a history of military planning.
5. Familiar odors came from the dormitory kitchen.
6. A burglar stole a calendar by error.
7. A senior's grammar should be superior.
8. The traitor's humor was vulgar.
9. The rumor about the doctor's behavior is false.
10. It is customary for a tenor singer to receive a salary.
11. The motor and radiator are stationary.
12. Liars often display singular lapses of memory.
13. Why the stationery should be slippery is a mystery.
14. The secretary's behavior is peculiar.
15. The worker's illness is singular and imaginary.

A WORD LIST

Begin now to keep a list of unfamiliar words that you have come across in other areas and out of school. You should be able to find at least one new word a week, more if you are alert. Keep a record of how the word was used.

(The next special spelling unit is Unit No. 15, p. 57.)

UNIT THIRTEEN

TWELVE STRESS WORDS

WAYS AND MEANS

Which word from the list at the right goes best in each blank?

1. A telescope lens has a variable —?—.

2. Lincoln's face on a penny is a —?—.

3. A special agent of the FBI is after a —?—.

4. Puritan life in New England is famous for its —?—.

5. The king is a merry —?—.

6. Only a powerful person can issue a —?—.

(There are two possible answers to No. 2.)

The Twelve
First Six

1. culprit
2. decree
3. focus
4. impact
5. mettle
6. monarch

Second Six

1. profile
2. rebuff
3. refuge
4. rigor
5. semblance
6. tumult

STRESS WORDS—First Six

1. **CULPRIT** . . . . . . guilty person, wrongdoer, offender

    n The culprit was the boy in the third row with a silly look on his face.

    aj The fire was an accident, and no one was really culpable (blameworthy).

2. **DECREE** . . . . an order, command, edict

    n The union issued a decree that none of its members could work more than forty hours a week.

    v The emperor decreed that all spinning wheels must be destroyed.

3. **FOCUS** . . center (coming-together) of activity, or of attention

    n The focus for all eyes in the room was the bat on the wall.

    v Focus the field glasses on the chimney and you will see a hole in it.

    v Sam's attention was focused on a math problem.

    Focus is literally the point at which a lens projects a clear image: The microscope must be in *focus* before you can see the red blood cells.
    The *-ing* and *-ed* forms may be spelled with a double *s.* Which spelling conforms to the rule given in Unit 4, page 13?

4. **IMPACT** . . . . force, force exerted, striking

    n The impact of a person's deeds far exceeds the impact of his words.

    aj An impacted (forced inward) tooth is pushed to one side or down from its normal position.

5. **METTLE** . . . . courage, spirit

    n Football and basketball test a boy's mettle.

    aj Davy Crockett was a mettlesome (spirited) pioneer.

    aj He was also an intrepid (dauntless) adventurer.

6. MONARCH . . . . king, ruler, sovereign

   n Louis XVI was the French monarch beheaded in 1793.
   n The British Commonwealth of Nations is a limited monarchy.
   n Edward VIII was a British sovereign who abdicated.

STRESS WORDS—Second Six

1. PROFILE . . tracing or outline, side view (especially of a face)

   n The jagged profile of the mountain peaks looked ugly in the pale light of late afternoon.
   n Mr. Sawyer has a hatchet-shaped profile.
   n Most high schools and colleges make a profile of your personality, character, and mental capacities.

2. REBUFF . . . . rejection or setback

   n "Then, welcome each rebuff
   That turns earth's smoothness rough. . . ." (Robert Browning, *Rabbi Ben Ezra*)
   v Old Mr. Spitz rebuffed Agnes when she tried to sell him a box of Girl Scout cookies.

3. REFUGE . . . . . . place of safety, a shelter, sanctuary

   n Most National Parks provide a refuge for wild animals.
   n A family of refugees (persons seeking shelter) from Hungary live near us. They fled from their country to escape persecution.

   A **sanctuary** is a holy or sacred place, usually a church or shrine, sometimes a refuge for birds and wild life. Cf. **haven**.

4. RIGOR . . . . harshness, severity, strictness

   n Both boys found the rigor of the Minnesota winters bracing.
   aj The Pilgrim Fathers led a rigorous life.

   Cf. **rigid**, stiff, strict, difficult.

5. SEMBLANCE . . . . an appearance or seeming condition

   n George kept up a semblance of studying, but he was actually reading a comic book.

   n The resemblance (similarity) between the two men was striking.

6. TUMULT . . . . uproar, agitation, commotion

   n In the tumult of battle, Ernest forgot his promise.

   aj The spaceman got a tumultuous welcome on Broadway.

PRACTICE SET

Copy the italicized words and beside each write its meaning in the sentence.

1. The *culprit* showed his *mettle* by offering to make amends.
2. We awaited the *impact* of the *decree* to burn the books.
3. The boys took *refuge* in a cornfield, but it was too near the *focus* of the search.
4. George was dressed as the old *monarch* of the sea and those on the after deck saw a *semblance* of Neptune's court.
5. Her personality *profile* indicates that she could not endure the *rigor* of a trip to the moon.
6. The man who caused the *tumult* suffered a *rebuff*.

SHORT SHORT SHORT SHORT STORY

What base word from this unit fits best into each blank?

The __?__ had no choice but to mount the king's gallows. His grim __?__ was outlined against the sunrise. His misdeeds had caused a __?__ despite the king's __?__ that anyone who made trouble must die. The __?__ admired his jester's __?__, but there was no __?__ from the __?__ of a royal edict. Hanging the jester would give __?__ to the king's authority and demonstrate that it was not merely the __?__ of authority. The deed would serve as a __?__ to those who thought he did not mean what he said, and it would __?__ attention on that authority.

UNIT FOURTEEN

SPRINGTIME IN THE ROCKIES

Fill the blanks fittingly from the words at the right without using a word twice. It is better to leave the second blank until last.

SPRING

1. Compared to summer, winter is a —?— time.

2. There is only a —?— amount of sun and warmth then.

3. Soon, however, spring comes with its —?— array of flowers.

4. Gay —?— displays appear.

5. Joy is —?— at this time of year.

The Words

First Six

1. floral
2. fragile
3. gallant
4. lavish
5. meager
6. pagan

Second Six

1. rampant
2. remote
3. rustic
4. serene
5. somber
6. urgent

53

SPRINGTIME—First Six

1. **FLORAL** . . . . . . consisting of or pertaining to flowers

   aj A floral tribute was presented to the aviator.
   n A florist raises or deals in flowers.
   aj A florid face is red like some flowers.

   > What is *floriculture?* What are *florescent* trees? Do not confuse *florescent* with *fluorescent.*

2. **FRAGILE** . . . . readily breakable, delicate

   aj Old china is often fragile.
   aj Josephine has a fragile look.
   n The fragility of the chairs makes them impractical.

3. **GALLANT** . . . . brave, dashing, chivalrous

   aj Sir Galahad was a gallant knight.
   n The gallantry of the class president makes him popular.

   > Cf. *cavalier* (Part One, Unit 8) and the Spanish word *caballero* (Part Three, Unit 20).

4. **LAVISH** . . . . abundant, generous, bountiful

   aj Uncle George is lavish with praise when you do something the way he wants it done.
   av He gives away dimes more lavishly than dollars.

5. **MEAGER** . . . . scanty, scarce, sparing

   aj The Pilgrims had only a meager supply of food.
   aj The Hansons have good times despite a meager income.

6. **PAGAN** . . . . heathen(ish), non-Christian

   aj Putting unfit babies out to die of exposure was a pagan practice.
   n Was Roman society, with its paganism, so different from our own?

SPRINGTIME—Second Six

1. **RAMPANT** . . . . prevalent, unrestrained

    aj Disease and disorder were rampant in the stricken city.

    av Mobs paraded rampantly (unrestrainedly) through the Paris streets.

    n Trees were uprooted and buildings destroyed when six elephants went on a rampage (reckless behavior).

2. **REMOTE** . . . . distant, far removed

    aj The forest ranger's tower is located on a remote mountain peak.

    aj The chances of getting caught were less remote than Nick imagined.

    av Adolf was remotely aware that he might be recognized.

    n The remoteness of the desert outpost kept it from being attacked.

3. **RUSTIC** . . . . countrified, unrefined, plain

    aj Billy's rustic shyness made it hard to get acquainted.

    n The rusticity (crudeness) of Lincoln's birthplace makes it quite a contrast to most homes today.

    v City dwellers like to rusticate (live in the country) during the summer.

    aj Rustic furniture is sometimes made from tree branches—with the bark left on.

4. **SERENE** . . . . calm, peaceful, placid

    aj Grandfather's serene existence is unruffled by clocks.

    n Can a person have real serenity within when turmoil and confusion rage outside?

5. **SOMBER** . . . . dreary, gloomy, grave, depressing

    aj The village looked somber in the November twilight.

    n Thomas Hardy writes about the somberness of the moors.

6. **URGENT** . . . .   pressing, must be done at once

   a] The call for berry pickers was urgent.
   n The boy was dying, and Dr. Ulp knew the urgency of his errand.

PRACTICE SET

Copy the italicized words and beside each write its meaning in the sentence.

1. Fear was *rampant* among our *pagan* enemies before the battle.
2. *Floral* displays help to make a funeral a less *somber* affair.
3. The need to increase our *meager* supply was *urgent*.
4. Folk music has a *rustic* charm that may seem *remote* to some people.
5. Robin Hood was *gallant* toward the rich, but *lavish* with the poor.
6. The English cottage stood *serene* in the midst of *fragile* flowers.

IN THE ROCKIES

Write the base word from the unit that best fits each blank.

In autumn the peaks are brown and __?__, but during the winter blizzards are __?__ with snow and __?__ winds howl drearily. The food supply for birds is __?__ above timberline in any season, but the birds are jaunty, __?__ creatures. They do not worry.

In the mountains life is a truly __?__ as well as a __?__ existence, far from the larger towns. It is a rather __?__ existence, too, unless nature worship is a Christian exercise. One can be very __?__ in the calmer weather, and nothing is really __?__ except sudden illness or injury to one's human framework. One knows that the __?__ displays of spring will appear tame in contrast to the savage grandeurs of the winter.

UNIT FIFTEEN

AL-EL-IL

Al is an ending which appears on hundreds of English words. It makes adjective forms out of most of the words to which it is attached.

Many of the Al words function as nouns, however. These are words that once served as adjectives, but people began omitting the noun. As a result, the adjectives had to stand up alone, and thus act like nouns.

If you will recall, there were a number of words in Unit Twelve ending in -*ary* which were usable either as nouns or as adjectives. Such words as *auxiliary, boundary, military, revolutionary*, and *tributary* can be used both ways, although each word usually acts one way more frequently than the other.

It is the same way with words ending in -*al*. As a matter of fact there are a great many more examples of -*al* words used as either nouns or adjectives than was the case with the -*ary* words. Take *equal* for example. "The team met its equal last week," you say. You mean it met a team of equal ability. In the same way a general is really a general officer, but for some time he has been just a general. The principal teacher in a school is now simply the "principal," while the total amount of money in a fund is now known only as the total.

Read the following list of *-al* words several times, stressing the *-al:*

Group I

accidental	liberal	moral	rival
central	(*generous*)	normal	royal
equal	local	oral	rural
federal	loyal	physical	total
general	medal	practical	universal
internal	(*ornament*)	principal	vital
(*within*)	medical		
interval	mental		
(*time lapse*)			

EXERCISES

1. Compose sentences containing the words, and mark each as adjective, noun or verb according to the function it has in your sentence. Be careful to use the word precisely, in the part of speech you intended.
2. Which three are not used as adjectives?
3. Write the *-al* form of *crime, critic, economy, electric, fate, form, instrument* (music), *mechanic, music, ornament, nation, nature, politic, technic.* Now add *-ly* to each. Use six of these *-ly* words in sentences.
4. Write the *-al* form of *approve, arrive, bury, deny, refuse, renew.* What is the *-al* form of *globe? topic? type?* Can they also form *-ly* words?
5. Each of the following has an *-ial* form. See how many you can spell correctly. Two are tricky. Use the dictionary, if necessary, to get each one right: *artifice* (trick), *commerce, essence, finance, office, part, substance.* How do you explain the *i* which appears in each word? How would the pronunciation be affected if the *i* were not there?

Group II

The widely used words that end in *-el* are less numerous than the *-al* words. The *-el* words function most of the time as nouns or verbs. Read the following list several times—aloud, if possible—stressing the *-el:*

barrel	label	noel	parcel
cancel (-tion)	marvel (-ous)	novel (-ist)	travel
chapel	model	panel (-ist)	vessel
jewel (-ry)	morsel	*parallel	

EXERCISES

1. Write sentences using these words.
2. What other words ending in *-el* can you add to the list of words in Group II?
3. Write those which contain a double letter. In each case explain why it has a double letter, and trace it back to its root. See Unit Four for a review of endings.
4. Write the suggested form of the words which have a suffix in parentheses.
5. Compose a sentence for each of the words you listed in Quest number four.

Group III

-Il words and *-ol* words are relatively few in number, but they sometimes bother spellers. Read the following aloud several times, stressing the *-il* or *-ol*.

civil (*polite*)	pencil	control
devil	*stencil	patrol
evil	until	pistol

Use them in sentences. Look up the origin of each to discover why it has an *-il* or *-ol* ending.

SENTENCES FOR PRACTICE

Write the following sentences from dictation:

1. We were all ready to cancel the order for supplies.
2. It is vitally important that the principal valleys be open to commercial activity.
3. The equal lines on the stencil are parallel.
4. The jewel is a marvel of natural beauty.
5. People were wrapping parcels to celebrate Noel.
6. Be loyal, moral, liberal, and practical.
7. A pill is a medical morsel to be taken orally (by mouth).
8. During the interval a medal fell into the barrel.
9. The arrival of Federal troops proved to be vital.
10. The principal read a novel about mental illness.

(The next unit for spelling emphasis is Unit No. 18, p. 69.)

UNIT SIXTEEN

DO AND BE WORDS

HOW?

Which one of the words at the right would you use to obtain:

Do and Be Words

First Six

1. accede
2. allure
3. besiege
4. caress
5. congest
6. distort

1. A fire? —?—

2. A larger allowance? —?—

3. More school spirit? —?—

4. A chipmunk or bird for a pet? —?—

5. A foolish face? —?—

6. Release from an unjust penalty? —?—

Second Six

1. entreat
2. evade
3. ignite
4. incite
5. protest
6. revere

61

DO AND BE WORDS—First Six

1. **ACCEDE (to)** . . . . to comply (with), agree

   v The police chief would not accede to the mayor's request that the traffic lights stay on all night.

   n Do you have access (means of approach) to the president of the company?

   aj Freeways make downtown Los Angeles quite accessible (readily approachable).

   Other *yes* words: *affirm, assent, concur, acquiesce.*

2. **ALLURE** . . . . to attract, tempt, entice

   v Cheese will allure a mouse.

   n Candy has great allurement for children.

   v "If sinners entice thee, consent thou not." (Proverbs 1:10)

   n No enticement would induce the man to betray a trust.

3. **BESIEGE** . . . . to lay under prolonged attack, to beset

   v English armies undertook to besiege Orleans in France.

   v Gloria's friends besiege her with requests to sing for them.

   n The prisoner survived a long siege of illness.

   To *bombard* a city is to fire missiles at it. A *beleagured* city is one that is surrounded, or *blockaded,* or under siege. *Blockaded* is used more often of a port city or a country shut off by hostile ships, however.

4. **CARESS** . . . . to stroke or pat fondly

   v Millie likes to caress her cat.

   n Her caresses calmed the frightened child.

   The Latin root is *carus,* dear. *Carissimus* means *dearest.*

5. **CONGEST** . . . . to jam up, overcrowd

   v Vast throngs congest the stores at Christmas time.

   n Traffic congestion is an increasing problem in most cities.

   aj A head cold causes a congested condition of the sinuses.

6. **DISTORT** . . . . to twist, warp, misrepresent

   v Pain began to distort Judy's face as she was lifted into the ambulance.

   n The speaker distorts the facts about teenage behavior.

   v Hi-fi radio sets reduce distortion to a minimum.

DO AND BE WORDS—Second Six

1. **ENTREAT** . . . . to beg, beseech

   v "Entreat me not to leave thee," Ruth said to Naomi. (Ruth 1:16)

   n His wife's entreaties finally induced him to buy a new automobile.

   See *implore, supplicate, importune, petition.*

2. **EVADE** . . . . to avoid, slip away from, elude

   v A burglar always thinks he can evade the police.

   n Evasion proved to be more difficult than he expected.

   aj The witness gave an evasive answer to the judge's question.

3. **IGNITE** . . . . to set afire, kindle

   v One spark is all it takes to ignite a forest.

   n The ignition (spark-furnishing) system in the car was disabled by water in the distributor.

   aj Igneous rock is rock produced by fire or intense heat.

4. **INCITE** . . . . to arouse, stir up

   v The French were able to incite several Indian tribes to revolt against the British.

   n Higher pay is a means of incitement to greater exertions.

   Cf. *actuate, impel, spur.*

5. PROTEST   . . . . . .   to object, complain, expostulate

    v The woman tried to protest, but the judge waved her aside.
    n The Boston Tea Party was a protest by the colonists against being taxed without their consent.

6. REVERE   . . . .   to respect, hold in awe

    v We revere our forefathers for their faith and their courage.
    aj "A Scout is reverent."
    n Removing one's hat is often an act of reverence.

PRACTICE SET

Write the meaning of the italicized words in each sentence.

1. We will *besiege* the City Council with letters urging it to *accede* to the city manager's new parking plan.
2. He *entreats* his mother not to *caress* him as if he were a baby.
3. Did you *distort* your features just to *incite* laughter?
4. Football *allures* the crowds and they *revere* the best players.
5. You cannot *evade* the fact that crowds *congest* our town.
6. If a spark should *ignite* the building, it would be too late to *protest*.

AN EXTRA HOUR ON MONDAYS

What word from the unit best fits into each blank?

The company __?__s its employees not to __?__ the entrance at closing time. The employees will __?__ to the request to work an extra hour on Mondays, but they __?__ about working at all on Saturdays. Longer hours every day would __?__ their displeasure, and could __?__ them to strike, much as they admire the president of the company. The president would rather __?__ a tiger than argue with them and his face __?__s at the thought of a strike. He knows his employees will __?__ him with criticism if he asks them to work an extra hour any day but Monday. The overtime pay for that hour does __?__ them, and he knows they will not __?__ the proposal the next time it comes up.

UNIT SEVENTEEN

PERSONS AND DEEDS

INSIDE

What, from the list at the right, would you be most certain to find:

The List

First Six
1. alms
2. apprentice
3. barter
4. buttress
5. circuit
6. escort

Second Six
1. exploit
2. prophet
3. regent
4. safari
5. shrine
6. sorcery

1. In American frontier trade in the 1600's?
   __?__

2. In a wigmaker's shop in the 1700's?
   __?__

3. In a radio set?   __?__

4. In a beggar's cup?   __?__

5. In native African medical practices?
   __?__

6. In a cathedral or church pulpit?   __?__

65

PERSONS AND DEEDS—First Six

1. ALMS . . . . gifts to the needy

   n "Alms! alms!" the beggar cried.
   n Who benefits more from alms, the giver or the person who receives them?

   What was or is an *almshouse?* What is an *almoner?*

2. APPRENTICE . . . . . . one learning an art or trade

   n In colonial days an apprentice was a youth bound out to a tradesman for seven years at low wages.
   n Ben Franklin served an apprenticeship to his brother.

3. BARTER . . . to trade (item for item) without using money

   n Business dealings with the natives took the form of barter.
   v Bob offered to barter his watch for a camera.
   n Why is barter sometimes used in international trade?

4. BUTTRESS . . . . a brace, bolster, support

   n A plank propped against the bulging wall of the old house served as a buttress.
   v Builders in the Middle Ages used side supports of masonry to buttress the walls of their churches.

5. CIRCUIT . . . . a route, course, pathway

   n The scout made a circuit around the camp and went back to report.
   aj A circuit rider in Lincoln's day was a judge or preacher who went from place to place on a regular schedule.
   aj The trip up the mountain is slow and circuitous (round-about).

   Cf. *circle, circulate. Circuit* implies a circular route in the sense that a circuit leads back to its starting point. A radio circuit is the very complicated route that its electrical currents have to follow. What is a "short" circuit?

6. **ESCORT** . . . . a companion, protector, conductor, convoy

   n The mayor provided a police escort for the King of Sweden.

   v Philip had to escort (accompany and protect) his sister to the dance.

     Cf. *cortege,* a procession.

PERSONS AND DEEDS—Second Six

1. **EXPLOIT** . . . . . . a deed, adventure, feat of daring

   n Have you read about the exploits of FBI agents?

   v Labor unions make it harder to exploit (treat unfairly) workers than it used to be.

   n Exploitation of laborers was common in the 1890's.

2. **PROPHET** . . . . . a religious leader; one who predicts

   n Elijah was the prophet who dared to condemn Ahab.

   n Prophets today are called ministers or preachers.

   n The prophecy about a mild winter did not come true.

   aj *Twenty Thousand Leagues Under the Sea* was a prophetic story.

   v One hundred years ago no one dared to prophesy a trip to the moon.

     Cf. *predict, presage, prognosticate.*

3. **REGENT** . . . . . acting ruler, one of governing board

   n A regent ruled until the boy king came of age.

   n It was during this regency the French attack came.

   n One of the regents of the university died.

4. **SAFARI** (sə fär′i) . a trip or expedition, especially to hunt in Africa

   n Colonel Kinsky brought two lions back from his safari.

   n The young people are planning a safari to Yellowstone this summer.

5. **SHRINE** . . . . a holy or sacred place

   n Mt. Vernon is a well-known American shrine.

   n Every year thousands visit the shrine at Lourdes.

   v Sir Winston Churchill will long remain enshrined in the hearts of Americans and British alike.

6. **SORCERY** . . . . witchcraft, black magic

   n Faust was a legendary German who dabbled in sorcery.

   n Circe was a sorceress in the *Iliad*.

PRACTICE SET

Copy the italicized words and beside each write its meaning in the sentence.

1. A *shrine* is a good place to ask for *alms*.
2. The *regent* asked for an *escort* to the sacred mountains.
3. On the *safari* we obtained native costumes by *barter*.
4. A *prophet* warned us of *sorcery*.
5. The silversmith's *apprentice* told of his *exploit* in facing a bear.
6. Bill made a *circuit* around the cave while trying to find some way to *buttress* his courage.

THE TRAVELER

Which word fits best in each blank?

The prince __?__ of the land, because of the trouble foretold by the __?__, decided to make a pilgrimage to the __?__. He took so many people with him as an __?__ that the pilgrimage looked more like a __?__ into the jungle. In fact, the prince had to __?__ many goods to pay the soldiers.

When they arrived at the destination, the prince gave __?__ to an old beggar who crouched beside the __?__ that supported the cathedral. The beggar warned him of the evil __?__ of his uncle who was an __?__ to a great magician. Therefore, to escape his uncle, the prince performed the incredible __?__ of making a __?__ around his uncle's land in order to return home.

UNIT EIGHTEEN

PRONOUNCE THE SPELLING

Do you say "because" or "becuz"?

This is a word you will spell correctly if you pronounce it as it should be. There are dozens of other words more easily spelled if pronounced correctly. Practice out loud on the groups below. Be precise, or even exaggerate the pronunciation.

Group I: A Problems

The A that IS there:

*because	*-ant	*-ian	*-man	*-ally
kangaroo	fragrant	Christian	chairman	equally
liable	servant	physician	freshman	generally
Niagara	vacant	musician	human	usually
Satan				
(sā′tan)	*-ace	*-ade	*-age	*-ate
separate	furnace	comrade	image	accurate
standard	grimace	decade	message	candidate
temperament	(grĭ·mās′)	lemonade	shortage	chocolate
temperature	surface		storage	(chôk′əlĭt)
				celebrate
				decorate

1. Think of additional words having one of the endings in Group I.
2. Write sentences illustrating three words in each of the columns above.

69

Group II: E Problems

The E that IS there:

atheist	*-edy, -ety*	*-ent*
cruel	comedy	dependent
hundred	tragedy	different
hurried	remedy	parent
offering	piety	recent
opera	society	reverent
quiet	variety	student
specimen		talent
vegetable		

The E that ISN'T there:

-eous	
advantageous	* argument
beauteous	elm (*one*
bounteous	*syllable*)
piteous	film (*one*
outrageous	*syllable*)
plenteous	* athletics
	(*three*
	syllables)
	lightning
	(*two*
	syllables)

1. Add words to each group.
2. Devise sentences using two or three of the above words in each group.

Group III: I That *Is* There

anticipate	ancient	bulletin	horrid	justice
aspirin	brilliant	margin	livid (*grey-*	prejudice
* definite	client	satin	*blue*)	sacrifice
family	fiery	spirit	timid	service
* privilege	genius	victim	torrid	
sacrilege	Orient			
splendid				

1. Add words with similar endings to each column.
2. Compose six sentences using words from Group III. You should try to use at least one word from each column. One sentence will need two words.
3. Review the *-ian* words in Group I. Use each in a sentence that illustrates it.
4. Using a dictionary or a thesaurus, look up adjective forms for the words *brilliance, prejudice,* and *sacrifice.*

Group IV: O Problems

-ory	-ony	-od, -ot	-ion	-ous
history	agony	method	cushion	dangerous
ivory	alimony	period	champion	desirous
memory	harmony	ballot	opinion	grievous
theory	testimony	pilot	religion	humorous
victory				perilous

The O that IS there: sophomore.

1. List as many words of like endings for each column as you can.
2. For each of the five columns in Group IV devise a sentence that uses two words from that column.

Group V: U Problems

The U that IS there

accurate	pursue
glamour	regular
minute	sulfur
murmur	surge
purge	urge

The U that ISN'T there

curb	among
curt	color [1]
disturb	valor [1]
spurt	honor [1]
yogurt	

Group VI: Tricky Consonants

distinctly	recognize	across
environment	sandwich	college
(hit the first n)	secretary	drowned *(one syllable)*
government	surprise	partner *(it's a t)*
(hit the first n)	standard	until
library	whether *(say the h)*	
Wednesday	whither	

[1] These words are spelled *-our* in England but not in the USA. Note also that *glamour* becomes *glamorous*.

1. Divide *government, environment, Wednesday,* and *recognize* into syllables, using the dictionary to check your answers.
2. Compose sentences or a brief story of school life, using at least ten of the words in Group VI.

SENTENCES FOR PRACTICE

Read them aloud. Write them from dictation.

1. The history film is about religions of the Orient.
2. The Federal Government will share the cost equally with the states.
3. Students do not usually celebrate athletic victories on Wednesday.
4. The opera is about a quiet shepherd.
5. The pilot cast his ballot for the physician.
6. The musician has talents that are distinctly different from those of other artists.
7. The remedy, incidentally, depends on memory alone.
8. The champion lived in a quiet environment.
9. Full of spirit, the players hoped they were winning.
10. The mystery of the timid tapping was never solved.
11. Even timid servants deserve human, civil treatment.
12. Satan is fond of travel and hard to recognize.
13. Satin in quiet colors is often quite splendid.
14. The freshman's victim was buried beneath a filing cabinet.
15. The horrid tragedy occurred because the house was vacant.
16. Niagara Falls is a beauteous but dangerous place.
17. The two secretaries had an argument about which college was more glamorous.
18. The family wants a definite answer about having a separate room for a library.
19. My partner across the street does not anticipate being involved in the school balloting.
20. Joe likes sandwiches and chocolate milk but not vegetables or yogurt.

(The next unit for spelling emphasis is Unit No. 21, p. 81.)

UNIT NINETEEN

VARIED ACTIONS

A MYSTERY

Supply for each blank the most suitable word
from the list at the right.

Something began to —?— in the wastebasket. Our interest in the reading lesson
suddenly —?—d. The teacher was —?—d
for an instant about what to do. While we
began to —?— excitedly, she bravely seized
the wastebasket and marched out the door
with it. We all admired her presence of mind
and —?—d to be like her.

The Actions

First Six

1. baffle
2. chasten
3. clamor
4. dwindle
5. garble
6. hamper

Second Six

1. hover
2. resolve
3. retain
4. shrivel
5. smolder
6. sojourn

VARIED ACTIONS—First Six

1. **BAFFLE** . . . . to perplex, foil, balk

   v The poisoning case did not baffle the police very long.
   aj The elusive bandit left a baffling trail.
   n Do missing clothes ever cause bafflement at your house?

   Hi-fi and stereo speakers are mounted on a **baffle** or ***baffleboard*** to improve the sound and its carrying power. Why does a **baffle** help and how does the word apply?

2. **CHASTEN** . . . . to punish, discipline, refine (by suffering)

   v Parents usually do not chasten their children in public.
   aj Long illness had a chastening effect on Aunt Ruth.

3. **CLAMOR** . . . . to cry or complain noisily

   v Hungry pigs clamor for their food.
   n The clamor for better government grew ever louder in Hoodville.
   aj A clamorous crowd in the stadium cheered wildly when we made the first score.

4. **DWINDLE** . . . . . . to decrease, diminish, waste away

   v Why does the number of Indians in North America continue to dwindle?
   v Our 15-point lead soon dwindled to three points.

5. **GARBLE** . . . . to mix up, twist

   v Merlin is certain to garble the figures about his sales.
   v The newspaper version of the fist fight was somewhat garbled.

6. **HAMPER** . . . . to hinder, obstruct, impede

   v Rain will hamper the work on our new house.
   v Strikes inevitably impede production.

VARIED ACTIONS—Second Six

1. HOVER . . . . . .   suspend (oneself) over, hang above

    v In the picture the goddesses hover over the city.
    v Clouds hover over the Swiss mountain peaks for days.
    v Vultures hovered over the bodies.

    Hover implies *protection*, *pity*, and sometimes *threats.*

2. RESOLVE . . .   to pledge or decide, to unravel or analyze

    v Do you solemnly resolve that you will not be late again?
    v The problem of how to tell him without hurting his feelings
    is not easy to resolve.
    n The council passed a resolution condemning the sales tax.

3. RETAIN . . . .   to keep, hold back, engage

    v Though the man is past seventy, he retains his youthful
    vigor.
    v Margaret has a very retentive memory.
    v Mr. Piper will retain a lawyer to defend him against the
    charge of criminal negligence.

4. SHRIVEL . . . .   to shrink, grow smaller, wither

    v Pea seeds will shrivel as they dry out.
    v Grass clippings wither rapidly under a hot sun.

5. SMOLDER . . . . .   to give off smoke, burn very slowly

    v Oily rags may smolder for hours before they burst into
    flame.
    aj The boy's eyes revealed his smoldering hatred.

6. SOJOURN . . . .   to dwell, stay

    v The travelers decided to sojourn a few days on the edge of
    the desert.
    n After a sojourn in Illinois, the Latter Day Saints migrated
    to Utah in 1847.

FIRST PRACTICE SET

Copy the italicized words and beside each write its meaning in the sentence.

1. As leaves *smolder* they begin to *shrivel*.
2. If you *hover* over the baby you may *hamper* the process of feeding him.
3. Confessing does *chasten* one's soul and helps one *retain* one's honesty.
4. Dear teacher, we *clamor* for help because you give us problems that *baffle* us.
5. Let him *resolve* that he will never *garble* a story again.
6. Your water supply will *dwindle* if you *sojourn* long in the desert.

SECOND PRACTICE SET

Select words from the basic list given in this unit that fit the blanks in the sentences given below.

1. Watch the eagles as they __?__ over their nest.
2. The enemy tried to __?__ our communications by jamming.
3. What a __?__ arose on the roof when the sleigh descended.
4. No mystery could long __?__ the great Sherlock Holmes.
5. How long will you __?__ with us in our humble home?
6. He watched the fire __?__ up the edges of the letter.
7. I __?__ to be a better student in the new year.
8. Only a severe rebuke will really __?__ him.
9. The trapped miners watched their supplies __?__ day by day.
10. Rough seas may __?__ the rescue operation.
11. How do you manage to __?__ your good humor?
12. Finally, the fire was reduced to a few ashes that continued to __?__.

HOME HAPPENING

Write a paragraph about a mishap at home, using several of the base words from this unit.

UNIT TWENTY

MOODS AND COLORS

MATCHMATES

Which of the following words best describes:

Moods and Colors

First Six

1. A cloudless sky in June? __?__

2. A calm, sober, unruffled old lady? __?__

3. Bath water at or just below room temperature? __?__

4. A drink made, not from oranges, but from the chemicals contained in oranges? __?__

5. Drapes of soft pink coloring? __?__

6. Glass a deep green color? __?__

First Six
1. desolate
2. emerald
3. hazel
4. pastel
5. plastic
6. prior

Second Six
1. sapphire
2. scathing
3. sedate
4. synthetic
5. tepid
6. unwitting

MOODS AND COLORS—First Six

1. **DESOLATE** . . . . deserted, barren, forlorn

   aj St. Helena is the desolate island where Napoleon spent his last days.

   v The Black Death managed to desolate Europe in the 1300's more effectively than any army ever has since.

   n Atilla's armies spread desolation wherever they went.

   Cf. *devastate.* To *desecrate* a place is to do violence to its sacred or holy aspect.

2. **EMERALD** . . . . hard, dark green (precious stone)

   aj Ireland is called the Emerald Isle.

   n Little emeralds were scattered about.

   Cf. *jasper, jade, aquamarine.*

3. **HAZEL** . . . . a light brown (nut)

   aj Her hazel eyes were deep and lustrous.

   aj Taffy is often hazel-colored.

4. **PASTEL** . . . . . . soft, pale, "unsaturated" (in color)

   aj Bright colors are arresting, but pastel shades are soothing.

   n Many wall colors are now pastels.

5. **PLASTIC** . . . . readily shaped or moulded

   aj Glass becomes soft and plastic when heated to high temperatures.

   aj A child's nature is more plastic than an adult's.

   n Rubber retains much of its plasticity after it cools.

   Plastics, as they are called, are hard and smooth like glass but relatively springy. They take their name from the fact that the material is readily moulded when it is warm or partly dissolved. *Plastic surgery* is the science of repairing injured parts of the human body by grafting flesh and skin.

6. **PRIOR** . . . . earlier, before

    aj The German had a prior claim to the property.

    av Prior to 1912 Arizona was still a territory and not a state.

    n During World War II a manufacturer could obtain a priority on any materials needed for war purposes.

    Cf. *anterior* and *option.*

MOODS AND COLORS—Second Six

1. **SAPPHIRE** . . . . a deep, brilliant blue (precious stones)

    aj Broken pieces of a sapphire vase lay on the floor.

    n Her string of sapphires made her look like a goddess.

2. **SCATHING** . . . . cutting, scorching, heated

    aj George received a scathing rebuke for putting his feet on the coffee table.

    aj My uncle came through the war unscathed (unharmed).

    The base word, *scathe,* is seldom used.

3. **SEDATE** . . . . calm, sober, dignified

    aj Helen is very sedate and relaxed.

    n My class reflects the sedateness of the teacher.

    Cf. *placid, tranquil* and *serene* (Part One, Unit 14).

4. **SYNTHETIC** . . . artificial, made to resemble the "real" thing

    aj Synthetic rubber is superior to natural rubber in many ways.

    n Synthetics are numerous today—including synthetic gasoline, synthetic leather, and even synthetic orange juice.

5. **TEPID** . . . . lukewarm

    aj Tepid water makes poor tea.

    aj Mary Jane's feeling about turtles was indeed tepid.

    Cf. *insipid,* which means *tasteless.*

6. **UNWITTING** . . . . thoughtless, unintended, unintentional

aj Her unwitting remark made the boys think Elaine was afraid of ghosts.

aj Mark Twain was a witty (clever) writer.

n One of his famous witticisms was his remark that the report of his death was greatly exaggerated.

PRACTICE SET

Write the meaning in the sentence of words in italics.
1. He walked in a *sedate* manner into the *tepid* water of the lake.
2. *Prior* to irrigation, the desert land of Palestine was *desolate*.
3. An *emerald* lampshade would not look well with a *sapphire* lamp.
4. His *plastic* cuff links were *hazel* in color.
5. He had *scathing* remarks to make about the artist's work in *pastel*.
6. Nylon is a *synthetic* fiber, an *unwitting* discovery.

THE QUEEN

Which base word fits best in each blank?

She was a __?__ (calm) and a rather __?__ if not insipid queen who never got excited. __?__ to her death, she ruled over a __?__ forsaken part of Norway. She never said __?__ things that hurt people's feelings, and, being young, she was more __?__, i.e., more easily influenced than queens usually are.

Her tastes were quite __?__, for she liked artificial jewels and materials better than the real thing. She preferred soft, __?__ colors, and these went well with her greenish __?__ eyes, all except the rather striking dresses of __?__ hue, brighter than the sky in June, which she liked to wear. Her hair was __?__ or nut-colored, and she looked like a model of good taste except when she __?__ly wore a dress which did not match her eyes.

UNIT TWENTY-ONE

SHYNESS AND SILENCE

Talkative children sometimes become quiet adults. Wives sometimes let their husbands do most of the talking; often it is the other way around. In a similar way many words have pairs of letters, one of which does most of the talking.

Year is an example. A thousand years ago it was probably pronounced *YAY-air*, with prolonged vowel sounds, almost as a two-syllable word. But the *a* became more and more silent until now it serves only to make the *e* longer.

Each word in the groups below has at least one letter which no longer talks. Study the words carefully. Pronounce them as they should be. Mispronounce them somewhat to make the silent letters speak as they once did. Divide the longer words into syllables. Write five sentences, each containing one or more words from each group. For each group write a sentence using one or more words from that group.

Silent A

beard	beacon	deaf	dreary	beagle
heard	deacon	leaf	weary	eagle
beam	health	reason	decrease	cease
dream	stealth	season	increase	disease
stream	entreat	measure	creature	please
feat	retreat	pleasure	feature	villain
heat	threat	treasure	peanut	captain
sweat	board	hoar	boast	carriage
loan	hoard	roar(ed)	roast	marriage
moan	road	soar(ed)	toast	
roan				

81

Miscellaneous: endeavor, search, weapon, weather, parliament, diamond

1. Make new words in each group by changing first letters to different letters or groups of letters.
2. Which words come from or via Old English? Look up all the words in one row or group and report to the class.

Silent B

dumb	tomb	debt
plumb(ing)	comb	Cf. debit

1. By changing the first letter, add one or more words to each pair.
2. Check on the origin of each of these words.

Silent C

rescind	ascend	conscience	discipline	fascinate
scene	descend	conscious	disciple	scissors

1. What words can you add to each column?
2. Write the word for *act of ascending; act of descending.* Write the opposite of *conscious,* using a prefix; the word for a man whose vocation is science.

Silent D

badge	bridge	dodge	budge(t)
hedge	cartridge	hodge-podge	grudge
ledge	ridge	lodge	judge
pledge			

1. What words can you add in each column?
2. Write those words that result when the *d* and *e* are dropped out.

Silent E

bade (pron. *bad*)	bear(ing)	determine	pageant	*foreign
	tear(ing)	ermine	*vengeance	*forfeit
horde (PART ONE, UNIT 5)	wear(ing)			surfeit

niche (PART ONE, UNIT 5)	height	*ninety	luncheon
forestall	sleight		pigeon
foretell	(*of hand*)		surgeon
forewarn			

1. List ten words like *take*, with a silent *e* at the end. How does it affect the spelling? (See Part One, Units 1 and 4.) How is *bade* different? *ache?*
2. What is the effect of the silent *e* in vengeance?

Silent G

campaign	deign (*to come down to another's level*)	*foreign	gnash
design		*sovereign	gnaw
resign	feign (*pretend*)		gnome (PART ONE, UNIT 8)
sign	reign		

1. What words can you add to each list?
2. Trace the origin of the words in one column.

Silent H

ghost	anchor	architect	character	chasm
ghoul (PART ONE, UNIT 8)	shepherd	orchestra	chemistry	chord

1. From what language did most of these words come?
2. What words can you add?

Silent GH

bough	caught	bought	freight	sleight
dough	naughty	fought	* neigh(bor)	(*of hand*)
through	taught	sought	weigh(t)	* height
thorough		wrought		* straight

1. By changing the first letter of *bough,* form three words which end with the *f* sound. Obtain a fourth with two letters in place of the *b.*
2. Change the first letter of *taught* and find two additional words to add to the second column.

Silent I

bier (*coffin*)	brigadier	* business	bruise
pier (*a dock*)	cashier	efficient	juicy
tier (*layer*)	financier	sufficient	pursuit
	frontier		suit

1. What is the origin of the words in the second column? To which one or more of the columns can you add words?
2. Change one letter of *bruise* and get *a sea voyage.*

Silent K

* knowledge	knead	knife	knock	knack
knuckle	knee	knight	knoll	knave
	kneel	knit	knot	

Silent N

autumn	solemn	hymn
column	condemn	

At one time there was an extra syllable at the end—*autumn* was *autumnus.* From what word does each of the others come?

Silent P

psalm	*psychology	pneumatic	empty
psalter		pneumonia	tempt

1. From what language does each word come?

Silent T

depot	catch	match	trestle	thistle
mortgage	latch	watch	wrestle	whistle
fasten	chestnut	glisten	often	bustle
hasten		listen	soften	hustle

1. Add words to at least three of the columns.
2. Check the origins and write a sentence using one of the words in each column.

Silent U

guard	guest	biscuit	conquer	resource
guardian	guile	circuit (PART	exchequer	source
guarantee	(dis)guise	ONE, UNIT 17)	(treasury)	

1. Compose five sentences, each using at least one word from one of the columns.

Silent W

fallow	fellow	pillow	harrow	borrow
mallow	bellow	willow	narrow	sorrow
sallow	mellow	follow	barrow	morrow
wallow	yellow	hollow	sparrow	writ
knowledge	whole	wrench	wringer	writing
shadow	whoop	wrest	writhe (PART	written
window		wretched	ONE, UNIT 3)	

1. What is the source of the words *fallow, mallow, sallow,* and *wallow?*
2. Write a four-line poem in which two of the lines rhyme.

SENTENCES FOR PRACTICE

Read these sentences aloud, picturing each word as you do so. Write them from dictation.

1. The deaf deacon rode in a carriage.
2. Sweat is nobler than pleasure for human creatures.
3. He needs a weapon to guard his treasure.
4. The government debt began to soar.
5. The scissors lay on the ledge near the plumbing.
6. In the last scene George must descend into the tomb.
7. The financier was unconscious for ninety minutes.
8. A foreign sovereign began his reign.
9. She has written a pageant about a ghost.
10. The architect did not deign to notice the lady's sighs.

MORE SENTENCES FOR PRACTICE

1. The orchestra struck a solemn chord.
2. The cashier got bruises when he fought the intruder.
3. The surgeon sought the brigadier on the frontier.
4. The guest sang a psalm of sorrow.
5. "Feign a virtue if you have it not," the widow quoted.
6. Tomorrow's search will be very thorough.
7. Pneumonia threatens one's health.
8. The guard wants to toast a biscuit.
9. Is it bad psychology to resign the pursuit?
10. The widow's remarriage will take place in the autumn.

(The next unit for spelling emphasis is Unit No. 24, p. 95.)

UNIT TWENTY-TWO

SHIPS AT SEA

SEASCAPE

Which word from the list at the right goes in each blank?

1. Columbus crossed the Atlantic in a —?—.

2. A —?— marks an object dangerous to ships.

3. —?— is foam or spray.

4. The —?— side of a ship is the side away from the wind.

5. A —?— fears a —?—, though it consists only of air in motion.

6. One of the quietest places on the ocean is the —?—.

Sea Words

First Six

1. buoy
2. doldrums
3. fathom
4. frigate
5. galleon
6. keel

Second Six

1. lee(ward)
2. mariner
3. monsoon
4. mooring
5. starboard
6. spume

SHIPS AT SEA—First Six

1. **BUOY** . . . . a floating marker

    n The lighted buoy marks a shoal (shallow area) not far from the channel.

    aj A buoyant person floats lightly on the surface of things.

    n Cork has unusual buoyancy.

2. **DOLDRUMS** (dŏl′drəms) . . very calm area; listless boredom

    n The *Flying Cloud*, becalmed in the doldrums, could not get under way.

    n Does school ever seem like the doldrums?

    The **doldrums** is an area near the equator with only light, irregular breezes. Once in it, sailing ships could not readily escape. Now a person who feels listless and tired is said to be in the doldrums.

3. **FATHOM** . . . . six feet, a unit of sea depth

    n The ship sank in sixty fathoms of water.

    v No one could fathom (understand fully) the boy's strange actions.

    aj Space was once a fathomless mystery (too "deep" to be understood).

    Fathom comes from the Old English word *faethm,* meaning *both arms outstretched* (to embrace someone). A fathom is thus the "wingspread" of such arms. In the same way *foot* and other measuring units arose from parts of the body.
    A ship's speed is measured in *knots,* a knot being one sea mile (6,080.27 ft.) an hour.

4. **FRIGATE** . . . . a light (war)ship

    n A frigate is larger than a corvette and smaller than a destroyer.

    A **frigate** was once a ship propelled by both sails and oars.

    Cf. *schooner, yacht, dinghy, yawl, kayak.*

5. **GALLEON** . . . . a sailing ship of the time of Columbus

   n The Spanish galleon struck sail when it got into port.

6. **KEEL** . . . . . . bottom (lengthwise) beam (of a ship)

   n Laying the keel is the first step in building a ship.
   v A pirate ship would sometimes keelhaul a victim—that is, drag him under the keel of the ship.

SHIPS AT SEA—Second Six

1. **LEE(WARD)** . . side away from the wind (or protected from it)

   aj The leeward deck of the torpedoed ship was already awash.
   av The coral island was alee from our position.

   The *windward* side is the side toward the wind.

2. **MARINER** . . . . sailor, one who goes to sea

   n "My mariners . . . 'tis not too late to seek a newer world." (Tennyson, *Ulysses*)
   aj The book is about marine life far below the surface.

   Marines are seagoing soldiers—or are they land-fighting sailors?

3. **MONSOON** . a strong seasonal wind (of south Asiatic waters)

   n The sailing ship almost foundered in a monsoon.
   n A monsoon reverses its direction seasonally.
   Wind words: **hurricane, typhoon, sirocco.**

4. **MOORING** . act of tying up, that which holds a ship in place

   n Mooring the ship took half an hour.
   n The tanker's mooring gave away and set it adrift.
   v ". . . a band of exiles moor'd their bark on the wild New England shore." (Felica Hemans, *The Landing of the Pilgrim Fathers*)

5.   **STARBOARD** . .   the right-hand side (as one faces the prow)

> n We sighted an enemy submarine ten miles to starboard.
> aj The starboard engine of the plane caught fire.
> n Steer the ship more to port (left or larboard side).

6.   **SPUME** (rhymes with *fume*) . . . . . . spray or foam

> n Spume gives the salt air its tang.
> n "And all I ask is a windy day with the white clouds flying,
> And the flung spray and the blown spume, and the sea-
> gulls crying." (John Masefield, *Sea Fever*)

FIRST PRACTICE SET

Copy the italicized words and beside each write its meaning in the sentence.

1. The ship's *keel* was damaged by one of the channel *buoys*.
2. In the *doldrums* a *frigate* had advantages over a *galleon*.
3. A wise *mariner* keeps in the *lee* of that island.
4. The salty *spume* blew in over the *starboard* side.
5. The *monsoon* tore the ship loose from its *mooring* and it sank in sixteen *fathoms*.

SECOND PRACTICE SET

Fill each blank sensibly with a word from the unit. Do not repeat any words.

A __?__ was becalmed in the __?__s. The crew could hear the bell on a distant __?__, where a shoal of only six __?__s was marked. No __?__ came over the side to wet the faces of the __?__s because there was so little wind, and no __?__ was necessary. There was absolutely no danger of there being an Asiatic __?__.

A __?__ approached from the __?__ on the __?__ side and towed the ship to haven. The __?__s of the two ships cut silently through the water as they moved slowly southward.

UNIT TWENTY-THREE

UPLAND AND LOWLAND

THEIR LOCATION

Fill the blanks from the words on the right.

The Goodapples lived in a —?— in western Nebraska. The town was located on a rise or —?— on a high —?—, about four thousand feet above sea level. At night the —?— seems like a huge bowl bottom side up and heavily sprinkled with stars.

The northwestern corner of Nebraska touches Wyoming, and it is not far to Cheyenne and Laramie where the —?— is more irregular, with an occasional —?— deep enough to have a —?—, at least in the spring when the snow water is running off.

Base Words

First Six

1. avalanche
2. boulder
3. cataract
4. chasm
5. firmament
6. foliage

Second Six

1. hamlet
2. knoll
3. lagoon
4. morass
5. plateau
6. terrain

UPLAND AND LOWLAND—First Six

1. **AVALANCHE** . . . . a sliding or falling mass, landslide

   n An avalanche destroyed the house on the mountainside.
   n The button factory received an avalanche of orders.

2. **BOULDER** . . . . . a large rock, weatherworn, detached

   n Mike sat on a boulder and ate his lunch.
   n Large boulders line the Whitney trail as it climbs above timberline.

3. **CATARACT** . . . . . . waterfall (usually a large one)

   n Niagara Falls is a cataract which roars like a jet bomber.
   n A cataract in the eye makes the lens whitish like the white foam of a waterfall and thus makes seeing difficult.

   A *cascade* is a small or rippling waterfall (or series) or something resembling a waterfall in appearance.

4. **CHASM** (kăz'əm) . . . . a gap, gorge, or abyss

   n The chasm had great scenic beauty.
   n The mother tried to close the chasm between father and son.

   Chasm words: *cleft, canyon, fissure, rift, glen, dell.*
   Cf. A *channel* is a kind of gorge under water.

5. **FIRMAMENT** . . . . the sky or heaven

   n "The spacious firmament on high," they sang.
   n Evangeline was the only star in Gabriel's firmament.
   n The horizon is the apparent dividing line between the earth and firmament.

   Cf. *interstellar.*

6. **FOLIAGE** . leafy growth of trees and plants (including flowers)

   n The foliage in the East is fresh, green, and lovely in May.
   n Sagebrush is the foliage of the desert.

UPLAND AND LOWLAND—Second Six

1. **HAMLET** . . . . a small village

   n Murren is a Swiss hamlet high in the Alps, near the Jung-frau.

   n Stratford was a little-known hamlet on the Avon River in Shakespeare's day.

2. **KNOLL** . . . . a mound or hillock

   n Little Round Top is a rather large knoll in the Gettysburg battlefield.

   n The highest land in Florida is the rise or knoll on which the Bok Tower stands.

3. **LAGOON** . . . . a pond or small lake

   n Minnesota has many lakes and lagoons.

   n "Too many islands with dreamy lagoons," she sighed.

   Cf. *bayou.*

4. **MORASS** . . . . a swamp or marsh

   n The pilgrims got bogged down in a morass.

   n A savage's mind is a morass of ignorance and superstition.

   Cf. *quagmire,* soft, muddy, ground; a *bog.*

5. **PLATEAU** . . . . a high tableland

   n Most of New Mexico and Arizona is a high plateau.

   n Production peaked and then settled to a plateau in April.

   In statistics a plateau is a sustained high level quite a bit above normal.

6. **TERRAIN** . . . . . ground, (kind of) land, tract or region

   n Rocky terrain is unproductive and poorly suited to any use unless it contains ore.

   n The prospector studied the terrain thoughtfully.

PRACTICE SET

Copy the italicized words and beside each write its meaning in the sentence.

1. The train was wrecked by a *boulder* and buried by an *avalanche.*
2. Year by year the *cataract* kept deepening the *chasm* it had cut.
3. The whole *firmament* seemed to come to a focus in the little *lagoon.*
4. The *foliage* on the *plateau* was luxuriant.
5. From a *knoll* we could see that the glade became a dank *morass.*
6. The *hamlet* called Sand Flats takes its name from the sandy *terrain.*

QUESTIONNAIRE

Which word in the unit is best described by each of the following phrases?

1. Deep and narrow? __?__
2. Miniature mountain? __?__
3. Star-pierced half sphere? __?__
4. Painful to toes? __?__
5. Crushing and crunchy? __?__
6. Very, very earthy? __?__
7. Refuge for canoes? __?__
8. Noisy and misty? __?__
9. Assortment of people? __?__
10. Leafy canopy rampant in May? __?__
11. Damp and unwholesome? __?__
12. Flat, high, and probably dry? __?__

A HIKE

Write several sentences or a paragraph about a walk or a hike you have taken or would like to take. Use at least eight of the words in this unit.

UNIT TWENTY-FOUR

EE-I-EE-I-OH!

Is it *ei* or *ie?* Study the two groups of words below and answer the questions which follow them.

List A	List B	
ceiling	achieve	apiece
deceive	believe	belief
deceit	mischief	*mischievous
conceive	brief	chief
*receive	field	fierce
receipt	fiend	frontier
perceive	grieve	grief
	piece	*niece
	relieve	priest
	retrieve	relief
	shield	shriek
	thief	siege
	view	tier
	review	hygiene
	pierce	yield

What is the letter before *ei* in List A? Do you find it before *ie* in any of the words in List B? How are both *ei* and *ie* sounded? Can you think of a simple rule to guide you when the *ei* or *ie* is pronounced *ee?*

*The following words are *exceptions* to the rule.

leisure   weird   seize   (n)either   deity

Note: *financier* is another exception, but it need not bother you because *-ier* is a word *ending*, and the rule was not intended for endings. *Species* also has a familiar and very normal ending. *Codeine*, a medicine, and *caffeine*, the stimulant in coffee, may be pronounced so as to be exceptions but are not widely used by pupils in their writing and may, with caution, be disregarded.

Here are some *ei* words in which the *ei* is not pronounced *ee:*

List C

feign (*pretend*)	deign	Sinn Fein
feint	reign	geisha (gā'shə, *a Japanese*
heir	skein (*coil*)	*dancing girl*)
height	sleigh	vein
neighbor	chow mein	weigh, weight

What words can you add to List C? How is *ei* pronounced in most cases? This fact will help you with *ei* pronounced like long *ā*. You will need to watch the words in which *ei* is pronounced like short *i* in sit:

List D

*foreign	*counterfeit
*sovereign	*forfeit

A few words such as *stein* and *kaleidoscope* have an *ei* pronounced like *i* in *wine*. These are usually German. It is helpful to remember that *ei* in German words or names is always pronounced like *i* in *wine* and *ie* in German words is pronounced like the *e* in *we*. This fact is a great help in spelling and pronouncing anything German. Practice it on the following:

List E

Names		Words

Names			Words
Turn Verein	Kiester	meister	Dienst (*worship*)
Weinstein	Bieber	(*master*)	liebe (*dear, beloved*)
Schneider	Lieber	geist (*ghost*)	liefer (*hand over,*
Enterlein	Gottlieb	mein (*my*)	*give*–Cf. *deliver*)
Peiper	Pieler	zeit (*time*)	lied (*song, ballad*)
		Krankheit	tief (*deep, profound*)
		(*illness*)	dieser (*this*)
		Stein (*stone*)	
		Arbeit (*work,*	
		labor)	

Few of the common words listed above are actually used very frequently in English-speaking countries, but you are likely to encounter the proper names. For this reason it may be very useful to understand the principles of pronouncing the *ie* and *ei* combinations.

List F

Among the *ie* words *not* pronounced *ee* are *friend, sieve* and such three-letter words as *die, fie, hie, lie, pie,* and *tie.* What others can you think of?

Do *friend* and *sieve* bother you? Pronounce *friend* as *fry-end* and *sieve* as *si-eve* a few times and the sounds you get will help you remember.

SENTENCES FOR PRACTICE

Write the following sentences from dictation to measure your mastery of *ie* and *ei* words:

1. Do you believe in signing a receipt for a neighbor?
2. He perceived that the thief would seize the chow mein.
3. The ceiling fell during the brief reign of Catherine.
4. Conceit kept him from yielding to the besiegers.
5. The fierce fiend shrieked and ran across the field with a skein of yarn.
6. His heir tried to feign insanity, but he deceived no one.
7. The thief failed to retrieve either the sieve or the handkerchief.
8. Neither the financier nor his friend could find the sleigh.
9. The priest saw a weird view of a human vein.
10. Each tier weighs ten tons and was shipped by freight to the receiving station.

BLANK-FILLING EXERCISE

Which goes in each blank—*ie* or *ei?*

1. Studying hyg_?_ne.
2. Gaining w_?_ght.
3. Devising misch_?_f.
4. Naming the spec_?_s.
5. Using one's L_?_sure.
6. The tower's h_?_ght.
7. Rev_?_wing for exams.
8. A charming n_?_ce.
9. Meeting g_?_sha girls.
10. A long r_?_gn.
11. Letters you rec_?_ve.
12. Misch_?_vous children.
13. Riding in a sl_?_gh.
14. A p_?_ce of cake..
15. A counterf_?_t coin.
16. Arturo Rubenst_?_n.
17. The English sover_?_gn.
18. Mr. Emil Schn_?_der.
19. Dr. Gottl_?_b. (GOTT-leeb)
20. A p_?_rcing scream.

NAMES

Make a list of people's names that you encounter in which there is an EI or an IE in the spelling. Write down the name and indicate also how it is pronounced.

UNIT TWENTY-FIVE

IT'S FUNNY

COMIC RELIEF

Can you find for each blank a word which fits aptly, from the list at the right?

By overdoing their looks or traits, animated cartoons offer a —?— of people we all know. Such cartoons often make animals —?— human beings. They are full of the outlandish behavior we call —?— and the sheer nonsense we call —?—. They move about in silly —?—s, and sometimes they give voice to the kind of rhyme, imitating a famous poem, which we call —?—.

Words

First Six

1. banter
2. caper
3. caricature
4. gambol
5. jest
6. mimic

Second Six

1. buffoon
2. drivel
3. farce
4. frivolity
5. hoax
6. parody

99

IT'S FUNNY—First Six

1. **BANTER** . . . to make sport of (in a good-natured manner)

   v Sue likes to banter her brother about his girl friends.
   n The two spent an hour in light-hearted banter yesterday.

2. **CAPER** . . . . to romp, frolic, cavort

   v Monkeys like to caper in their cages.
   n Kitten capers are fun to watch.

3. **CARICATURE** . to portray in a laughingly exaggerated manner

   n The comic scene is a caricature of a sword fight.
   v Cartoonists like to caricature celebrities.

   Caricature may take the form of a drawing, a description, or a dramatic imitation.

4. **GAMBOL** . . . . to leap about playfully

   v Goats gambol solemnly in the pasture.
   n The gambols of the brown bears attracted a crowd to their cage.

   Note: **Gambol** and **caper** have about the same meaning except that capers are perhaps lighter and less dignified than gambols.

5. **JEST** . . . . to joke, make witty remarks

   v It is bad taste to jest about sacred subjects.
   n What comedian's jests do you enjoy the most?

6. **MIMIC** . . . . . to imitate, especially for humorous effect

   v Dick sometimes mimics his sister's way of using the telephone.
   n He is a skillful mimic.
   v A talent for mimicry makes enemies as well as friends.

   Note that *mimicry* is actually a rather subtle and precise form of imitation.

IT'S FUNNY—Second Six

1. **BUFFOON** . . . . a clown or jester

   n Uncle Herb is quite a buffoon at family affairs.
   n Jim's boys enjoy his buffoonery especially.

   Cf. *harlequin.*

2. **DRIVEL** . . . . nonsense, silly talk, twaddle

   n Petroleum V. Nasby's "wisdom" was mostly drivel.
   v Horses drivel (drool, slobber) when they run fast.

   Note: **Drivel** literally is saliva flowing from one's mouth or the foam around a horse's bridle. Cf. *drool.*

3. **FARCE** . . . . something absurd or ridiculous

   n The trial of the spies was a farce.
   aj Sir John Falstaff is a farcical character in two of Shakespeare's plays.

   Note: **Farce** is also a term for a light, humorous, exaggerated play.

4. **FRIVOLITY** . . . . light-hearted fun

   n Frivolity makes a party enjoyable.
   aj Girls are often frivolous (giddy, fond of trifling).

   Note: **Frivolity** is gayer and not so empty as *drivel.*

5. **HOAX** . . . . a trick or fraud meant as a joke

   n The telephone call about Sally's being arrested was a hoax.
   v George was hoaxed by a pal who dressed up as a girl.

6. **PARODY** . . humorous imitation, especially of a song or poem

   n Sue knows a clever parody of "Jingle Bells."
   n The colonel's takeoff of Kipling's "If" shows he is a skillful parodist.

QUESTS

1. Does *gambol* differ from *gamble* in pronunciation?
2. Change a letter in *caper* and get *to provide food or meals*, especially for hire.
3. List the words you can get by changing the first letter of *banter*. Of *jest*. Of *hoax*.
4. Can you name six other words besides *caricature* which end in *-ture?*
5. What is the source of *farce?* of *parody?* of *hoax?*

PRACTICE SET

Copy the italicized words and beside each write its meaning in the sentence.

1. Uncle Joe likes to *banter* his nieces and *mimic* their actions, but he does not *caper* with them.
2. It is bad taste to *jest* about or *caricature* a religious rite.
3. The two jolly *buffoons* from Buffalo added to the *frivolity* by showing how an elephant *gambols* in a china shop.
4. The campaign for longer vacations was a *farce,* and the arguments mostly *drivel.*
5. The *parody* on "John Brown's Body" is part of a *hoax.*

A MOCK BALLET

What words from this unit fits best in each blank?

The mock ballet is a __?__ of a fairy dance. A fullback weighing 250 pounds __?__ across the stage, and a basketball center weighing 150 pounds who is six and a half feet tall __?__ about, __?__ing the fullback. His __?__s amuse the audience because he is a good __?__ even though what he says is merely__?__ and not so light-hearted as __?__ really should be. The fullback recites a __?__ entitled "The Barefoot Boy" and fixes up a little __?__ to scare the tall boy and make him wince. The whole act is a __?__. Neither one can dance at all, but the fullback can __?__ an elephant cleverly.

FINAL TESTS ON INDIVIDUAL UNITS

Unit 1

Write from dictation:

1. The man stroked the lion's mane in a humane way.
2. She took a bath clothed in a bathing suit.
3. The actress wore a sheath dress when dining out.
4. He paused by the gate, then went to the door in haste.
5. The man picked up a cone from beneath the pine tree.
6. The man spat and turned to scan the site with spite.
7. It was the fate of Dan, the Great Dane, to bite a rat.
8. The bird will pine away on the mat where his mate sat.
9. He was not loath to pin a Christmas wreath to the door.
10. She looked cute in her new hat made of pale blue satin.

Unit 2

Write on separate paper the word that goes in each blank:

1. A miser will __?__ (greedily accumulate) money and __?__ (drive out) all visitors.
2. __?__ (cling) to your beliefs, __?__d (subdue) your worries, and you will __?__ (gather in small quantities) happiness.
3. Eleanor __?__d (flinched) as the car __?__ (changed course).
4. The earth began to __?__ (rise up) as the earthquake struck, and many buildings were __?__d (destroyed).
5. He began to __?__ (wander) aimlessly but was unable to __?__ (contend) with hardships.
6. Water commenced to __?__ (soak through) under the floor.

Unit 3

Write on separate paper the word that goes in each blank:

1. __?__ (search out) deeply into the matter; do not __?__ (shrink away) at the results.
2. __?__ (put in its case) your knife and __?__ (hide) it away.
3. If his interest should ever __?__ (decrease) he will __?__ (twist in pain) with boredom.

4. You must __?__ (wrap) the baby in blankets lest the flames __?__ (scorch) him.

5. Do you wonder that I __?__ (detest) him and __?__ (suffer great agitation) over his meanness.

6. The Spanish had to __?__ (yield) the island, but they continued to __?__ (fret) at such injustice.

Unit 4

Write the word, correctly spelled, which goes in each blank:

1. You gripe, you are __?__, you __?__ed about your homework.
2. You __?__, you are slapping, you __?__ your chest.
3. You __?__, you are __?__, you gripped the golf club.
4. You care, you are __?__, you __?__ for the baby.
5. You __?__, you are __?__, you won the chess game.
6. He commits, he is __?__, he __?__ the crime.
7. You __?__, you are __?__, you dimmed the lights.
8. You worship, you are __?__, you __?__ in the church.
9. You __?__, you are __?__, you slid down the hill.
10. You __?__, you are flipping, you __?__ the pancakes.

Unit 5

Write on a separate paper the word that goes in each blank:

1. He will protect his __?__ (coat-of-arms) from any __?__ (break) of honor.
2. A __?__ (swarm) of ants milled about the dead __?__ (male bees).
3. Her body was wrapped in a __?__ (covering for a dead person) and placed in a __?__ (hollowed-out place) in the canyon wall.
4. The cat dashed with a loping __?__ (pace) after its hapless __?__ (victim).
5. The object of the man's __?__ (search) was a suitable __?__ (brace) for his crippled son.
6. In a __?__ (slip) of memory, the actor could not find his diamond __?__ (small projection).

Unit 6

Write on a separate paper the word that goes in each blank:

1. His strength remained __?__ (unharmed), but his hope was __?__ (dead).
2. Long imprisonment had given his face a __?__ (yellowish), __?__ (deathly pale) appearance.
3. A lonely, __?__ (desolate, dismal) life made him __?__ (brief, curt) in his speech.
4. The __?__ (stretched flat) figure could not be seen through the heavily painted and therefore __?__ (not letting light through) glass.
5. Gloria was so __?__ (conceited) that her life was __?__ (empty) of both friendship and sympathy.
6. The population of Northern Alaska is __?__ (thinly distributed), and the inhabitants are practically __?__ (inactive) during the winter.

Unit 7

Write the words that are incomplete, filling in the missing letters and making the changes necessary to make the noun plural or complete the verb in the present tense with -s or -es.

1. She always polish_?_ her glass_?_ after she washes the dish_?_.
2. They strummed their banjo_?_ as they sat on their porch_?_.
3. The turkey_?_ planned gruesome tortur_?_ for their human enem_?_.
4. The hero_?_ phone number was two two_?_ and three zero_?_.
5. A marine biologist search_?_ in the shadow_?_ for rare fish_?_.
6. Dick hid in the bush_?_ by the two church_?_ to watch the coach_?_ go by.
7. The rebellious colon_?_ broke their treat_?_.
8. Moss_?_ grew in large bunch_?_ on the galler_?_.
9. This book tells the dut_?_ of secret societ_?_.
10. Conflicting testimon_?_ upset the theor_?_ of the attorney_?_, and the case ended in a hung jury.

Unit 8

Write on a separate paper the word that goes in each blank:

1. He mistook the __?__ dwarf for a __?__ (ghost).
2. The __?__ (hawker, peddler) dreamed he was a __?__ (gay, gallant gentleman).
3. Though a __?__ (poor person), he finally got to Africa as a __?__ (illegal passenger) in a freight ship.
4. A __?__ (member of male religious order) admonished the __?__ (wanderer) about his bad habits.
5. The __?__ (pirate) was enchanted with the graceful __?__ (fairies) he found in the forest.
6. The __?__ (fiend) murdered an innocent __?__ (wayfarer).

Unit 9

Write on a separate paper the word that goes in each blank:

1. Boris would __?__ (show anger) when a friend __?__d (dared) to suggest that he wash his neck.
2. __?__ (treat with fondness) your ideals, and __?__ (fight, struggle) with those who try to change them.
3. Joe will always __?__ (enjoy) a good joke; but he is able at any time to __?__ (shake) his friends with rage.
4. He will not __?__ (encourage) the stock market venture even if circumstances __?__ (justify) it.
5. He liked to __?__ (lean back) at his ease reading for days at a time, and he almost seemed to __?__ (devote) his life to it.
6. If you __?__ (alter) your voice more when you speak, the complaints will __?__ (cease).

Unit 10

Write on a separate paper the word that goes in each blank:

1. Joe's __?__ (daily record) told of his visit to a __?__ (home for cows).
2. Your ring is __?__ (not tight); fasten it or you will __?__ (suffer loss of) it.

3. Our janitor, who had an incurable __?__ (illness), is now __?__ (dead).

4. Please disregard the __?__ (piece of gossip) you heard about our __?__ (boarder).

5. Submit your idea to the __?__ (group of advisers), and one of them will __?__ (advise) you on it.

6. He was awarded a __?__ (decoration) made of __?__ (cold, shiny material) for his display of __?__ (courage).

7. They waited for their __?__ (final course of a meal) until they had crossed the __?__ (barren stretches of sand).

8. It is easier to use __?__ (writing paper) in a dwelling that is __?__ (fixed, immovable).

9. The __?__ (introductory statement) to the book says we must go __?__ (ahead).

10. Even at the __?__ (place to offer religious services) it was not too late for them to __?__ (change) their plans.

Unit 11

Write on a separate paper the word that goes in each blank:

1. To __?__ (hold back) him with needless instructions is to __?__ (weaken) his energy.

2. "I __?__ (rebuke) you because you want to __?__ (trespass) upon my rights," he said.

3. Unless we __?__ (replace with better) our present method, the campaign will soon __?__ (break down).

4. Mayor Hootson did not __?__ (refuse) the chance to __?__ (cut) the ribbon and thus open the new highway.

5. Summer need not __?__ (drive away) books or the knowledge that will __?__ (seep) through them into the reader's mind.

6. Does wealth always __?__ (debase) those who __?__ (desperately want) it?

Unit 12

Write the words that are incomplete, filling in the missing letters.

1. Jim coll_?_ed a burgl_?_ in the cell_?_.
2. The schol_?_ paid his sec__?__ (letter-writer) a very small __?__ (wage).
3. The act_?_ was very popul_?_ with direct_?_s.
4. The past_?_ observes the custom_?_ rules of gramm_?_ in his sermons.
5. The bachel_?_ checked the calend_?_, and discovered that he was in err_?_ about the date.
6. If my mem_?_y is correct, a doc_?_ solved the myst_?_y.
7. Are you famil_?_r with the pecul_?_r ways of this particul_?_r edit_?_?
8. Cel_?_y has a flav_?_r the janit_?_r likes.
9. The trai_?_r has slip_?_y ways of reporting hist_?_y.
10. The conduct_?_r displayed terr_?_r as we crossed the bound_?_y into enemy territ_?_y.

Unit 13

Write on a separate paper the word that goes in each blank:

1. The hermit's sharp __?__ (side view) suggested the __?__ (severity) of his solitary life.
2. The bugler had the __?__ (spirit, responsiveness) to defy the king's __?__ (order).
3. A wounded knight sought __?__ (sanctuary) from the wrath of the __?__ (ruler).
4. The __?__ (offender) kept up a __?__ (appearance) of innocence.
5. If you __?__ (center) your attention on the spot, you will feel the __?__ (force) of the explosion.
6. Her __?__ (act of rejection) to the king caused a __?__ (uproar) at court.

Unit 14

Write on a separate paper the word which goes in each blank:

1. She is __?__ (generous) with praise even for __?__ (sparing) efforts.
2. George's __?__ (unrefined) manners make him seem unnaturally __?__ (gloomy, grave).
3. Her manner was __?__ (peaceful, placid) but very __?__ (distant).
4. The __?__ (delicate) __?__ (pertaining to flowers) design drew lavish praise.
5. The __?__ (dashing, brave) cavalier was as much a __?__ (heathen) as any of the islanders with whom he fought.
6. The epidemic ran __?__ (unrestrained), and the doctor was deluged day and night with __?__ (pressing) calls.

Unit 15

Write the words that are incomplete, filling in the missing letters.

1. The gener__ called to canc__ the meeting with his riv__.
2. The lab__ on the barr__ was marked "norm__" in penc__.
3. Rur__ boys are civ__ and loy__.
4. The attractive mod__ was awarded a med__ for scholarship by her gallant princip__.
5. A little stage fright is norm__ unt__ you l_se contr__.
6. Take a physic__ exam before you trav__ in the centr__ area.
7. I await your approv__ of my nov__, but try not to be too critic__.
8. She sat in the chap__ and listened to a mor__ discourse.
9. This jew__ is artific__, and therefore only ornament__.
10. Patr__ the gates with a pist__; shoot at the Dev__ if you see him.

Unit 16

Write on a separate paper the word that goes in each blank:

1. I __?__ (beseech) you not to __?__ (twist) the truth.
2. It is better to __?__ (slip away from) the dangers which __?__ (entice) you.
3. To __?__ (arouse) an outburst like the Boston Tea party was to __?__ (kindle) a full-scale rebellion.
4. You __?__ (comply) to his demand but __?__ (object to) its severity.
5. To __?__ (lay under long attack) a dog with threats is less effective than to __?__ (pat fondly) him gently.
6. Crowds __?__ (overcrowd) the stores in December, but not because they __?__ (hold in awe) the stores or their owners.

Unit 17

Write on a separate paper the word that goes in each blank:

1. The __?__ (one who is learning a trade) offered to __?__ (trade) his watch for a rifle.
2. The pilgrim brought __?__ (gifts to the needy) to the __?__ (religious leader).
3. The __?__ (acting ruler) has a fear of __?__ (witchcraft).
4. Col. Beardsley's __?__ (expedition) paused before the ancient __?__ (holy place).
5. Joan will need an __?__ (conductor) for her __?__s (adventures) as a spy.
6. The inspector made a __?__ (route) around the old church to check its __?__ (supports).

Unit 18

Fill in the missing letters of the words that are incomplete.

1. We us____ly (ordinarily) call a ph_____ (doctor) be_____ (for the reason that) we might be held li____ (subject to) for damages.

2. Pre_____ (bias against) does def_____ (distinct) harm to soc____ (people generally) and to standards of just____ (fair play).

3. The vict_m wore sat____ (a glossy, silk fabric) at the time of the tra____y (catastrophe).

4. Col____ (school above high school) gener____y begins on W_____day.

5. It is dang_____ (risky) and disadvant_____s (detrimental) to p_rs____ (follow) a fire engine.

6. It is a gr__vous sacr_l____ (blasphemy) to follow Sat_n's standard.

7. The cand____te (one seeking office) drank ch_____ (cocoa drink) at Niag____ Falls.

8. A Christ____ is rever____ about his relig____.

9. Com____y (humor) and a hum____s (funny) spir_t often have a medical value like asp____n.

10. The champ__n gained glam__r by his rec_nt vict__ry.

Unit 19

Write on a separate paper the word that goes in each blank:

1. Crowds __?__ (cry noisily) and fires still __?__ (burn very slowly) in the devastated city.

2. Try not to __?__ (mix up) the reports of your __?__ (stay) in Antarctica.

3. Did you __?__ (hold back) part of your savings or do they continue to __?__ (diminish)?

4. To __?__ (puzzle) an enemy is to __?__ (hinder) his plots.

5. The threat of doom __?__ing (suspended, hanging) over her did not serve to __?__ (punish, refine) her.

6. He __?__d (pledged) not to let them __?__ (shrink) and die.

Unit 20

Write on a separate paper the word that goes in each blank:

1. His __?__ (light brown) eyes showed his __?__ (calm sober) nature.
2. __?__ (a deep, brilliant blue) is hardly a __?__ (soft, pale) shade.
3. Putty is __?__ (readily shaped) __?__ to (before) hardening.
4. The __?__ (dark green) islands of the South Seas are rarely __?__ (barren, forlorn).
5. __?__ (scorching) criticism is no more maddening than __?__ (lukewarm) praise.
6. Dr. Chool expressed an __?__ (unintentional) preference for __?__ (artificial) foods.

Unit 21

Write the words that are complete, filling in the missing letters.

1. If that cr__ture thr__tens you, use wool as a w__pon.
2. Their d__nt (climb down) into the t__ (grave) was sol__ and dignified.
3. The for__gn dancer wore ermi__ in the pag__nt.
4. Our __chology (science of behavior) teacher is ill with __eumonia, and we fear for his h__lth.
5. The surg__n fell from a le__e (rocky shelf) and suffered a bad br__se.
6. The g____l (fiend) terrorizing the nei__borhood was never cau__t.
7. His con____ce told him the vill__n deserved to forf__t his veng__ce.
8. The capt__n's carr__ge waited near the br__ge (structure over a river) for a fr____t train.
9. The g__t (spectre) a__nds (comes up) from the c__sm (deep fissure) to buy bisc__ts and br__d.
10. Ni__ty d__cons (church officials) will be present at the mar__ge of their sover__n.

Unit 22

Write on a separate paper the word that goes in each blank:

1. The __?__ (bottom beam) of the __?__ (sailing ship) broke on the rock.
2. A __?__ (light warship) was sighted to __?__ (the right side of a ship).
3. The desperate crew made their __?__ (place of tying up a ship) next to the __?__ (floating marker).
4. Almost no __?__ (spray) was produced by the ship as it sailed through the __?__ (calm area).
5. Look to __?__ (side away from wind), my __?__ (sailors)!
6. The ship foundered in the __?__ (Asiatic seasonal wind), sinking in 100 __?__ (units of 6 feet) of water.

Unit 23

Write on a separate paper the word that goes in each blank:

1. The high __?__ (waterfall) was hidden by __?__ (heavy growth).
2. An __?__ (landslide) deposited this __?__ (large rock) on the lawn.
3. There is a __?__ (low mound) in the middle of the __?__ (swamp).
4. Only a narrow strip of the __?__ (sky) can be seen from the bottom of the __?__ (gorge).
5. There is a __?__ (small village) on the far side of the __?__ (small lake).
6. A __?__ (high tableland) often has a rocky __?__ (kind of land).

Unit 24

Write the words that are incomplete, filling in the missing letters:

1. Father will go to p___ces when he discovers that you dec___ved him about his n___ce.
2. Our n___ghbor is eating chow m___ with a g___sha girl.
3. She f___gned illness to gain l___sure, but her misch___f was soon discovered.
4. I perc___ve that you rec___ved the pr___st with a br___f speech.
5. R___n in the horses; this sl___gh is going too fast.
6. She heard a w___rd shr___k from a f___ce f___nd while trying to find rel___f.
7. S___ze a s___ve for Herr Gottl___b and his financ___rs.
8. Did you ach___ve the bel___f in hyg___ne class that caff___ne is harmful?
9. An ath___st will not d___n to recognize the D___ty.
10. The h___t of the c___ling affords a v___w of the whole n___ghborhood.

Unit 25

Write on a separate paper the word that goes in each blank:

1. Do you like to __?__ (make sport of) your friends and __?__ (imitate) your elders?
2. Elephants __?__ (leap about playfully) in the circus ring while clowns __?__ (joke) lamely.
3. Puppies like to __?__ (frolic) on the lawn, and children love unrestrained __?__ (light-hearted fun).
4. A __?__ (clown) likes to __?__ (mock by imitating in an overdone manner) important people.
5. The __?__ (humorous imitation) of the school song made education appear to be a __?__ (something absurd).
6. The girl's __?__ (silly talk) convinced me that she was a party to some kind of __?__ (joke, fraud).

PART **II**

ROAD SIGNS

You will find one of four symbols beside each illustrative sentence in the regular units, thus:

v to mark a *verb* form of the base word or a synonym of the base word

av to mark an *adverb* form of the base word or a synonym of the base word

n to mark a *noun* form of the base word or a synonym of the base word

aj to mark an *adjective* form of the base word or a synonym of the base word

In the spelling units a number of the most troublesome words are marked with a red star, thus: *

ROAD SIGNS

UNIT ONE

WORDS HAVE FAMILIES

Words, like animals and human beings, come in groups, much like families. Each word has relatives, and these relatives resemble each other in important ways. Take the word *kind* as an example. One of its family members is *kindness*. Another is *kindly*. *Kindliness* is close of kin to *kindly*.

The *kind* family also has relatives that are just the opposite in temperament. *Unkind* is one, and *unkindness* is another. *Unkindly* is a third.

Now consider the *fierce* family—*fierce, fierceness, fiercely*. All have the same six letters, *f-i-e-r-c-e* at the beginning, with *i* before *e*, and the sound is *ee*.

Meeting words in families helps you understand them. You would probably know what a *kindless* villain is without looking in the dictionary. *Superfierceness*, if there were such a word, would mean fierceness beyond anything you ever saw before.

Meeting words in families helps spell them, too. In each word of the *fierce* family, *i* comes before *e*. In fact *i* usually comes before *e* except after *c* when the sound is *ee* (Part One, Unit 24).

Group I

How well do you know the families of everyday words? Can you fill each of the blanks below? Copy the guide words and go to work:

Example:	glad	gladness	gladly
1.	__?__	madness	__?__
2.	__?__	__?__	sadly
3.	__?__	loudness	__?__
4.	clear	__?__	__?__
5.	__?__	cleanness	__?__
6.	*__?__	__?__	fiercely
7.	cautious	__?__	__?__
8.	__?__	awfulness	__?__
9.	__?__	happiness	__?__
10.	__?__	__?__	holily

QUESTS

1. Words 9 and 10 require a slight change in spelling to get from the *-ness* form to the base word. What is the change? What other words can you think of, like *weary*, that make the same change?
2. What two-letter prefix in front of *clear* makes it just the opposite? Place the same prefix in front of Nos. 5, 9, 10 and write the three forms for each. Change the first letter of the prefix, apply it to *cautious*, and write the three forms and then use them in sentences.
3. Write the three forms of *strange, prompt, clever,* and *empty* in columns as done in the exercise above.
4. For each of the three forms of the words that you found in Quest No. 3, write sentences showing how the meaning changes as the form changes.
5. Write another noun form of *clearness.* What is the basic spelling change that has occurred?

Group II

Fill in the blanks in the table below. In each case the second form will end in *-ment* and the third in *-able*. In two cases, however, the *e* at the end of a word in the first column is omitted in the second column. Do not write in this book.

1.	agree	__?__	__?__
2.	pay	__?__	__?__
3.	__?__	__?__	employable
4.	__?__	*government	__?__
5.	__?__	encouragement	
6.	__?__	*argument	__?__
7.	__?__	judgment	
8.	manage	* __?__	* __?__
9.	__?__	__?__	replaceable
10.	__?__		*noticeable

QUESTS

1. Why do the last three keep the *e* in the *-able* form? (Hint: What is the consonant in front of the *e* in each case? What would happen to the pronunciation of this consonant if the *e* were dropped?)
2. Write the *-ment* form of:

advance	assign	develop	fulfill
adjust	attach	*disappoint	improve
amuse	commence	entertain	induce
appoint	command	equip	postpone
*arrange	conceal	establish	require
			settle

3. *Acknowledge*, like *judge*, has a missing *e* in the *-ment* form. Write this form of the word in a sentence to illustrate the way it is used.
4. What happens to the *-ed* form and the *-ing* form of *club, equip, ship, worship, kidnap?* Can you explain why? (See Part One, Unit 4)

5. Summit question: By using the proper prefix, write the opposite of each of five of the *-able* words above in Group II. Five use *un-*, one takes *dis-*, and one requires *ir-*. Can you explain the *ir-*?
6. Compose a paragraph using ten or more words in this group.

DICTATION

Write the following sentences from dictation:
1. The tone is clear and loud.
2. The man hoped for happiness as well as holiness.
3. The lion's fierceness made the trainer cautious.
4. They worked for the establishment of good government.
5. We will need new equipment for replacing the old tools.
6. It is a room in which to entertain notables.
7. She is too excitable and disagreeable for the job.
8. The boy's good judgment made him employable.
9. There was a noticeable change in the settlement.
10. We were disappointed because the boat proved unmanageable.

SUMMIT EXERCISE

Write the proper form of the word in parentheses.

1. Do you like her __?__ (arrange) of the flowers?
2. Mules are noted for their __?__ (stubborn).
3. Her __?__ (cautious) kept her out of trouble.
4. The dog barks __?__ (fierce) at strangers.
5. The man's directions were __?__ (not clear).
6. Her goal in life is the pursuit of __?__ (happy).
7. The account is now due and __?__ (pay).
8. Avoid an __?__ (argue) if you can.
9. The bonds are __?__ (retire) in ten years.
10. Have you an __?__ (acknowledge) of your order?
11. A reliable man is __?__ (can't replace him) on this job.
12. A careless man is __?__ (can't employ him) at any price.

(The next word-building unit is Unit No. 5, p. 133.)

UNIT TWO

DO WORDS

WISE WAYS TO ACT

What, in terms of the words at the right, would you do with:

1. A bomb? __?__ it. Why?

2. A murderous maniac? __?__ him.

3. An unjust law? __?__ it.

4. A war hero? __?__ him.

5. A taste for sweets? __?__ it.

6. A murder clue? __?__ it.

7. An empty wardrobe? __?__ it.

The Words

First Group

1. emit
2. exhort
3. extol
4. immerse
5. indulge
6. invoke
7. modify
8. qualify
9. recede
10. verify

Second Group

1. obviate
2. pulsate
3. replenish
4. rescind
5. segregate

121

DO WORDS—First Group

1. **EMIT** . . . . to give forth, to voice

   v A foghorn emits a sleepy grunt.
   n Soup-eating noises are unpleasant emissions.
   n Ultraviolet rays are one of the sun's emissions.

2. **EXHORT** . . . . to urge, entreat

   v "I exhort you to be patient," the speaker pleaded.
   n The teacher's exhortations about health scared Martha.

3. **EXTOL** (ĭk·stōl′) . . . . to praise, laud, glorify

   v We extol the courage of George Washington.

4. **IMMERSE** . . . . to dip, plunge into a fluid

   v Immerse the bearing in kerosene.
   n What is baptism by immersion?
   aj Are you ever immersed in a book?

5. **INDULGE** . . . . to yield to (a desire); enjoy

   v Does Gracie often indulge her fondness for fudge?
   aj An indulgent parent usually lets you do what you please.
   n Wide reading is an indulgence that makes Jack do better work.

6. **INVOKE** . . . . to call upon (for aid), appeal to

   v The judge will invoke an old law to hold the man for trial.
   n The invocation comes at the beginning of a church service.

7. **MODIFY** . . . . to change somewhat

   v He had to modify his plans for the building.
   n Rain caused modification of the plan for the picnic.
   n An adjective is a modifier.

8. **QUALIFY** . . . . **to make or render (oneself) fit; to limit**

    v Only a high school graduate can qualify for the job.
    v An Eagle Scout is well qualified for officer training.
    n Good eyesight is one of the qualifications of a pilot.

9. **RECEDE** . . . . **to go or move back**

    v The flood waters began to recede.
    aj Uncle Henry has a receding hair line.
    n The organ played a recessional.

10. **VERIFY** . . . . **to confirm, make certain**

    v Did you verify the figures about employment?
    n The court will demand verification of each claim.

Second Group

1. **OBVIATE** . . . . **to remove, take out of the way**

    v A big breakfast will obviate the need of stopping for lunch.
    aj The crack in the chimney is obvious (evident, easy to see).

2. **PULSATE** . . . . . **to throb, beat, vibrate (with rhythm)**

    v The woods fairly pulsate with new life in the spring.
    n The pulsations of the engine ceased suddenly.

3. **REPLENISH** . . . . . . **to (re)fill, make complete again**

    v The plane crashed before it could replenish its fuel supply.
    n Replenishment of exhausted soil is part of the program.

4. **RESCIND** . . . . **to cancel, annul, make void**

    v We voted to rescind the motion raising the dues.
    v The coaches refused to rescind the ruling.

5. **SEGREGATE** . . . . . . **to separate, isolate, set apart**

    v Doctors always segregate patients who have scarlet fever.

FIRST PRACTICE SET

Write the meaning of the italicized words in the sentences.

1. The fifes *emit* a shrill sound as the players *recede*.
2. The coach *exhorts* his players not to *indulge* in midnight feasts.
3. He must *immerse* himself in the work if the boys *invoke* his aid.
4. Jane may *qualify* as a nurse if she will *modify* her behavior.
5. The President never fails to *verify* his facts. Even his enemies *extol* his accomplishments.
6. No one can *obviate* the danger of trying to *replenish* the food supply under enemy fire.
7. The law will *segregate* the criminal from society.
8. You could feel the strings *pulsate* as he plucked them.
9. The town council will *rescind* its order.

SECOND PRACTICE SET

Place a base word of the unit where it fits best.

1. A girl confronted by a mouse will __?__ a yell.
2. One is tempted to __?__ the doughnut in the cup of coffee.
3. The train will __?__ as it leaves the station.
4. A legislature will __?__ a bad law it has passed.
5. A minister or priest will often __?__ his people to live right and to __?__ divine aid in doing so.
6. A Republican orator is likely to __?__ Abraham Lincoln.
7. A noisy office girl needs to __?__ her behavior.
8. A boy who hears he can win a $10,000 prize will __?__ the offer and then __?__ for it.
9. A girl with a quart of ripe strawberries will __?__ her fondness for them.
10. A man about to start for Mars will __?__ with excitement.
11. A hiker with an empty canteen will __?__ it.
12. Police will __?__ a killer and thus __?__ the danger.

UNIT THREE

WHAT IS (S)HE LIKE?

SELLING THINGS

How would you fill the blanks?

    The competition is —?—, but if I am very —?— and —?—, I feel sure I shall succeed. I must not be —?— about meeting prospects, and I should not be too —?— when they tell me how poor they are. Women customers are said to be more —?— than men, but I have found them more —?—.
Discuss the different answers that may be given, either before or after you study the unit.

Traits

First Group

1. charitable
2. congenial
3. consistent
4. haughty
5. impulsive
6. pliable
7. prudent
8. ruthless
9. stolid
10. wayward

Second Group

1. affable
2. boisterous
3. diligent
4. gullible
5. timorous

TRAITS—First Group

1. **CHARITABLE** . . . kindly (in judging), help-giving (to needy)

   aj Marvin takes a charitable view of his mother's actions.
   aj CARE is a charitable activity which sends food abroad.
   n The organization depends on charity for its support.

2. **CONGENIAL** . . . . similar in tastes, agreeable

   aj The two boys are congenial because they both like sports.
   aj Writers like the congenial climate of Southern California.
   n Salesmen have to cultivate congeniality.

3. **CONSISTENT** . . . agreeing (with itself), in harmony, uniform

   aj Are your actions consistent with your beliefs?
   n The consistency of the gravy (uniform thickness) is good.
   aj The two accounts of the crime are inconsistent.

4. **HAUGHTY** . . . . proud, disdainful

   aj "Pride goeth before destruction, and an haughty spirit before a fall." (Proverbs, 16:9)
   n Alice's haughtiness irritated her girl friends.

5. **IMPULSIVE** . . . . quick to speak or act, very responsive

   aj Peter is in the "doghouse" because he was impulsive.
   n Is it impulsiveness which makes him offer to do the work?
   n Joyce's impulsiveness makes her say or do things hastily.

6. **PLIABLE** . . . . easily influenced, flexible

   aj Stan's father is more pliable than his mother.
   n Her pliability got her into too many activities.

7. **PRUDENT** . . . . wise, cautious, discreet

   aj It was prudent of Connie to ask for advice.
   n His prudence kept Jim from entering the cave.

8. RUTHLESS . . . . merciless, cruel, pitiless

   aj The dictator's troops waged ruthless warfare.
   n The ruler's ruthlessness caused a revolt.

9. STOLID . . . . impassive, not easily excited

   aj Though accused of murder, the prisoner remained stolid.
   aj Elephants are stolid as well as immense.

10. WAYWARD . . . . unruly, disobedient, contrary

   aj The teachers found Sandra very wayward.
   n Waywardness is willfulness that often winds up woefully.

Second Group

1. AFFABLE . . . . pleasant, friendly, amiable

   aj George is an affable companion when he feels well.
   n His affability makes him popular.

2. BOISTEROUS . . . . noisy, disorderly, violent

   aj The two newsboys are a boisterous pair.
   n Their boisterousness broke up the Scout meeting.

3. DILIGENT . . . . hard-working, industrious

   v "Seest thou a man diligent in his business? He shall stand
   before kings." (Proverbs 22: 29)
   n Diligence was one of Benjamin Franklin's traits.

4. GULLIBLE . . . . . too willing to believe, easily deceived

   aj Quack doctors get rich on people who are gullible.
   n Sideshows exploit (take advantage of) one's gullibility.

5. TIMOROUS . . . . nervously afraid, timid

   aj A timorous mouse darted under the baseboard.
   n The lady's timorousness was very amusing.

FIRST PRACTICE SET

Copy the italicized words and beside each write its meaning in the sentence:

The catcher is *affable,* but the pitcher is rather *haughty* at times. He is *ruthless* when in good form but *prudent* about arguing with the umpire. The first baseman is *impulsive* and *pliable.* The shortstop is *stolid* like a bull; nothing gets by him. The third baseman is *consistent* at bat and *diligent* in chasing balls. The second baseman is rather *boisterous* and *gullible* off the field. The coach keeps everybody at his best by being *congenial.* He chides us about our *timorous* playing at times, and he is not very *charitable* when we play badly. However, the *wayward* antics of the batboy keep us in good spirits.

SECOND PRACTICE SET

Which of the base words in this unit applies most readily to each of the following? Answer first the ones you are sure about and later rearrange as necessary. Use each word only once.

1. Modeling clay? __?__
2. Boys in a reform school? __?__
3. An ox? __?__
4. The Community Chest? __?__
5. A cautious banker? __?__
6. A bold gangster? __?__
7. The climate of the South Sea Islands? __?__
8. A lordly peacock? __?__
9. The team that always wins? __?__
10. Quick generosity? __?__
11. A Halloween party? __?__
12. A hesitant driver? __?__
13. A painstaking worker? __?__
14. A believer in Santa Claus? __?__
15. A friendly pilot? __?__

UNIT FOUR

HOW DOES (S)HE ACT?

ATTITUDES

Use a word from the list at the right to describe the state of affairs at the left.

1. Cruelty to prisoners —?—

2. An intentional insult —?—

3. Sneaking past the sentry —?—

4. A puppy punished for seizing a sandwich —?—

5. An off-hand manner —?—

6. Stamping one's foot angrily —?—

Manner Words
First Group
1. callous
2. casual
3. deliberate
4. irate
5. passive
6. peevish
7. resolute
8. stealthy
9. surly
10. wistful

Second Group
1. contrite
2. demented
3. despondent
4. flippant
5. hysterical

HOW DOES (S)HE ACT?—Manner Words

1. **CALLOUS** . . . . unfeeling, hardened
   aj Could anyone be callous in the presence of starvation?
   n Callousness toward suffering is criminal.

2. **CASUAL** . . . . offhand, occurring by chance
   aj A casual inspection of the car showed that the frame was bent.
   n The casualness of her refusal irritated him.

3. **DELIBERATE** . . . . intentional, intent of purpose, unhurried
   aj His remark about Sue's slowness was a deliberate insult.
   aj The teacher's explanation was careful and deliberate.
   v Judge Hawkins will need a week to deliberate (reflect unhurriedly) on the case.
   n After hours of deliberation, the coaches adopted the rule.

4. **IRATE** . . . . angry, enraged, indignant
   aj My refusal to lie about the mistake made him irate.
   n The dog's ire (wrath) was aroused by a cat.

5. **PASSIVE** . . . . inactive, indifferent
   aj In the rush for seats, Dad remained passive.
   aj A cow is a rather impassive (stolid) creature.

6. **PEEVISH** . . . . fretful, irritable, cross
   aj Illness made Aunt Mazie peevish and demanding.
   n Peevishness destroys many friendships.

7. **RESOLUTE** . . . . . determined, having a fixed purpose
   aj Columbus was resolute when his men wanted to turn back.
   n Joan of Arc never wavered in her resoluteness.

8.   STEALTHY . . . . sly, sneaky, secret

   aj A stealthy footstep was heard in the kitchen.
   n The thief's stealth(iness) did not save him.

9.   SURLY . . . . crabby, snappy, ill-natured

   aj A surly answer makes the coach irate.
   n One guard's surliness cost him his life when the prisoners broke loose.

10.   WISTFUL . . . . thoughtful, wishful, yearning

   aj His wistful eyes stared off into space.
   n Ellen's wistfulness is one of her charms.

Second Group

1.   CONTRITE . . . . . . deeply sorry (for a sin or wrong)

   aj "A broken and a contrite heart, O God, thou wilt not despise." (Psalms, LI, 17.)

2.   DEMENTED . . . . insane, unbalanced

   aj The Persian violinist was apparently demented.
   n Senile dementia is the "madness" of old age.

3.   DESPONDENT . . . . discouraged, disheartened

   aj Losing the race made Randy despondent for a while.
   n His despondency was short-lived.

4.   FLIPPANT . . . . . . silly, frivolous, not serious enough

   aj Doctors dislike flippant remarks about painful illnesses.
   n Teachers do not like flippancy.

5.   HYSTERICAL . . . . highly excited

   aj A mouse made Rose hysterical.
   n War spreads panic and hysteria.

FIRST PRACTICE SET

Copy the italicized words and beside each word write its meaning in the sentence.

1. The old wise man was *passive* and *wistful*.
2. The Nazi general was *resolute* and *callous*.
3. The cat was *stealthy* and *deliberate* as she waited.
4. Mr. Orne became *irate* at his son's *surly* manner.
5. Such a *casual* remark shouldn't make you so *peevish*.
6. Junior is very *contrite* about the *flippant* letter.
7. The man is *demented*.
8. A policeman made a woman driver *hysterical*.
9. The news of the accident made her *despondent*.

A PRANK

Write the word that is appropriate for each blank in the anecdote below, putting in first those words you are sure about.

"You must have been __?__ when you bought it!" Sue exclaimed when she saw Sammy's new purple suit. Her manner was __?__ and unconcerned to the point of being __?__. Sammy, who was in an active, not a __?__ mood, decided to punish Sue, and he was very __?__ in his purpose.

After a long search, he found a snake in a ditch, made a __?__ entry into his sister's room, and, with __?__ care, arranged it in her favorite chair. Sue became __?__ when she found it and ran away so fast she collided with Dad, knocking him downstairs.

Dad, his glasses broken, was really __?__. Sammy suddenly became very __?__ when he saw what had happened and rather __?__ too, for he thought his father was hurt badly. Sue, however, acted __?__ and even __?__ because Dad did not get out of her way. Mother, realizing Dad was not hurt, made a __?__ remark but cast a __?__ look on the broken glasses.

UNIT FIVE

SOME FAMILIES ARE LARGE

The *Mercy* family, which came to the English language from Latin (*merces - mercedis*) by way of French (*merci*), is one of the larger families:

mercy—merciful—mercifully—mercifulness—unmerciful— merciless—mercilessly, mercilessnesss, and so on.

Many common words belong to large families, and each member of the family is sometimes a help in saying exactly what one wants to say, without using long pauses, delays, or verbal detours.

Group I

Copy the guide words and fill each blank:

Noun Form	Adjective Form	Adverb Form	Noun Form
1. __?__	awful	__?__	__?__
2. skill	__?__	__?__	__?__
3. __?__	__?__	__?__	trustfulness
4. __?__	__?__	willfully	__?__

Group II

Copy the guide words below, and fill each blank:

Noun Form	Adjective Form	Adverb Form	Noun Form
1. defense	__?__	__?__	__?__
2. __?__ (*luck*)	hapless	__?__	__?__
3. __?__	__?__	senselessly	__?__
4. __?__	__?__	__?__	witlessness

Group III

Ishness isn't always admirable, but it runs in some families. Can you place it in the following?

Noun Form	Adjective Form	Adverb Form	Noun Form
1. fool	__?__	__?__	__?__
2. __?__	girlish	__?__	__?__
3. __?__	__?__	mannishly	__?__
4. __?__	__?__	__?__	peevishness

Make an Ish family of *ghoul, clan,* and *style.*

What is the root and root meaning of *fool?* From what source do the other three words in Group III come?

WORD-BUILDING EXERCISE

Write the most suitable form of the word in parentheses.

1. The thief took advantage of the girl's __?__ (no defense).
2. Elaine was stubborn and __?__ (will).
3. George Washington is famous for his __?__ (truth).
4. The man failed because of his __?__ (no tact).
5. His __?__ (peeve) makes him unpopular.
6. The __?__ (plenty) of supplies was encouraging.
7. Hubert is __?__ (clan) and unsociable.
8. The explorer's __?__ (no fear) was much admired.
9. Her income was __?__ (pity) small.
10. Her account was highly __?__ (fancy).

(The next word-building unit is Unit No. 9, p. 147.)

UNIT SIX

FACING THE MULTITUDE

"SHORTY"

Which words fit the blanks?

"Shorty," the captain of the basketball

team, is six feet four inches tall. Naturally

he plays center because of his —?—. The

coach often —?—s him for his —?—, with

—?— as a result. His —?—, like his height,

is amazing. He suffers pangs of strong —?—

whenever the team loses a game.

Words

First Group

1. assert
2. beguile
3. commend
4. confide
5. confront
6. fortify
7. imply
8. surmise

Second Group

1. agony
2. contempt
3. egotism
4. prowess
5. remorse
6. stamina
7. stature

135

FACING THE MULTITUDE—First Group

1. **ASSERT** . . . . to declare, state, put forward

   v Father will assert his authority if the fight continues.
   n Are all of the pilot's assertions true?

2. **BEGUILE** . . . . to charm, deceive, ensnare

   v Can we beguile you into mowing the lawn?
   n The stranger's beguilements induced him to leave.

3. **COMMEND** . . . . . . to praise, approve, compliment

   v We commend Columbus for his bravery and perseverance.
   n A hero does not usually ask for commendation.

4. **CONFIDE** . . . . to entrust (secrets)

   v A boy can confide in his father.
   v The woman to whom the general confided was a spy.
   n The sick man had unlimited confidence in his doctor.

5. **CONFRONT** . . . . to face, oppose

   v American justice permits a man to confront his accuser.
   v "Let us confront our enemies boldly," the leader cried.

6. **FORTIFY** . . . . to make strong

   v Neither side could fortify Boston in the Revolutionary War.
   v The makers of cereals fortify them with vitamins.
   n The Maginot Line was a French fortification.

7. **IMPLY** . . . . to hint, indicate without saying

   v If you run away, you imply that you are afraid.
   n Clouds contain the implication that a storm is coming.

8. SURMISE . . . . to guess, suppose, infer

    v I surmise from the way you dress that nights are cool here.
    n The idea that trees attract lightning is more than a surmise.

Second Group

1. AGONY . . . . extreme suffering, acute anguish

    n The woodsman endured the agony of his crushed legs as well as he could.
    aj An agonized shriek awoke us.
    v Mrs. Gibson continues to agonize over her sister's death.

2. CONTEMPT . . . . low opinion, disrespect, scorn

    n People treated Larry with contempt when they found he could not be trusted.
    aj A contemptuous smile formed on Sally's lips.

3. EGOTISM . . . . . . (sense of) self-importance, conceit

    n The sophomores accused the four freshmen of egotism.
    n To some readers Walt Whitman sounds like an egotist.
    aj George makes the egotistical claim that he is the best player on the team.

4. PROWESS . . . . superior skill, bravery, valor

    n Custer is famous for his prowess in Indian warfare.
    n Bill admires the prowess of a jet pilot he knows.

5. REMORSE . . . . sorrow for one's sins, regret

    n The killer showed no remorse when he was caught.
    aj Hitler was a remorseless ruler.

6. STAMINA . . . . power of resistance, endurance

    n Civil servants must have the moral stamina to refuse bribes.
    n Mountain climbing tests a person's stamina.

7.   STATURE   .   .   .   .   .   .   (bodily) height, size or grandeur

  n Pigmies are men of small stature.
  n Governor Harris is a man of great political stature.

PRACTICE SET

Copy the italicized words and beside each write its meaning in the sentence.

1. You did not *assert* yourself enough for the scoutmaster to *commend* you.
2. The message seems to *imply* that Mr. Whybegood will *fortify* himself with all the facts before he *confronts* his audience.
3. Alfred would not confide to anyone his *agony* of guilt.
4. Your *egotism* is without end.
5. Zacchaeus, a man of small moral *stature,* felt little genuine *remorse* for his dishonest ways.
6. Delilah was able to *beguile* Samson into revealing the secret of his *stamina.*
7. I *surmise* that Tarzan was a man of real *prowess.*
8. Do not show *contempt* for the man who *confides* in you.

CAPTAIN SPOTTYWOODE

Which of the base words fits best in each blank?

Captain Spottywoode, a man of ample waistline, but short __?__, was nevertheless a man with unbounded __?__. He disguised his lack of __?__ on the march by his ability to fool his commanding officer and to __?__ the opposite about himself. He would __?__ the general with tales of his own ability to __?__ the enemy with a smile of __?__ on his lips. Once he even tried to __?__ that only he knew best how properly to __?__ a town. But, the general had begun to __?__ the truth about Spottywoode. Pretending to __?__ him for his ability, the general ordered him to hold an easy position from the enemy. Spottywoode's failure led to an __?__ of shame for him and he felt __?__ that he had ever boasted. No longer did he __?__ in the general about his __?__.

UNIT SEVEN

UNTIRING VIGILANCE

HISTORIC FACTS

Which word from the list at the right fits best in each blank?

1. The Chinese worship their —?—s.

2. The Mayflower was tossed upon the —?—s.

3. Nathan Hale faced his —?— bravely.

4. The Declaration of Independence resulted from a —?— in American affairs.

5. The British lost much of their —?— when Cornwallis surrendered.

6. Americans have always regarded George III as a somewhat demented —?—.

Words
First Group

1. ancestor
2. beacon
3. billow
4. chivalry
5. crisis
6. domain
7. obstacle
8. ordeal
9. rampart
10. tyrant

Second Group

1. attire
2. eloquence
3. maneuver
4. revel
5. vigil

UNTIRING VIGILANCE—First Group

1. ANCESTOR . . . . forefather, forbear

    n Queen Elizabeth I was an ancestor of Queen Elizabeth II.
    n One of his ancestors came to America on the *Mayflower*.

2. BEACON . . . . a signal or warning (light)

    n The old lighthouse served as a beacon to mariners.
    n Mount Fujiyama serves Tokyo as a beacon by land, sea, and air.

3. BILLOW . . . . a huge wave, swell, surge

    n "All thy waves and thy billows are gone over me." (Psalms 42:7)
    v Smoke began to billow from the burning tanker.
    aj Petticoats make a party dress balloonlike and billowy.

4. CHIVALRY . . . . knighthood, courtesy to women

    n Sir Galahad was a model of chivalry.
    aj Carrying the girls' books was a chivalrous act.

5. CRISIS . . . . turning point, critical situation

    n A crisis came when Don had to decide whether to go to college or go to work.
    n The sinking of the *Lusitania* in 1915 brought on a crisis.

6. DOMAIN . . . . one's territory, estate, sphere of activity

    n A county was once the domain of a count.
    n The British long regarded the seas as their special domain.

7. OBSTACLE. . . . . . . hindrance, barrier, impediment

    n A tree trunk was the obstacle that blocked the trail.
    n George Washington Carver faced life with courage.

8. **ORDEAL** . . . . . a severe trial, very trying experience

 n Going to the dentist is a familiar ordeal.
 n Football is an ordeal if one does not enjoy it.

9. **RAMPART** . . . . . . a protecting barrier or bulwark

 n The steep hill served as a rampart for the village.
 n "Guard well the ramparts of American freedom!"
 n "O'er the ramparts we watched," sang the chorus.

10. **TYRANT** . . . . a ruthless ruler, dictator

 n George III was a tyrant who goaded the Americans to rebel.
 aj Elizabeth Barrett had a tyrannical father, according to biographers.

Second Group

1. **ATTIRE** . . . . clothing, apparel

 n Spring calls for gay attire.
 v Janet should attire herself more suitably.

2. **ELOQUENCE** . . . . speaking power and skill

 n Daniel Webster's eloquence stirred the nation.
 aj Bill can be eloquent when he wants to use the family car.

3. **MANEUVER** . (tricky) operation, shrewd act, piece of strategy

 n Parking parallel to the curb is a difficult maneuver.
 v By offering to do his homework, Sally tried to maneuver George into taking her to the party.

4. **REVEL** . . . . merrymaking, a celebration

 n The witches' revel began in the mountains at midnight.
 v Joan revels in the thought that summer is almost here.
 n Why does revelry usually take place at night?

5. VIGIL . . . . wakeful watching

n The anxious vigil at Lincoln's bedside lasted all night.
a| The vigilant watchman heard strange noises.
n Vigilance is necessary where rattlesnakes abound.

PRACTICE SET

Copy the italicized word and beside each write its meaning in the sentence.

1. The ghost of one of his *ancestors* appeared on the *rampart*.
2. Billow rose upon *billow* but none was high enough to blot out the *beacon*.
3. Equal rights for women created a *crisis* for *chivalry*.
4. No *obstacle* discourages a *tyrant*.
5. Defending their *domain* was a costly *ordeal* for the citizens.
6. The king's *eloquence* had magical power throughout the land.
7. The captain wore military *attire* to the *maneuvers*.
8. Sounds of *revel* disrupted the *vigil* in the chapel.

THE WAR

Fill each blank with the most appropriate base word from this unit. Do not write in the book.

His __?__ had lived in England. One had been a knight, well versed in the code of __?__, but now he himself had the spirit as well as the homespun __?__ of an American. He became a bright __?__ light of patriotism and courage, undaunted by the might of British power. In the __?__ that resulted after the Boston Tea Party, he joined in the __?__ to protect American liberties. He spoke with great __?__ and fought with great bravery.

He was wounded in the __?__s at Bunker Hill. There his men set up such an __?__ for the British that the battle was more an __?__ than the rout they had expected it would be. The redcoats that swarmed in __?__ up the hill never were able to overrun the American __?__s and heavy losses spoiled their nightly __?__s. The __?__ who had sent them to fight the colonists could not hope to win, and his __?__ lost a bright pearl.

UNIT EIGHT

OBJECTS AND ACTIONS

MOSQUITOES

Fill each blank wisely from the list at the right. Do not write in the book.

We —?— the mosquitoes which —?— us. Somehow they —?— the screens and annoy us so that we cannot —?— on the game we are playing. Smoke and spray —?— their numbers for only a short time, and we therefore cannot —?— this method of dealing with them. Perhaps putting oil on the ponds were they breed will —?— their numbers.

Actions and Objects

First Group

1. combat
2. concentrate
3. confound
4. diminish
5. distinguish
6. encumber
7. endorse
8. obstruct
9. penetrate
10. restrict

Second Group

1. replica
2. residue
3. specimen
4. venison
5. vortex

143

ACTIONS AND OBJECTS—First Group

1. **COMBAT** . . . . to fight against, oppose

    v The new drugs help doctors to combat disease.
    n The millionaire's son was killed in combat.
    aj The boy displayed a combative attitude when police questioned him.

2. **CONCENTRATE** . focus one's forces or powers, gather together

    v During the Battle of Britain Churchill decided to concentrate the British army along the shores of Southern England.
    n Walter's powers of concentration are remarkable.

3. **CONFOUND** . . . . . to throw into confusion, perplex

    v Gideon's men employed a strange maneuver to confound their enemies.

4. **DIMINISH** . . . . . . to lessen, decrease, make smaller

    v Kay's mistakes will diminish as her skill in typing grows.
    aj The price of stocks will vary, but the dollar value of a bank account remains undiminished.

5. **DISTINGUISH** . . . . . to see clearly, observe differences

    v With field glasses, we could distinguish three figures on the ridge of the roof.
    v It is often difficult to distinguish between courage and foolhardiness.
    aj Jim had a distinct (clearly seen) feeling he had said the wrong thing.

6. **ENCUMBER** . . . . to burden, weigh down

    v Why let bad habits encumber you?
    n Excess weight is a needless encumbrance.
    aj Armor was very cumbersome (burdensome).

7. ENDORSE (INDORSE) . . . . to approve, sign over

    v I heard Fred endorse your candidate.
    v His endorsement must imply that he will help elect the man.
    v Did you endorse the check? Your endorsement is necessary before it can be cashed.

8. OBSTRUCT . . . . to block or hinder

    v It took more than a tornado to obstruct the work.
    n Obstructions on the road included boulders a foot high.

9. PENETRATE . . . . to pierce, cut, or spread through

    v Most bullets will not penetrate a tank's armor.
    n Prof. Sawmill is a man of unusual penetration.

10. RESTRICT . . . . to limit or confine

    v During the war we had to restrict the use of gasoline.
    n The city imposes numerous restrictions on the use of guns.

Second Group

1. REPLICA . . . . . a copy, reproduction (of a work of art)

    n East Springfield, Illinois, is a replica of the village where Lincoln lived in the 1830's.
    n This paperweight is a replica of the Lincoln Memorial.

2. RESIDUE . . . . that which remains

    n Ashes are the residue of a fire.
    aj Soot is a residual deposit in a furnace or fireplace.

3. SPECIMEN . . . . a sample, typical example

    n Experts examined a specimen of the handwriting.
    n Here is a set of specimen leaves to identify.

4. VENISON . . . . deer meat

    n Pioneers like Daniel Boone ate venison.
    n Venison is a delicacy much sought after by hunters.

5. VORTEX . . . . a whirlpool, eddy

     n The crate whirled a while on the edge of the vortex.

     n The roaring vortex of the tornado veered toward the house.

PRACTICE SET

Write the meaning in the sentence of each italicized word.

1. If a student will *concentrate* on his math problems, they will not *confound* him.
2. *Combat* the fires with a spray and thus *diminish* the fire area.
3. Debts *encumber* a person and *restrict* the fun he can have.
4. Can you *distinguish* what it is that *obstructs* the entrance?
5. You would not *endorse* the man if you could *penetrate* his reasons for wanting the job.
6. The *venison* we ate was merely a *specimen*.
7. The *residue* of the fund will be spent upon a *replica* of a Ben Franklin stove.
8. Sherry could not hold her own in the *vortex* of school activities.

THE HIKE

Write words that fill each blank properly.

Darkness came, but we kept on. We had flies to __?__ and fallen logs to __?__ our path. It was difficult to __?__ trail markers because our eyes would not __?__ the cone-like __?__ of whirling fog that seemed to lie ahead. We had heavy packs to __?__ us, too, and sheer weariness served to __?__ our zeal.

The maze of paths began to __?__ us, and the more we would __?__ on finding the right one, the more bewildered we were. Only a __?__ of our courage was left. We had no more dried __?__ or any other food, only a kind of crude __?__ of food in the form of a picture of peaches on the can containing our bacon grease.

The failure of our only flashlight helped to __?__ us further and make us aware that we could not __?__ the kind of light of which it had been a source.

UNIT NINE

USING THE PRECISE WORD

Sometimes you think of a word you want to use, but it does not fit. For example, you want to say that you lost the ball game yesterday because Joe wasn't there. You could say:

"Joe's absence made us lose the game."

Or you could say:

"Joe's not being there made us lose the game." Or,

"We lost the game because Joe was absent."

If you want to report that Daddy talked last night as if his mind were on something a long way off, you could say it in three words:

"Daddy talked absently."

This unit is an activity in thinking of several different forms of a word and spelling them correctly. Copy the guide words and for each blank supply a word that ends like the other words in the column:

Group I

Adjective Form	*Noun Form*	*Adverb Form*
Example: absent	absence	absently
1. abundant	__?__	__?__
2. convenient	__?__	__?__
3. __?__	distance	__?__
4. __?__	__?__	evidently
5. __?__	magnificence	__?__
6. __?__	__?__	obediently
7. patient	__?__	__?__
8. __?__	__?__	presently
9. __?__	permanence	__?__
10. __?__	__?__	violently

147

QUESTS

1. From what language do the first five of these words come?
2. What is the basic verb form for *defiantly, excellently, obediently, presently, silently,* and *violently?* the usual adjective and noun form for *instantly, defiantly,* and *excellently?*
3. Write the opposite of the adjective form in lines 4, 6, 7, and 10 of Group I by putting *in-, im-, dis-,* or *non-* in front of the word.
4. Write the *-cy* noun form for *agent, recent, accurate, decent.*

Group II

Fill each blank in the following.

Verb Form	-ing Form	Noun Form
1. admire	__?__	__?__
2. *__?__	__?__	cancellation
3. confirm	__?__	__?__
4. __?__	__?__	explanation
5. initiate	__?__	__?__
6. __?__	observing	__?__
7. __?__	__?__	organization

QUESTS

1. What is the noun form ending in *-(a)tion* for: *accuse, combine,* consider, consult, examine, declare,* destine, expect, explore, identify,* imagine, inform, inspire,* install, invite, irrigate, limit, oblige, prepare, register, quote, represent, reserve, salute, situate, tempt?** for *expedite ** and *render?*
2. Make a person or agent noun from the starred verbs in the first question above by adding one letter. Example: *give—giver.* In the same way change the verb form for lines 1, 6, and 7 of Group II to a person word by adding one letter.
3. Write the past tense of *cancel, consider, limit, examine, organize, prepare, oblige, register, quote, render, represent.*
4. Write the form ending in *-able* or *-tive* for lines 1, 4, and 6 of Group II; for *imagine, inform* and *quote?*

Group III

Can you fill all the blanks correctly?

	Verb Form	*Person or Agent*	*-ion (Noun) Form*
1.	* __?__	celebrator	__?__
2.	__?__	competitor	__?__
3.	__?__	communicator	__?__
4.	__?__	__?__	cultivation
5.	__?__	decorator	__?__
6.	demonstrate	__?__	__?__
7.	generate	__?__	__?__
8.	__?__	__?__	navigation
9.	operate	__?__	__?__
10.	* __?__	__?__	solicitation

QUESTS

1. What is remarkable about the endings of the words in the second column? Is there anything in Part One, Unit 12 which would lead you to expect this?
2. Write the verb form for *association, affection, appreciation, anticipation, collection, completion, cooperation, conviction, desperation, devotion, distribution, education, elimination, graduation, imitation, indication, investigation, location, population, prohibition, visitor.*
3. Write the form ending in *-tive* for five of the verbs in Group III and for five of the words in Quest No. 2 above.

SENTENCES FOR PRACTICE

Write the following from dictation:

1. A lending organization will investigate the plan to irrigate.
2. Your cooperation in keeping silent is much appreciated.
3. The speaker at graduation quoted an explorer.
4. Did you observe the location of the Indian reservation?
5. There was an abundance of appreciative celebrators.

6. "I want to set up a permanent agency," he declared.
7. Evidently they are excellently prepared.
8. She is patient, affectionate, and obedient.
9. He was tempted to cancel the plan to operate a bus.
10. A letter confirmed the conversation with his competitor.

WORD-BUILDING EXERCISE

Fill each of the blanks correctly, using any correct form of the word in parentheses. Do not write in the book.

1. The captain yelled __?__ (defy). There was a __?__ (defy) look on the halfback's face.
2. House-to-house __?__ (solicit) is prohibited.
3. There is a law against __?__ (not decent) books. The Legion of D__?__ (decent) opposes bad movies.
4. His father was once the __?__ (navigate) of a big bombing plane.
5. *Bungalow* has a Hindu __?__ (derive).
6. The __?__ (devastate) was hard to believe.
7. The serpent was the __?__ (tempt) in the Garden of Eden.
8. My __?__ (inform) was a nurse at the hospital.
9. From the mountain one can see __?__ (no limit) stretches of prairie land.
10. They lived in hourly __?__ (expect) that the ship would founder.

(The next word-building unit is Unit No. 13, page 163.)

UNIT TEN

BUSINESS WORDS

FINANCE

What word from the lists at the right best
fits in each blank?

1. Q: What do you do when you impose a
   new tax?
   A: You __?__ it.
2. Q: How do you find out whether you are
   making a profit?
   A: You consult the __?__.
3. Q: How do you buy a $1,000,000 factory
   when you have only $100,000?
   A: You borrow $900,000 on a __?__.
4. Q: How can you keep the owner from selling the factory to someone else while you
   are making up your mind?
   A: You take or buy an __?__ on it.
5. Q: What does the factory become, once
   you own it?
   A: It becomes an __?__.
6. Q: What do you need to start in business?
   A: You need __?__.
7. Q: What does interest do?
   A: It __?__s.

First Group

1. arrears
2. asset
3. capital
4. ledger
5. lien
6. mortgage
7. option
8. rebate
9. revenue

Second Group

1. accrue
2. assess
3. consign
4. exempt
5. inflate
6. levy

151

BUSINESS WORDS—First Group

1. **ARREARS** . . . . amount overdue

   n Your loan is $1200.00 in arrears.
   n The Grays are trying to pay up the arrears on their car.

2. **ASSET** . . . . something of value that one has

   n Land and money in the bank are material assets.
   n Courage, brains, and tact are all intangible assets.

3. **CAPITAL** . . . . wealth (invested or to invest)

   n You must have capital to start a business.
   n That bank has a capitalization of $9,000,000.

4. **LEDGER** . . . book for recording money received and spent

   n The ledger in the desk drawer is posted to March 1.
   n If the debits exceed the credits in the ledger, the business is losing money.

5. **LIEN** . . . . a claim on property (to secure a debt)

   n A tax lien makes it possible for the city or county to take over the property if you do not pay your taxes.

6. **MORTGAGE** . paper pledging property as security for a debt

   n You give the owner a mortgage to secure a loan on a house.
   v You can mortgage your car if you need money.

7. **OPTION** . . . . . . choice, prior right to buy something

   n You have the option of buying the rugs on consignment.
   aj Headrests are optional equipment on certain cars.

8. **REBATE** . . . . return of part of amount paid

   n Do your parents get a rebate on their income tax payments?
   n You can get a rebate on your airplane ticket.

9.   REVENUE . . . .   income, proceeds (from business or taxes)

    n The revenue collected by ten-cent stores is tremendous.
    n You pay your income tax to the Bureau of Internal Revenue.

Second Group

1.   ACCRUE . . . . . .   to be added (as a normal growth)

    v Interest on deposits accrues at the rate of 3% per year.
    n Accrual (accruement) at this rate (semiannually) will double
      the amount deposited in 23 years.

2.   ASSESS . . .   to set a value on, impose a charge or penalty

    v The bank will assess the house and tell you how big a loan
      its value warrants.
    n The tax assessment is $500 on the assessed value of $30,000.
    n The county assessor says the land is worth more now.

3.   CONSIGN . . . . . .   to hand over, assign, deliver

    v If Uncle Herb goes, he will consign Sylvia to my care.
    n A consignment of rugs came in Saturday.

4.   EXEMPT . .   to excuse, release from (a duty to which others are
                                                  subject)

    v The law exempts churches from taxation.
    n The man next door requested exemption from jury duty.
    aj Certain kinds of bonds are tax exempt.

5.   INFLATE . . . . . .   to expand, fill with air or spirit

    v Winning the state championship will inflate Gary's ego.
    n Why does price inflation reduce the value of a dollar?
    aj Raising wages can have an inflationary effect on prices.

6.   LEVY . . . .   to impose (a tax, fine, etc.)

    v The 1920 Congress voted to levy an income tax.
    n The levy brought in more money than was expected.

FIRST PRACTICE SET

Copy the italicized word and beside each write its meaning in the sentence.

1. George III tried to *levy* unjust taxes, but he got an entirely unexpected kind of *"revenue"* from them.
2. Charges *accrue* if you do not pay promptly, and a *lien* can be placed on your goods.
3. You had an *option* on the land, but you had to let it lapse because your *assets* were not sufficient to take it up.
4. The *ledger* shows that you had *arrears* due last year.
5. Does the government *exempt capital* invested abroad from taxation?
6. Take out a *mortgage* on the house and I will *consign* it to you.
7. The state will *assess* any *rebate* that dealers give.
8. Why does loaning too much money tend to *inflate* prices?

SECOND PRACTICE SET

Fill all the blanks correctly, using each base word in this unit once. Do not write in the book.

1. The state will __?__ an income tax this year.
2. Does that __?__ show both income and expenses properly?
3. Interest on bonds begins to __?__ at once.
4. Those who are in __?__ on their taxes have their names published in the paper.
5. All __?__ from ticket sales goes to charity.
6. Will they ever be able to pay off the __?__?
7. __?__ that lot to the warehouse.
8. An __?__ is something you have on the credit side of the balance.
9. A __?__ was placed against his car until he paid the tax.
10. Mrs. Skimp received a tax __?__ this year.
11. You need __?__ in order to start a business.
12. Spiraling wages and prices __?__ the value of the dollar.
13. The town will __?__ you for street repairs.
14. No one is __?__ from paying that tax.
15. An __?__ to buy gives you first call on that property.

UNIT ELEVEN

SOUP TO NUTS

THE BANQUET

Can you fill each blank edibly?

1. The —?— potatoes looked like a set of pick-up sticks.

2. The —?— on the lemon pie was at least two inches thick.

3. The weather is too cold for a —?—.

4. Coffee was served —?—.

5. Potatoes —?— are made with cheese.

6. Instead of a frozen dessert he chose an —?—.

7. Stale peanuts taste —?—.

Dishes and Ways

1. au gratin
2. demitasse
3. éclair
4. fricassee
5. julienne
6. lyonnaise
7. meringue
8. mousse
9. sauté
10. soufflé

Taste and Fitness

1. brackish
2. edible
3. potable
4. rancid
5. saline

DISHES AND WAYS—First Group

1. **AU GRATIN** (ō′grä′tən)   .   .   covered with browned bread crumbs
   - **aj** Au gratin potatoes were listed on the menu.
   - **av** Oysters are sometimes served au gratin.

2. **DEMITASSE** (dĕm′ĭ·tăs)   .   (in) a small cup (of or for black coffee)
   - **av** Mrs. Boodles served coffee demitasse.
   - **n** "Demitasse with dessert," the program said.

   Demitasse literally means half cup.

3. **ECLAIR** (ā·klâr′)   .   bun-shaped shell filled with cream; cream puff
   - **n** The bakery sells fresh éclairs.
   - **n** Bobby bought an éclair on the way home from school.

4. **FRICASSEE** (frĭk′ə·sē)   .   meat cut in pieces and cooked in gravy;
   a kind of stew
   - **n** Do you like fricassee of veal?
   - **n** Fricassee of chicken is fried chicken pieces.

5. **JULIENNE** (jōō·lĭ·ĕn′)   .   .   cut in thin strips; soup containing thin
   strips of vegetable
   - **av** The carrots were served julienne (in slender strips).
   - **aj** The first course that day was soup julienne.

6. **LYONNAISE** (lĭ·ə·nāz′) . . . . cooked with onions
   - **aj** Men like lyonnaise potatoes.
   - **av** Liver is usually served lyonnaise.

   The word **lyonnaise** in French means *as in Lyon.*

7. **MERINGUE** (mə·răng′)   .   .   frothy egg-white-and-sugar covering
   - **n** She ate the meringue off the pie first.
   - **n** A meringue looks like whipped cream.

8. **MOUSSE (mo͞os)** . . . a frozen mixture of gelatin and cream

   n For dessert one could have either a chocolate eclair or a strawberry mousse.

9. **SAUTÉ (sō·tā′)** . . fried lightly all over (and turned frequently) in a little fat

   aj Jim liked onions sauté.
   aj Sautéed liver is delicious.

10. **SOUFFLÉ (so͞o·flā′)** . . . . a spongy baked dish

    n Do you know how to fix cheese soufflé?
    n An omelet is a soufflé of eggs.
    n A soufflé is ordinarily lightened with beaten egg whites.

TASTE AND FITNESS—Second Group

1. **BRACKISH** . . . . flat, somewhat salty

   aj The water from the spring turned brackish.
   n Because of the brackishness of the well water, summer visitors buy spring water.

2. **EDIBLE** . . . . fit to eat, suitable for food

   aj Horse meat is edible if not appetizing.
   n Scientists are discussing the edibility of seaweed.
   aj Dog flesh is considered inedible.

3. **POTABLE (po′tə·bəl)** . . . . fit for drinking

   aj River water is not potable as a rule.
   n A potage (pō·täzh′) is a thick soup.

4. **RANCID** . . . . having a "strong" or stale taste

   aj Butter becomes rancid in hot weather.
   n Rancidity occurs in nuts, too.

5. **SALINE** (sā′līn) . . . . salty

    aj Gargling a saline solution helps a sore throat.
    n The Dead Sea water has excessive salinity.

        Explain the name **Salina** Street in Syracuse, N. Y.

FIRST PRACTICE SET

Copy the italicized words and beside each write its meaning in the sentence:

1. The *julienne* soup, oysters *au gratin*, cheese *soufflé*, and strawberry *mousse* made a splendid meal.
2. Susie ate the *meringue* off the pudding and helped herself to an *éclair*.
3. We ordered *fricassee* of lamb and *lyonnaise* potatoes.
4. Kippered herring has a fishy, *saline* taste and is for many persons not very *edible*.
5. Swamp water is not *potable* until it has been purified.
6. Olive oil sometimes becomes *rancid*, and stale ginger ale could be called *brackish*.
7. *Sautéed* mushrooms make a tasty dish; a *demitasse* is a bracing beverage.

SECOND PRACTICE SET

Write the word that goes in each blank.

1. Potatoes may be eaten __?__ (with cheese), __?__ (in thin strips), or __?__ with onions.
2. Meat may be cooked __?__ (diced with gravy) or __?__ (fried lightly all over in butter).
3. For dessert, you can have an __?__ (a frozen cream) or __?__ (frothy pudding).
4. That which is __?__ (stale) or __?__ (too salty), or __?__ (flat and salty) is not __?__ (fit to eat).
5. A large dinner in the evening often ends with a __?__ (half cup of strong coffee).
6. Cheese __?__ is a light, puffy dish.
7. I do not call this soup __?__ (fit for drinking).

UNIT TWELVE

LASTING DEEDS

WORD PICTURES

A Summer Evening

We like to watch the waves splash along the shore while we __?__ about the stars and wonder what __?__s on Mars. We'd like to __?__ some of our pennies into gold coins and forget forever the __?__ which says, "A penny saved is a penny earned." Tomorrow's work in an __?__ called a school will come all too soon to __?__ these pleasant fancies. This work is a way to __?__ some of the world's knowledge and wealth.

First Group

1. adage
2. apostle
3. bounty
4. compact
5. courier
6. edifice
7. minimum

Second Group

1. inherit
2. protrude
3. ratify
4. reinstate
5. speculate
6. supplant
7. transmute
8. transpire

LASTING DEEDS—First Group

1. **ADAGE** . . . . wise saying, proverb, maxim

   n "Murder will out" is a familiar saying.
   n "Haste not, rest not" is a German adage.

2. **APOSTLE** . . . one sent to promote an idea or undertaking

   n Paul was an apostle to the Gentiles.
   n The Senator toured Asia as an apostle of good will.
   aj An apostolic delegate was sent to the conference.

3. **BOUNTY** . . . . free giving, gift, reward

   n Spring flowers are one form of Nature's bounty.
   aj Autumn often brings bountiful harvests.
   n The government once paid a bounty to those who killed
   wolves and other harmful animals.

4. **COMPACT** . . . . a solemn agreement or contract

   n The Mayflower Compact was an agreement the Pilgrims
   made before they landed.
   aj Portable radio sets are very compact (small in size).

5. **COURIER** . . . . runner, messenger

   n The courier arrived at dawn.
   n The Marines on Iwo Jima communicated by couriers.

6. **EDIFICE** . . . . (large) building or structure

   n Though in ruins, the Colosseum in Rome is still an impos-
   ing edifice.
   n The Empire State Building is New York's tallest edifice.

7. **MINIMUM** . . . . the smallest allowable amount

   n Illness reduced Mr. Johnson's strength to a minimum.
   v It would be very foolish to minimize the danger of a war.

Second Group

1.   INHERIT   .   .   .   .   .   .   to receive by birth or bequest

    v As an only son, Philip will inherit all his father's property.
    aj The inheritance tax will amount to $50,000.
    v Claire inherited her father's red hair and his hot temper.
    n Freedom of religion is part of the American heritage.

2.   PROTRUDE   .   .   .   .   .   .   to thrust out, jut out, project

    v The ladder will protrude from the rear of the car.
    n One's nose is a facial protrusion.

3.   RATIFY   .   .   .   .   to approve or confirm

    v The Senate would not ratify the Covenant of the League of
      Nations.
    n Ratification of the new trade agreement may reduce the
      price of cars.

4.   REINSTATE   .   .   .   to restore to the original place or standing

    v The company discharged a man but had to reinstate him.
    n The court ordered his reinstatement.

5.   SPECULATE   .   .   .   .   .   .   to guess, wonder, theorize

    v Martha likes to speculate about life on Mars.
    n Speculation in stocks is buying on the expectation or theory
      that the stock will go up in value.

6.   SUPPLANT   .   .   .   .   supersede, displace

    v The Confederate government in Richmond tried to sup-
      plant the Federal government in Washington.
    v Why can't love supplant hate in all of our lives?
    n Jacob was called "The Supplanter."

7.   TRANSMUTE   .   .   .   to change into something finer, transform

    v The alchemists tried to transmute baser metals into gold.
    n Transmutation of fear into courage is a stirring feat.

8. TRANSPIRE . . . to happen, come to pass, become known

> v It transpired that the king's chief adviser was actually in league with the enemy.

PRACTICE SET

Copy the italicized words and beside each write its meaning in the sentence:

1. Jesus promised that each *apostle* would *inherit* eternal life.
2. All but two unions were ready to *ratify* the *compact*.
3. Why *speculate* about what the *courier* will bring?
4. The *bounty* on buffaloes was reduced to a *minimum*.
5. No matter what *transpires*, the board will *reinstate* him.
6. An *adage* says that necks which *protrude* may get broken.
7. A new management will *supplant* the present one when the new *edifice* is completed.
8. Will you *transmute* your good will into good deeds?

QUIZ

Place each word where it fits best, using each of the base words in this unit once. Do not write in the book.

1. The __?__ about going "from pillar to post" involves objects that __?__, especially the post.
2. He was called "the __?__ of freedom" because he arranged a __?__ providing for equal rights.
3. Buckingham Palace is a London __?__. What __?__s there is front-page news.
4. The company will __?__ the guarantee it discontinued or __?__ it with a better one if the directors __?__ the new plan.
5. The actor did not want to __?__ with the stocks included in the __?__ from his father.
6. The __?__ who told the news got a __?__ from the King.
7. A healthy human body with a __?__ of discomfort can __?__ plain food into beautiful eyes and lovely hair.

UNIT THIRTEEN

ITY

"Are you sure?" the reporter asked.

"Certain," she replied.

Her knowing without any doubt about the depth of the pool saved everybody a lot of trouble.

What word could be used in place of *knowing without any doubt,* assuming that she *was* certain and not merely positive about it? The word is *certainty.* Noun, verb, or adverb forms of common adjectives will often save time-wasting verbal detours.

Sometimes you need only to add *-y* or *-ty* to an adjective form to get a noun form. More often *-ity* is required. Frequently the final *e* on the adjective becomes the *i* or *ity.* What word goes in each blank below?

	Adjective	Adverb	Noun
1.	__?__	certainly	__?__
2.	__?__		difficulty
3.	honest	__?__	__?__
1.	__?__	absurdly	__?__
2.	minor		__?__
3.	__?__	__?__	personality
4.	public	__?__	__?__
5.	__?__	__?__	solemnity
1.*	curious	__?__	__?__
2.	__?__	humbly	__?__
3.	__?__	__?__	profanity
1.	able	__?__	__?__
2.*	__?__	__?__	probability
3.	__?__	nobly	__?__

163

QUESTS

1. Explain the spelling changes. Consider the root as well as the problem of pronouncing.
2. Write the -*ly* (adverb) and -*ity* (noun) forms of *acid, active, *electric, equal, false, fatal, fraternal, immense, modern, modest, native, necessary, original, possible, real, reliable, responsible, sane, secure, severe, simple, *sincere, vain.*
3. Under what conditions does a double *l* appear in the -*ly* (adverb) forms? Note that the final *e* of an adjective is usually not dropped in forming the adverb. What is the -*ity* form for *captive? liable? major? prior? senior?*
4. List five familiar prefix-formed opposites of the base forms in the tabulation of the preceding page and ten from the words in No. 2 above.

WORD-BUILDING EXERCISE

For each blank supply the correct form of the word in parentheses:

1. Railroad men have __?__ (senior) in their jobs.
2. The __?__ (not probably) of the tale was apparent.
3. The Labor Day weekend brought many __?__s (fatal).
4. His __?__ (vain) was apparent to everyone.
5. A person who is __?__ (not responsible) is not __?__ (necessary) insane.
6. It is __?__ (not noble) to be __?__ (not sincere).
7. The contractor was worried by the __?__ (immense) of the task and the __?__ (not certain) regarding obtaining materials.
8. The __?__ (severe) of the storm created a feeling of __?__ (solemn).
9. His __?__ (humble) is sometimes mistaken for __?__ (not able).
10. Treating a man __?__ (fraternal) gives him a feeling of __?__ (secure).

US AND US-NESS

Another word pastime consists of collecting families that belong to a tribe known as the *-oussians* (pronounced "us-sians"). Supply the word which goes into each blank in the following lines and spell it correctly:

Base Form	Adjective—Adverb Form	Noun Form, -ness
1. danger	__?__	__?__
2. humor	__?__	__?__
3. __?__	perilous(ly)	__?__
4. __?__	poisonous(ly)	__?__
5. __?__	__?__	vigorousness
6. ★__?__	__?__	villainousness

The following have slight variations in spelling. Be vigilant and, if necessary, use the dictionary as you write down the guide words and fill the blanks:

1. __?__	__?__	famousness
2. __?__	__?__	gloriousness
3. __?__	gracious(ly)	__?__
4. harmony	__?__	__?__

QUESTS

1. Why is the *i* added in *gracious?*
2. Expand each of the following into a line like the ones above, using the dictionary if you are doubtful: *ambition, bile, continue, curiosity, envy, fury, industry, injury, marvel, *mystery, nerve, prosper, ridicule, space, study, treachery, vary. Bile* behaves like *grace* even though it does not have a *c.* Write the prefix-opposite of five of the adjective forms.
3. Write a line like the ones above for *advantage* and *courage,* remembering that a *g* needs an *e* to keep it soft. Do *conscience,* remembering *essential* on page 158. What is the *-ous* form of *anxiety? courtesy? generosity?*
4. What *-ous* word means *before? delightful to taste? huge?*
5. What is the prefix-opposite of *gracious? glorious? harmonious?*

A FINAL FLING

Write the word which goes in each blank:

1. __?__   sparkled   __?__
2. __?__   __?__   tackling
3. tickle   __?__   __?__

Construct a similar table from *grumbling, handle, resembled, ruffling, sampling, stumbling, tangled, trembling, trifled,* and *tumble.*

Write the *-le* word for the name of a holy book; a finger cover used in sewing; a place of worship; a write-up in a magazine.

WORD-BUILDING EXERCISE

Write for each blank the correct form of the word in parentheses:

1. Murder is a __?__ (villain) crime.
2. "I won't do it!" is an __?__ (not grace) remark.
3. The __?__ (poison) of the drug is so great that one drop will kill a man.
4. The __?__ (space) of the new library pleased us.
5. An attack of __?__ (bile) kept him out of school.
6. The letter was a __?__ (humor) account of our trip.
7. __?__ (not harmony) sounds are very disturbing.
8. The runner was __?__ (tackle) behind the goal line.
9. __?__ (study) habits will help you in college.
10. The new method proved quite __?__ (advantage).

(The next word-building unit is Unit No. 16, p. 175.)

UNIT FOURTEEN

WORKADAY WORDS

PROJECTS

Fill each blank with the word that best fits using the list at the right.

Wood is —?—. It will —?— only if exposed to the weather without paint for many years. Brick is more —?—, but it is less —?—. It will not —?— as readily as new wood or a painted surface. —?—d brick will not absorb moisture and is therefore not —?—.

The Words

First Group

1. anneal
2. baste
3. bevel
4. congeal
5. erode
6. fuse
7. glaze
8. gyrate
9. tarnish

Second Group

1. acrid
2. durable
3. ductile
4. porous
5. resilient
6. viscous

WORKADAY WORDS—First Group

1. **ANNEAL** . . . . . to toughen, temper by heat treatment

    v We anneal each frame to make it less brittle.
    aj Education is a mind-annealing process.

2. **BASTE** . . . . to sew loosely (with long stitches); to moisten (roasting meat); to hit, strike or beat

    v Mother bastes a dress before sewing it on her machine.
    v Roast turkey should be basted with melted fat from the pan.
    v Joe threatened to baste his brother for telling on him.

3. **BEVEL** . . . . to cut on a slant or at an angle

    v Be sure to bevel the baseboards along the top.
    n Mark the bevel clearly where you want it cut.

4. **CONGEAL** . . . . to freeze, stiffen

    v Does a murder story congeal your blood?
    aj Zero weather has a congealing effect on the grease in a car.
    n Congealment of jelly requires pectin.

5. **ERODE** . . . . to wear away, eat away

    v Soft teeth erode rapidly.
    n The hills are barren because of soil erosion.

6. **FUSE** . . . . to melt (together), to blend by heat

    v Sugar crystals will fuse when heated.
    v Sand and soda fuse to form glass.
    n Marriage is a fusion of two lives.

7. **GLAZE** . . . . to coat with glass, become glassy

    v To glaze porcelain is to coat it with glass.
    aj His eyes were glazed (glassy) after the knockout punch hit him.

8. GYRATE . . . . to whirl, revolve

     v The dancer gyrates gracefully on one foot.
     v A gymnasium fairly gyrates with activity.
     n The pitcher's gyrations were intended to confuse the batter.

9. TARNISH . . . . . . to discolor, lose luster, besmirch

     v Stainless steel will not tarnish readily.
     v Silverware tarnishes rapidly.
     v The singer's reputation began to tarnish.

Second Group

1. ACRID . . . . sharp, bitter, biting

     aj Vinegar has an acrid taste.
     aj Acrid remarks make enemies.

2. DUCTILE . . . . easily drawn out

     aj Copper and gold are ductile metals.

3. DURABLE . . . . lasting, long-wearing

     aj Canvas is a durable material.
     n The speaker discussed the durability of our friendship with
     England.

4. POROUS . . . having tiny openings (that allow water and
                                                moisture to seep into)

     aj Unglazed earthenware is quite porous.
     n The porousness of a sponge makes it very useful.
     n The usefulness of a filter depends on its porousness.

5. RESILIENT . . springy, returning readily to its original shape

     aj Rubber pads are very resilient.
     n The resiliency of the springs saves much discomfort.

     Cf. *elastic* (flexible, springy): rubber bands are very elastic.

6.   VISCOUS   .   .   .   .   .   .   sticky, not flowing freely, thick

     aj Molasses is very viscous.

     n Heavy oil has a high viscosity.

PRACTICE SET

Copy the italicized words and beside each write its meaning in the sentence.

1. An *annealing* oven is hot enough to *fuse* glass.
2. *Bevel* the cloth and then *baste* it.
3. Silver is *ductile* and quite *durable*.
4. Rain will *tarnish* a metal roof; in time it will *erode* a shingle roof.
5. Sponge rubber is both *porous* and *resilient*.
6. The dessert will *congeal* and take on a *glazed* appearance.
7. The *viscous* stuff in the jar gives off an *acrid* odor.
8. The winds *gyrate* ceaselessly around the peak.

TWELVE REMARKS

Fill each blank correctly. Use each base word once. Rearrange if necessary. Do not write in the book.

1. Milk on a zero morning will __?__.
2. Frost will often __?__ the pond in late October.
3. Cheap mirrors __?__ quickly.
4. __?__ a casting to toughen it.
5. Rocks __?__ slowly through the centuries.
6. The bantams __?__ as they fight.
7. A boy's clothes must be extremely __?__. Summer underwear should be very __?__.
8. Wooden bleachers are more __?__ than brick would be.
9. Medicine usually tastes __?__, and cough medicine with honey in it is quite __?__.
10. Red-hot blocks of the metal have a tendency to __?__, and glass is more __?__ than most persons realize.
11. Rafters and molding must be __?__ed to fit.
12. __?__ the meat two or three times every hour.

UNIT FIFTEEN

VILLAINY

JESSE JAMES

Fill each blank appropriately with words chosen from the column at the right.

He was a famous b—?— who repeatedly committed the crime of —?— on a large scale. People began to —?— the feeble efforts of the police to catch him. Finally, when he held up seven victims in a single night, the people determined to —?— themselves upon him and halt the —?—s of this hated —?—.

Villainy Words

First Group
1. assault
2. avenge
3. denounce
4. pilfer
5. ravage

Second Group
1. brigand
2. depredation
3. infamy
4. larceny
5. marauder
6. turpitude

Third Group
1. blaspheme
2. encroach
3. impugn
4. malinger

VILLAINY—First Group

1. **ASSAULT** . . . . to hit, strike, attack

   v Did you see the hobo assault the barber?
   n The suspect was charged with assault and battery.

2. **AVENGE** . . . . to repay, retaliate for exact punishment

   v Orestes undertook to avenge the murder of his father.
   n Hamlet was also an avenger.

3. **DENOUNCE** . . . . . . to condemn, cry down, accuse

   v Mr. Boop likes to denounce his political enemies.
   n The Russian editorial is a denunciation of American policies.

4. **PILFER** . . . . to steal (small quantities)

   v Sam was arrested for trying to pilfer fruit from a market.
   n A pilferer was arrested—and charged with pilferage.

5. **RAVAGE** . . . . to lay waste, destroy

   v Epidemics began to ravage Europe.
   n Stone houses resist the ravages of time.

Second Group

1. **BRIGAND** . . . . robber, bandit, plunderer

   n John Dillinger was a notorious brigand.
   n Brigandage was rampant on the highways in England.

   Cf. ***desperado,*** a reckless or especially daring lawbreaker.

2. **DEPREDATION(S)** . . . . despoilment, pillage

   n The depredations of the rats ruined the stored food.
   n *Gone With the Wind* tells about the depredations by Sherman's army.

3.   INFAMY . . . .   disgrace, dishonor, reproach

   n Long will the attack on Pearl Harbor live in infamy.
   aj Two atomic spies were executed for the infamous crime of treason.

4.   LARCENY . . . .   (legal term for) theft

   n The man was charged with larceny.
   n Petty or petit larceny involves a small sum.

5.   MARAUDER . . . .   one who raids and plunders

   n A skunk in a chicken house is a marauder.
   n The sheriff's men trailed the marauder all night.

6.   TURPITUDE . . . . . .   baseness, shameful wickedness

   n Was it turpitude or weakness that made Judas betray Jesus?
   n The crimes of the Nazis mark the depths of human depravity.

   Cf. *depravity,* which is used more of one's moral condition, **turpitude** more of specific actions.

Third Group

1.   BLASPHEME . . . . . .   to curse, swear, utter profanity

   v "Do not blaspheme," the stranger warned.
   n The Third Commandment forbids blasphemy.
   aj A blasphemous retort escaped the prisoner's lips.

2.   ENCROACH . . . .   to trespass, intrude

   v Does Ellen ever encroach upon her brother's rights?
   n He will find a way to punish her encroachments.

3.   INPUGN (ĭm·pūn') . . . . . .   to assail, call in question

   v Why do you impugn the actor's honesty?

   Impugn literally means *fight against.*

4. MALINGER   .   .   .   to pretend illness (to avoid duty), to shirk

   v The new secretary seems inclined to malinger on Mondays.

   n Physical weakness makes her a malingerer.

PRACTICE SET

Copy the italicized words and beside each write its meaning in the sentence.

1. The *brigand* was a coward to *assault* an old man.
2. He was determined to *avenge* the losses he suffered at the hands of the *marauder*.
3. The accusation of baseness *impugns* my honor and *encroaches* upon my civil rights.
4. *Pilfering* pennies is a form of *larceny*.
5. Great *infamy* lay in planning to *ravage* a neutral country.
6. Is it *turpitude* that makes a man be willing to *blaspheme* and *malinger* in his duties?
7. To *denounce* their continued *depredations* is the only answer.

A CRIMINAL

Fill the blanks, using each base word once, where it best fits.

1. At the age of six Tommy began to __?__ candy from a store and to __?__ a neighbor's peach tree.
2. Later, he learned to __?__ the honesty of his parents and to __?__ upon the rights of other pupils.
3. He thought it was manly to __?__ his employer harshly for unfairness and to __?__ when he was supposed to be working.
4. Tommy was a petty __?__ in his own neighborhood before he became __?__ robbing banks.
5. He liked to __?__ loudly and dared to __?__ a policeman when he was arrested for grand larceny.
6. Prison put an end to his __?__ but not to the __?__ or __?__ of his nature.
7. He kept saying he had tried to __?__ the injustices of society.

UNIT SIXTEEN

WORD CONSTRUCTION AHEAD

The leading characters in this unit are Ance and Ence. Each is the head of a tribe which includes several families or parts of families. Each is proud of his tribal traits and eager to cleave to them.

In the table below are eight families of Ance words. If you can find a simple, sure rule to distinguish them from the Ence words, you will have achieved a notable feat.

Table I

Copy the guide words below accurately and fill all the blanks correctly. Use a dictionary, if necessary, to find the words and spell them correctly.

	Verb Form	Noun Form	Adjective Form	Opposite
1.	accept	__?__	__?__	__?__
2.	allow	__?__	__?__	__?__
3.	__?__	avoidance	__?__	__?__
4.	__?__	__?__	endurable	__?__
5.	__?__	__?__	__?__	uninsurable
6.	__?__	__?__	*resistible	__?__
7.	rely	__?__	__?__	__?__
8.	__?__	variance	__?__	__?__

QUESTS

1. Read the completed tabulation of the Ances, exaggerating the endings to fix them in mind for your ear as well as your eye.
2. Write the Ance form of *annoy, assist, comply, guide, enter, grieve, convey, maintain, observe, persevere, resemble.*

3. What is the noun form and the past tense prefix-opposite of *assist, remember, sever* (cut), *acquaint, appear, apply, attend, issue, perform, persevere,* and *suffer?* Two lose an internal *e.*

Table II

The Ances are less numerous than the Ences. The families are smaller and lack many of the forms in the table above or the table below. The Ances vary more. Quite a few are formed on simple, everyday words that come from Old English or Old French like *clear, guide,* and *hinder.* Others are rather remote, like *resonance* and *consonance.*

The table below presents the Ant branch, whereas Table I was concerned with the Ables. It is not easy to find many Ance-Ant words that commonly use all three forms. Write the guide words and complete the table. Watch No. 1 and No. 6 for spelling irregularities and No. 3 for a form simpler than Ance:

	Base Form	(Noun Form — *Ance*)	(Adjective Form — *Ant*)
1.	*appear	__?__	
2.	__?__	__?__	assistant
3.	*descend		__?__
4.	__?__	dominance	__?__
5.	__?__	__?__	ignorant
6.	__?__	significance	__?__
7.	tolerate	__?__	__?__

QUESTS

1. What is the spelling irregularity in No. 1 and No. 6?
2. Do all the Ant forms have the same function in sentences? Do all of the Ant words function at times as adjectives? Which ones rarely or never function as nouns?
3. Write the Ance form of *abundant, brilliant, clear, *disappear, elegant, endure, inherit, remember.*
4. Which words in No. 3 have an Able form?

Table III

The Ence families are larger and more regular. They include the Sist words—all but two, *Resistance* and *Assistance*. The Here words are Ences. So are the Ven words, the Verge words, and the Pend words. The Fer words are numerous and familiar, while the Cel words and the Fici words make up in frequency what they lack in numbers. Here are ten Ence words from ten different root families. Jot down the guide words and fill the blanks.

	Root	Base	ENCE	Ent Form
1.	*here*	cohere	__?__	__?__
2.	*ven*	convene	__?__	__?__
3.	*verge*	__?__	convergence	__?__
4.	*spond*	★__?__	__?__	correspondent
5.	*fide*	__?__	__?__	__?__
6.	*pend*	depend	__?__	__?__
7.	*fer*	★__?__	difference	__?__
8.	*fict*	(effect)	efficiency	__?__
9.	*cel*	__?__	__?__	excellent
10.	*sist*	__?__	__?__	__?__

QUESTS

1. Make a line like those above but omitting the last column for each of the following: *adhere* (stick to), *consistent*, *diffidence* (timidity, shyness), *defer* (show respect), *deficiency* (lack), *divergence, existent, persist, preferent* (-ial), and *provide*. One has no Base. Indicate the family in each case.
2. Write the family name and Ence form of *confer, despond* (Unit 4, page 131), *refer, sufficient* (cf. *efficient*).
3. Using a prefix is often the best way to give a word its opposite meaning. The prefix-opposite form of *confide* is *unconfident*. Write the prefix-opposite form of *cohere, convene, depend, differ, effect, excel,* and *insist*.
4. Write the family root, *Ence* form, *Able* form, and prefix-opposite form of *transfer*.

Table IV

The Ence tribe also includes several other small families included in the table below. Copy the guide words and fill the blanks.

	Family	Base	ENCE	Ent
1.	*tin*	__?__	__?__	abstinent
2.	*cide*	coincide	__?__	__?__
3.	*con*	__?__	__?__	concurrent
4.	*dulge*	__?__	indulgence	__?__
5.	*vel*	prevail	__?__	__?__
6.	*curr*	__?__	__?__	recurrent
7.	*side*	__?__	residence	__?__
8.	*vere*	revere	__?__	__?__
9.	*fice*	__?__	sufficiency	__?__
10.	*lat*	(__?__)	__?__	violent

QUESTS

1. Write the Ence forms of *consequent, diligent, eminent, equivalent, intelligent, magnificent, patient, penitent, permanent, present, prominent.*
2. Write the Ency form for *current, decent, proficient, resilient.*

WORD-BUILDING EXERCISE

Build the right word for each blank:

1. The two are at __?__ (vary) over a trifling matter.
2. The new janitor is __?__ (can't be relied upon).
3. Her __?__ (insist) on a new trial won out.
4. A fishing license for __?__s (not residents) costs more.
5. A man with heart trouble is __?__ (can't get insurance).
6. The ticket is not __?__ (can't be transferred).
7. The original document is no longer in __?__ (exist).
8. __?__ (comply) with the new law is very difficult.
9. The accident was __?__ (couldn't be avoided).
10. Tony is __?__ (not acquainted) with American ways.

(The next word-building unit is Unit No. 21, p. 195.)

UNIT SEVENTEEN

"YOU'RE IN THE ARMY NOW"

QUESTIONNAIRE

Which words from the column best answer each question? Use no word more than once.

1. What are you when you report to the Army? A —?—.

2. Where do you live? In a —?—.

3. What in the Army makes the most noise? —?—.

4. What do soldiers wear to distinguish rank or role? —?—.

5. What are the foot soldiers called? —?—.

6. Large guns are often mounted in a —?—.

First Group

1. artillery
2. barracks
3. battalion
4. cadet
5. cavalry

Second Group

1. hostage
2. infantry
3. insignia
4. recruit
5. turret

Third Group

1. decode
2. deploy
3. induct
4. infiltrate
5. muster

ARMY WORDS—First Group

1. **ARTILLERY** . . . . mounted guns, ordnance

    n Our planes attacked the enemy artillery.
    n Several artillerymen were killed.

2. **BARRACKS** . . . . . living quarters for military personnel

    n "We like our barracks nice and clean," runs the song.
    n One recruit was told to stay in the barracks until he knew the town better.

3. **BATTALION** . . large army unit, a large number (of troops)

    n Only one battalion escaped the battle.
    n One of Masefield's themes is "The men of the battered battalion which fights till it dies."

4. **CADET** . . student training to be an officer in the armed forces

    n A cadet was killed in an auto accident.
    n General Matthews served his cadetship at West Point.

5. **CAVALRY** . . . . . motorized (formerly mounted) troops

    n In Cromwell's day, the cavalry units made up the sides or flanks of an army in the field.
    aj Winston Churchill was a cavalry officer in his youth.

Second Group

1. **HOSTAGE** . . . . person held as a guarantee

    n The bandits held the banker's wife as a hostage.
    n The Austrians held the enemy commander as a hostage.

2. **INFANTRY** . . . . foot soldiers

    n Air power can disable but only infantry can occupy.
    n It takes many weeks to train infantrymen thoroughly.

3.   INSIGNIA . . . .   badges or emblems

    n Military insignia show a man's division and his rank.
    n Why don't more civilians wear insignia? (What are some kinds they do wear?)

4.   RECRUIT . . . . . .   newly enlisted soldier, new member

    n A recruit has to start as a private.
    n Recruitment of additional teachers is necessary each year.

5.   TURRET . . . .   small tower (to mount guns)

    n The tank has several gun turrets.
    n A shell hit one of the ship's gun turrets.

Third Group

1.   DECODE . . . . . .   to translate, make understandable

    v The recruit did not know how to decode the flag signals.
    v The sergeant could encode and decode radio messages.
    aj It was his duty to destroy the code books if capture seemed near.

2.   DEPLOY .   to spread out (a military force), take positions for battle

    v The 89th was ordered to deploy and surround the village.
    n The deployment of our artillery followed a novel pattern.

3.   INDUCT . . . . . .   to bring in formally, install, initiate

    v The Army Air Forces will induct a thousand recruits.
    v When will the club induct its new officers?
    n The induction will take place next week.

4.   INFILTRATE . . . . .   to slip through or into (gradually)

    v Enemy troops in American uniforms tried to infiltrate our lines and disrupt our defenses.
    n Each plant must guard against Communist infiltration.

5. **MUSTER** . . . .   to assemble, summon, gather

    v The troops will muster at dawn.

    v Shirley could not muster the courage to speak.

FIRST PRACTICE SET

Copy the italicized words, and beside each write its meaning in the sentence:

1. The *artillery* was too near the *barracks*.
2. The *cadet* found himself in the wrong *battalion*.
3. The enemy held one of the officers in the *cavalry* as a *hostage*.
4. The spy who tried to *infiltrate* our unit wore the *insignia* of the wrong *infantry* corps.
5. A *recruit* sought safety in the *turret*.
6. *Decode* the message and find out how we are to *deploy*.
7. We had to *induct* the men into the service before we could *muster* them.

UNHORSED

Fill the blanks, using each base word just once—where it fits best. Do not write in the book.

1. The __?__ who came to live in our __?__ today is an ex-jockey.
2. He wanted to join the __?__ and ride in a jeep, but he found himself on foot in a __?__ of __?__ instead.
3. He wanted to get into the __?__ and fire the big guns, but he could not __?__ the courage to go near them.
4. When a corporal called to him from the __?__ of a tank to tell him to __?__ to the east, he stumbled and fell down.
5. He could not __?__ the simplest flag signals, and he did not grasp the __?__ of rank the officers wore.
6. He would never have dared to __?__ an enemy position or seize an enemy officer as a __?__.
7. "Why did we ever __?__ him into the army?" his officer, a former West Point __?__, kept asking.

UNIT EIGHTEEN

"ANCHORS AWEIGH"

I F

Fill in the blanks properly.

1. If a storm comes up, we may have to —?— part of the cargo.

2. As the —?— water rises in the hull, it must be pumped out.

3. To watch the flying fish, we lean over the —?—.

4. The compass is housed in the —?—.

5. If we want to go on a voyage, we must first —?—.

6. Food is prepared in the ship's —?—.

First Group
1. armada
2. barge
3. bilge
4. binnacle
5. boatswain

Second Group
1. ensign
2. galley
3. gunwale
4. gyroscope
5. sextant

Third Group
1. convoy
2. embark
3. jettison
4. navigate
5. procure

''ANCHORS AWEIGH''—First Group

1. ARMADA (är·mä′də) . . an array of armed ships, large fleet

    n The enemy armada sailed toward Midway.
    n The Spanish Armada went down to defeat.

2. BARGE . . . . a large, flat-bottomed ship

    n The barge was loaded with iron ore.
    v He barged (pushed his way) in ahead of me.

3. BILGE . . . . . . dirty water in the hull; bottom of hull

    n Bilge splashed back and forth as the ship rolled and tossed.
    aj A loose bilge plate let in water.

4. BINNACLE . . . . case containing ship's compass

    n The binnacle is near the ship's wheel.

5. BOATSWAIN (bō′sən) . . a non-commissioned, or petty officer
    who has charge of rigging, anchors, and cables

    n The boatswain uses a "pipe" to call the crew to duty.

Second Group

1. ENSIGN . . the national flag; lowest rank of commissioned
    naval officers °

    ° Except for a few commissioned warrant officers.

        n Officers and men always salute the national ensign as they
        board or leave a ship of the navy.
        n The officer of the day on a small ship might be an ensign.

2. GALLEY . ship's kitchen; ancient one-decked ship driven by oars

    n The captain spent too much time in the galley.
    n Ben Hur escaped from the galley when it sank.

3. GUNWALE (gŭn′əl) . .   deck railing, upper edge of ship's side

    n Three seasick passengers bent over the gunwale.
    n Originally the gunwale served as a support for the guns.

4. GYROSCOPE .   fast-whirling wheel used as a balancing device

    n A large vertical gyroscope will keep a ship from rolling.
    aj A gyroscopic compass is surer than a magnetic compass.

5. SEXTANT . . .   instrument for measuring angular distances

    n A navigator needs a sextant to find his ship's position.
    n When Captain Ahab threw away the ship's sextant, he
    threw away his means of finding his way home again.

Third Group

1. CONVOY . . . . .   to conduct or escort (for protection)

    v Corvettes used to convoy ships through the danger zone.
    n A large convoy of Army trucks assembled.

2. EMBARK . . . .   to set sail, leave port

    v "And may there be no sadness of farewell when I embark."
    n Le Havre was the port of embarkation.

3. JETTISON . . . .   to throw overboard

    v As the storm got worse, we had to jettison the cargo.

4. NAVIGATE . . . .   to sail, plot one's course

    v No ship could navigate in such shallow water.
    aj With the aid of a few canals the entire length of the St.
    Lawrence River is now navigable.

5. PROCURE . . . .   to obtain, get, acquire

    v The chairman has to procure food for the picnic.
    n The Office of Officer Procurement interviewed candidates
    for commissions.

PRACTICE SET

Copy the italicized words and beside each write its meaning in the sentence.

1. The *boatswain* of the damaged merchantman ordered the crew to *jettison* the cargo.
2. The light near the *binnacle* could be seen from the *gunwale* of the *barge*.
3. The warship sent to *convoy* the tanker could not *navigate* in such shallow water.
4. The *ensign* tried to *procure* enough reading matter for the entire crew.
5. Each ship of the *armada* was pumping out *bilge*.
6. The men in the *galley* could not feel the vibration of the *gyroscope*.
7. The captain would not *embark* without a *sextant*.

ALL AT SEA

Which of the base words of this unit goes in each blank? Use each once—where it fits best.

1. ___?___ swishes about on the hull's bottom. The ___?___ is located in the pilothouse.
2. A corvette can be used to ___?___ a merchant ship, but is not large enough to fight a battleship; a ___?___ is not a fighting ship at all, and is awkward to ___?___ in a narrow channel.
3. Our huge ___?___ will have to ___?___ much of its equipment in order to outrun the enemy.
4. Before sailing, the captain had to ___?___ a ___?___ to chart the ship's position.
5. A young ___?___ passed down the order to ___?___ from the island port.
6. The ___?___ was overweight because he spent too little time on the rigging and too much in the ___?___.
7. A weary landsman leaned over the ___?___.
8. He kept wishing the ship had a ___?___ to keep it from rolling in the waves.

UNIT NINETEEN

"WILD BLUE YONDER"

FLYING

Which word from the column at the right best fits in each blank?

1. The main framework of a plane is its —?—.

2. An airplane banks one way or the other according to the way one sets the —?—s.

3. If a pilot flies up into the —?— without being in a pressurized cabin, he may suffer from —?—.

4. Long before a plane touches the runway, the pilot must begin to —?—.

5. If you pull a certain lever in a jet fighter, a mechanism will —?— you from the cockpit, seat and all.

6. The man in a spaceship is known as an —?—.

First Group
1. aileron
2. altimeter
3. anoxia
4. fuselage
5. turbine

Second Group
1. amphibian
2. astronaut
3. gyropilot
4. stratosphere
5. supersonic speed

Third Group
1. compute
2. decelerate
3. eject
4. propel
5. stabilize

''WILD BLUE YONDER''—First Group

1. **AILERON** (ā′lə·rŏn′) . hinged wing section for banking a plane

   n One of the ailerons jammed while the plane was in the air.

2. **ALTIMETER** . . . . instrument measuring height (of a plane above the ground)

   n A sextant may be used as an altimeter.
   n A barometric altimeter gives the height above sea level.

3. **ANOXIA** . . . . lack of oxygen

   n A pilot flying at very high altitudes without oxygen may suffer from anoxia.
   n The first symptom of anoxia is giddiness.

4. **FUSELAGE** . . . . the main frame of a plane

   n An explosion damaged the fuselage of the transport plane.
   n The fuselage of a model plane is often made of balsa wood.

5. **TURBINE** . engine driven by blast on curved blades fixed to a rotating cylinder

   n The new generator is driven by a steam turbine.

Second Group

1. **AMPHIBIAN** . . . . aircraft operating from land or water

   n An amphibian plane went down in the ocean.
   aj Frogs are amphibious (living both on land and in water).

2. **ASTRONAUT** . . . . space traveler

   n A trip to the moon will be easy for astronauts of the future.
   aj Weightlessness is a problem of astronautical travel.

3. GYROPILOT . . . . automatic pilot

    n The gyropilot keeps a plane on its course by resisting any change of direction.

    n A gyrocompass is more than a magnetic compass.

4. STRATOSPHERE . . the upper atmosphere, about 7-25 miles up

    n Jet liners fly in the stratosphere.

5. SUPERSONIC SPEED . . . . . beyond the speed of sound

    aj Jet planes frequently fly at supersonic speed.

    aj Bats emit supersonic squeaks which dogs can hear.

Third Group

1. COMPUTE . . . . calculate

    v It takes the pilot only a moment to compute the true air speed from his air-speed indicator.

    n By means of complex computation the navigator can plot the course of the plane.

2. DECELERATE . . . . to lose speed, slow down

    v The plane began to decelerate as it headed in for a landing.

    n Either deceleration or failure to attain sufficient speed will cause a plane to stall.

3. EJECT . . . . to cast or hurl out

    v Sam ejects anybody who bothers him when he is working.

    n Ejection of the pilot takes place automatically.

4. PROPEL . . . . to drive forward

    v It takes more power to propel a boat than a car.

    n Jet propulsion revolutionized the design of aircraft.

5. STABILIZE . . . to make steady or firm; keep from moving or changing

    v Gyroscopes are used to stabilize ships.

    aj Prices were very stable (unchanged) for several years.

    n That airplane has a gyro-stabilizer.

FIRST PRACTICE SET

Copy the italicized words and beside each write its meaning in the sentence.

1. One of the *ailerons* broke off from the *amphibian* plane.
2. The *altimeter* was wrong, and the pilot did not recognize the symptoms of *anoxia*.
3. The *fuselage* was not strong enough for the strain of *supersonic speed*.
4. Somehow the *gyropilot* became deranged in the *stratosphere*.
5. If the spaceship does not *decelerate* when it re-enters the atmosphere, the *astronauts* inside will be roasted alive.
6. Only an engineer can *compute* the speed at which the *turbine* operates.
7. Once it attains its orbit, a satellite will *stabilize* itself. It needs a rocket, not to *propel* it, but to *eject* the capsule it carries.

SPACE VOYAGE

Fill in the blanks below with words from the unit which fit best.

1. We are __?__s, bound for the moon, traveling at the __?__ of 20,000 miles per hour. It took a huge rocket to __?__ us into orbit.
2. Our spaceship has no __?__s since there is no atmosphere.
3. The __?__ of our ship has to be sturdy to stand the strain of launching, and it uses rocket engines instead of a __?__ with curved blades.
4. We passed through the __?__ a few seconds after blastoff, and we are now trying to __?__ our speed.
5. A spaceship needs no __?__ to keep it on its course, and the speed tends to __?__ it in its orbit.
6. Our ship is an __?__ because it can land on water or land if we ever get back.
7. We will die of __?__ if our oxygen fails.
8. Our retro-rockets will __?__ the ship to 1000 miles per hour when it reenters the atmosphere.

UNIT TWENTY

INDUSTRY AND FINANCE

PUBLIC AFFAIRS

Can you fill the blanks correctly?

1. What about the school system? —?— it, and find out what it needs.

2. What do discontented people like to do? —?—.

3. How do many of our citizens get to work? They —?—.

4. What about new industries? Encourage an —?—.

5. To pay for the schools, towns —?— a tax on property.

6. People who give to charity can —?— part of it from their income tax.

First Group

1. agitate
2. appraise
3. deduct
4. emerge
5. impose

Second Group

1. commute
2. comprise
3. deteriorate
4. eradicate
5. espouse

Third Group

1. anguish
2. gravity
3. impetus
4. influx
5. lineage

191

INDUSTRY AND FINANCE—First Group

1. AGITATE . . . . to stir up, excite

   v Fears agitate Mrs. Whipple so she cannot sleep.
   n An agitator came to stir up trouble in the town.
   n There is agitation for a 13-month calendar.

2. APPRAISE . . . . to estimate the value of

   v Ask the new dealer to appraise our car.
   n The appraiser shook his head sadly.
   n The appraisal was disappointing.

3. DEDUCT . . . . to subtract

   v A salesman forgot to deduct the value of the old typewriter.
   n There is a deduction of 2% if you pay cash.
   aj Gifts are deductible on an income tax return.

4. EMERGE . . . . to appear, come forth, rise from

   v Frank watched a dark figure emerge from the bushes.
   n The emergence of spring is very gradual.

5. IMPOSE . . . . to put (an undue burden) upon

   v Her husband's relatives impose upon her by coming for
     dinner every Sunday but never offering to help.
   n He does not regard these visits as an imposition.

Second Group

1. COMMUTE . . . to reduce or lessen (a sentence); to travel
                 regularly (especially to and from one's work and home)

   v Governor Mason will not commute the murderer's sentence.
   v The chef lives in Bugleville and commutes to the city.
   n He has been a commuter for thirteen years.

2.   COMPRISE . . . .   to make up, include, embrace

   v Ten towns comprised the region known as Decaoplis.
   v Guns taken from criminals comprise the FBI collection.

3.   DETERIORATE . .   to become corrupt, lose value, or cease to
                                   function properly

   v Machines deteriorate if they are not kept oiled.
   n Each year a manufacturer deducts from his income the deterioration of his equipment.

4.   ERADICATE . . . .   to remove, wipe out

   v Can we ever eradicate prejudice?
   n An ink eradicator is often useful.
   n Eradication of crime is difficult.

5.   ESPOUSE . . . .   to support, advocate, take as one's own

   v Lafayette was one of the first Frenchmen to espouse the American cause.
   n The President's espousal of the "common man" helped him win the election.

Third Group

1.   ANGUISH . . . .   intense suffering

   n Miriam had the anguish of seeing her brother run over.
   n A person comes into the world "on the wings of anguish."

2.   GRAVITY . . . .   seriousness, solemnity

   n The gravity of the world situation worries many persons.
   n The President spoke with great gravity.

3.   IMPETUS . . . .   momentum, drive, incentive

   n The impetus of the Confederate attack carried the fort.
   n Under the impetus of a new idea, the inventor worked day and night.

4.   INFLUX . . . .   inflowing, inpouring

   n The new factory brought an influx of metal workers.
   n An influx of settlers followed the opening of the Louisiana
   Territory.

5.   LINEAGE (lĭn′ē·ĭj) . . . .   line of descent

   n Karen traces her lineage to Priscilla Alden.
   n Mary was a maiden of the lineage of King David.

   Lineage (lĭn′·ĭj) is the number of lines devoted to something,
   usually in advertising: Each year classified advertising surpassed
   the previous year in lineage.

PRACTICE SET

   Copy the italicized words and beside each write its meaning
in the sentence.

1. We had the bank *appraise* the house.
2. Uncle George could not *eradicate* from his mind the notion
   that he could *deduct* his carfare from his income tax.
3. Will an *influx* of new pupils *agitate* the teacher?
4. Will the governor *commute* the sentence of the man who
   espoused the gangster trio?
5. The *gravity* of the danger should *impose* caution.
6. His experiences *comprise* a fine training for the sales job, and
   his self-confidence will *emerge*.
7. Mr. Morton suffered *anguish* when his health began to *deteriorate*.
8. The *impetus* of the movement grew when people understood
   its *lineage*.

UNIT TWENTY-ONE

KNOTTY KNOTS

A combat is a fight, and a person who takes part in a fight is a combatant or participant. Anyone who is not a fighter or refuses to fight becomes a *noncombatant* or *nonparticipant*. Thus a three-letter prefix *non-* has changed a fighter into a person who does not fight. Prefixes are an easy, swift, and efficient way of making words fit our needs when we want to say something a trifle complicated.

The English language has many prefixes that in some sense negate or give an opposite meaning to words to which they are attached. This unit presents twelve such prefixes and shows how they work.

OPPOSITES

Make each sentence reverse its meaning by inserting in each blank the correct prefix from the list at the right.

Prefixes of Opposition

1. anti-
   contra-
   counter-
2. non-
   un-
   in-
3. mis-

Prefixes of Separation

1. ab-
2. de-
3. dis-
4. ex-   ec-
5. se-

1. The material was —?—usable.

2. The dog is —?—contented in the house.

3. This book is strongly —?—-Communist.

4. Do you ever —?—spell the word rhythm?

5. Public executions are —?—grading.

6. Gandhi believed in —?—violent resistance.

KNOTTY NOTS—PREFIXES OF OPPOSITION

1.   ANTI-, CONTRA-, COUNTER-   .   .   against, opposing, opposite

   n   An *anti*toxin works *against* a poison.
   n   An *ant*onym is the *opposite* of a word.
   n   An *anti*septic works *against* infection.
   v   To *contra*dict a person is to say the *opposite*.
   n   A *counter*claim is an *opposite* or *opposing* claim.
   n   A *counter*balance is an *opposite* force or weight.

   Note: Quite often **ob-** means **against** as in **object, obsess, obstruct, opponent, obtrude.**

2.   NON-, UN-, IN- . . . . not

   n   A *non*resident does *not* reside where he happens to be
       living or working.
   aj An *un*wanted visitor is one who is *not* wanted.
   aj An *in*eligible person is one who is *not* eligible.

   Other examples: **nonsense, nonunion, nonexistent, unrealized,
   undesirable, unattached, ungovernable, incautious, infrequent,
   indecisive, inconvenient, inattentive.**
   Note 1: Sometimes **un-** carries the idea of reversing as in **un-
   twist, untangle,** and **undress,** but this meaning is less common
   and will seldom be confusing.
   Note 2: **In-** becomes **im-** before *m* and *p*, *il-* before *l*, *ir-* before
   r, as in **immovable, illogical,** and **irreligious.** It often means *in*
   or *into* instead of *not.* **Insert, induce,** and **inform** are examples.

3.   MIS- . . . . wrong(ly), incorrect(ly)

   v   *mis*behave—behave *wrongly.*
   v   *mis*calculate—calculate *incorrectly.*
   n   *mis*conduct—*wrong* conduct.
   v   *mis*read—read *incorrectly.*
   v   *mis*quote—quote *incorrectly.*
   v   *mis*judge—judge *wrongly.*
   v   *mis*manage—manage *badly.*

PREFIXES OF PARTING
AND SEPARATION

1. AB- . . . . away (from)
2. DE- . . . . down (from)
3. DIS- . . . . not, opposite
4. EX-, EC- . . . . out (from)
5. SE- . . . . apart (from)

v To *ab*duct is to lead *away from* or kidnap.
v If you *ab*hor something, you shrink *from* it.

v *de*populate—take the inhabitants *from*
v *de*press—push *down*
v *de*scend—climb *down*
v *dis*miss—send *away from*
v *dis*arm—take arms *from*

v *ex*clude—shut *out from*
v *ex*communicate—cut *off from* (membership)
n *ef*fusion—a pouring *out*
v *ec*lipse—a going *out of* sight, n shut *out of* sight

Note: **Ex-** is reduced to *e* before *d, g, l, m, n, r, v,* and one or two other consonants. It becomes *ef* before *f* and sometimes *es-* or *ec-*. Cf. *edict, educate, egress, elude, emit, elect.*

v *se*cede—go *apart from,* separate
aj *se*cure—without (*apart from*) care
v *se*gregate—gather *apart* or separately

QUESTS

1. Make a list of 25 words using any one of the prefixes in this unit. Consult the dictionary to get ideas and to check spellings.
2. Write the opposite of each of the following, using the right prefix: *ability, certain, comfortable, continue, courage, definite, ease, pleasant, reasonable, satisfactory, sense, understand, use.*
3. What *in-* word means *harmless* or *guiltless?* What *dis-* word means an *argument? far off?*

FIRST PRACTICE SET

Supply for each blank the meaning of the italicized prefix.

1. To *mis*guide a person is to guide him __?__.
2. An *un*identified person is one __?__ identified.
3. A *non*descript person is one who is __?__ readily described.
4. An *anti*tank gun is one used __?__ tanks.
5. An *in*sufficient supply is __?__ enough.
6. To *ex*tract a tooth is to draw it __?__.
7. To *se*clude is to shut __?__.
8. An *ab*erration is a wandering __?__.
9. To *de*duct a sum is to take it __?__ the original amount.
10. To *dis*pel the mist is to drive it __?__.

SECOND PRACTICE SET

Think of the word for each blank. Form it from the word in parentheses.

1. The performance was __?__ (not satisfactory).
2. The boy was very __?__ (not polite).
3. The reporter was __?__ (incorrectly informed).
4. The book contains __?__ (not American) ideas.
5. Most cars use __?__ (knock-preventing) gasoline.
6. Traffic moves around the circle in a __?__ (opposite-to-the-hands-of-a-clock) direction.
7. Father and mother sometimes __?__ (opposite of agree).
8. Newspapers will sometimes __?__ (represent incorrectly) the actual facts.
9. Bad habits __?__ (draw down) from one's chances of success.
10. The king threatened to __?__ (drive out) all the foreign emissaries.

(The next special unit is a spelling-emphasis-type review, No. 24, p. 207.)

UNIT TWENTY-TWO

A DAY IN COURT

ARE YOU GUILTY?

Which word goes in each blank?

1. Should you be charged with a crime, the court will —?— you.
2. If you can get —?— posted, you will not have to go to prison until you have been convicted.
3. You will need an —?— to defend you.
4. A —?— investigates every death which might have resulted from a crime.
5. Either the judge or the jury renders a —?—.
6. If you serve a prison term, good behavior may get you out on —?— ahead of time.

First Group
1. attorney
2. bail
3. coroner
4. deputy
5. felony
6. legacy
7. misdemeanor
8. parole
9. verdict

Second Group
1. arraign
2. attest
3. extradite
4. prosecute
5. refute
6. waive

A DAY IN COURT—First Group

1. **ATTORNEY** . . . . lawyer

   n The defense attorney began to question his client.

2. **BAIL** . . . money or security as a guarantee (that one will
   appear for trial if released)

   n The suspect was released on $5,000 bail.
   aj If the charge is murder, the prisoner is not bailable (not eligible for bailment).

3. **CORONER** . medical official who determines the cause of death

   n The coroner conducted an inquest and found that the singer had been poisoned.
   n Who is the coroner in your locality?

4. **DEPUTY** . . . . representative, agent

   n The sheriff's deputy was hurt fighting outlaws.
   aj The six men were deputized (authorized as agents) to form a posse and search the woods for the kidnapper.

5. **FELONY** . . . . a major crime

   n Murder, arson, and grand larceny (major theft) are felonies.
   n A felon was shot when he tried to escape.
   aj The neighbor whom Joe Hooker beat up charged him with felonious assault.

6. **LEGACY** . . . . something inherited, a bequest

   n A legacy from an uncle put George through college.
   n The inheritance made him a legatee.

7. **MISDEMEANOR** . . . . a minor offense

   n Driving too fast is a misdemeanor.
   n The penalty for a misdemeanor is usually a fine or a short term in a local jail.

8. PAROLE . . . . . early, conditional release from prison

   n Seven of the prisoners are out on parole. They must avoid bad company and report regularly to the Parole Board.

9. VERDICT . . . . decision, judgment

   n The jury's verdict of "guilty as charged" means that the killer will go to the electric chair.
   n After a careful probe, the doctor announced his verdict.

Second Group

1. ARRAIGN . . . . to call before a court, summon for trial

   v The court will arraign the boy on a speeding charge.
   n His arraignment followed his arrest.

2. ATTEST . . . . . to testify, state under oath, depose

   v The father was eager to attest his son's innocence.
   n The attestations of six witnesses were recorded.

3. EXTRADITE . to transfer a wanted person from another state or authority (by legal process)

   v Illinois will extradite the man wanted for forgery in Ohio.
   n Extradition papers were prepared in Columbus.

4. PROSECUTE . . . . to subject to trial at law

   v The state tried to prosecute the man for starting fires.
   n The prosecution had very little evidence.

5. REFUTE . . . . . . to disprove, bring contrary evidence

   v No one could refute the prosecutor's evidence.
   n The bus driver testified in refutation of the charges.

6. WAIVE . . . . . . to forego, give up (a right or claim)

   v A person may waive the right of trial by jury.
   n She signed a waiver releasing the company from liability.

FIRST PRACTICE SET

Copy the italicized words and beside each write its meaning in the sentence:

1. We must *extradite* the man before we can *prosecute* him.
2. The *coroner* will *refute* the suicide theory.
3. Mr. Gluck received a *legacy* while on *parole* for a *felony*.
4. The suspect will *attest* his statement in the presence of both *attorneys*.
5. The prisoner will *waive* the right to be released on *bail*.
6. The marshal's *deputy* committed a *misdemeanor*.
7. A court would not usually *arraign* a criminal on one day and announce its *verdict* the next day.

AT LARGE

Fill the blanks, using each base word once. Fill first the blanks you are sure about. Do not write in the book.

1. A sheriff's __?__ sought the bandit who had jumped __?__.
2. He had crossed the line into Ohio, but state's __?__s in Indiana were planning to __?__ him.
3. They planned to __?__ for the serious __?__ he had committed in Indiana while on __?__ from a Utah prison.
4. Meanwhile, Ohio wanted to __?__ a claim it had on him as the result of a coroner's __?__ and would not __?__ its right to try him first.
5. Witnesses in Ohio were willing to __?__ his resemblance to the wanted man, and his lawyer was unable to __?__ their evidence.
6. The bandit had been arrested in the first place for a mere __?__ while trying to claim a small __?__ from a relative who had just died.
7. The __?__ of the Ohio jury was that the man was guilty of murder.

UNIT TWENTY-THREE

VARIED QUALITIES

A PLAY

Can you fill each blank sensibly?

1. Putting on a play is a highly —?— undertaking.

2. The director needs to be very —?— in handling the cast, and an —?— temperament is a distinct asset.

3. The actors were —?— on learning their lines.

4. The audience will be in a —?— mood.

5. The play should have a —?— plot.

6. If the play is to make money, we must not hand out too many tickets —?—.

First Group
1. adept
2. arbitrary
3. external
4. feasible
5. fervent
6. festive
7. flagrant
8. harrowing
9. intent

Second Group
1. arduous
2. assiduous
3. equable
4. garish
5. gratis
6. odious

VARIED QUALITIES—First Group

1. ADEPT . . . . highly skillful

   aj Uncle Joe is an adept fisherman.
   n His adeptness in pitching horseshoes won him a trophy.

2. ARBITRARY . . . . positive and unreasoning

   aj The referee's decisions seemed very arbitrary.
   n His arbitrariness often irritated the players.

3. EXTERNAL . . . . outside, outwardly apparent

   aj Rubbing alcohol is intended for external use only.
   aj If manners are merely external observances, they make a person seem hollow.

4. FEASIBLE . . . . practicable, readily carried out

   aj Use of roof tops for landing fields is feasible.
   n The feasibility of atomic aircraft was discussed.

5. FERVENT . . . . eager, glowing, ardent

   aj The boy has a fervent desire to climb Mount Whitney.
   n The speaker argued with great fervor for world brotherhood.
   aj A fervid radio appeal failed.

6. FESTIVE . . . . joyous, sportive, gay

   aj The crowd at the game was in a festive mood.
   n The May Day festivities began at noon.

7. FLAGRANT . . . . glaring, notably bad

   aj Playing in the street is a flagrant violation of safety rules.
   n The flagrancy of McClellan's behavior toward President Lincoln is hard to believe.

8. HARROWING . . . . tormenting, agonizing

   aj Torture by fire was a harrowing experience.
   n A harrow is a spike-toothed farm machine that levels and stirs up ploughed ground.
   v Good bottom soil harrows well.

9. INTENT . . . . fixed earnestly, engrossed

   aj Stan is intent on becoming a doctor.
   n Several teachers noticed Susie's intentness in her studies.
   n The intent (intention) of the law is to keep children in school longer.

Second Group

1. ARDUOUS . . . . trying, difficult, laborious

   aj Shell racing is one of the most arduous sports.
   n The story shows the arduousness of a lumberman's life.

2. ASSIDUOUS . . . . diligent, patient, unremitting

   aj As a piano player Judy is very assiduous, but assiduousness is not enough.
   av Practicing assiduously is important to attaining perfection.

3. EQUABLE . . . . . . even, tranquil, not varying much

   aj Florida has a very equable climate.
   n Mr. Lee's equability is one of his fine qualities.

4. GARISH . . . . . . gaudy, showy, extravagantly gay

   aj Mrs. Birdwood's purple dress was a garish mistake.
   n *Quo Vadis* shows the garishness of a Roman dinner party.

5. GRATIS (grā′tĭs) . . . . . free, costing nothing, gratuitous

   aj The publisher sent the book to the teacher gratis.
   aj A gratuitous compliment is one given willingly; a gratuitous insult is one not deserved or justified.

6. ODIOUS . . . . hateful

> aj Benedict Arnold is a name odious to Americans.
>
> n The odiousness of the man's crime did not prevent his receiving a fair trial.

FIRST PRACTICE SET

Copy the italicized words and beside each write its meaning in the sentence:

1. The Governor displayed *adept* handling of *external* affairs.
2. A good secretary is *intent* on conserving her boss's time.
3. An *arbitrary* answer as to whether the plan is *feasible* will not satisfy us.
4. Can one be *fervent* and *festive* at the same time?
5. The story is *harrowing* and full of *flagrant* historical errors.
6. Making a lawn, an *arduous* task, is *odious* to a lazy person.
7. The painter gave away his most *garish* work *gratis*.
8. Mr. Gudge was known for his *equable* handling of those who were most *assiduous* in seeking party jobs.

''TUBBY''

Fill the blanks appropriately, using each base word once.

We call him "Tubby" because his __?__ appearance is smooth and round like a ripe grapefruit. Stiff tennis matches are __?__ to his muscles, but he is __?__ at playing checkers. He has a rather musical voice and is very __?__ and patient in collecting stamps. His mistakes of grammar are really __?__, but by __?__, almost fiery, application he has managed to improve.

Tubby can be quite __?__ on holidays, and he will sing __?__ when asked. He is __?__ on space travel and believes a trip to the moon will be __?__ in a few years, but that it will be a(n) __?__ adventure nevertheless and hair-raising rather than merely __?__. Most Christmas displays he considers __?__. He is really very __?__ in his judgments, but quite __?__ in dealing with his friends.

UNIT TWENTY-FOUR

ABLE AND IBLE

Once there were two salesmen, Able and Ible. They became great rivals, and each went to work to see how many words he could enroll. Below are some of the familiar members each gained.

Able I	Able II	Ible I
agreeable	adorable	contemptible
available	advisable	convertible
commendable	comparable	discernible
considerable	desirable	perceptible
eatable	durable	resistible
	(page 169)	(page 175)
enjoyable	imaginable	
explainable	irritable	
fashionable	likable	**Ible II**
favorable	miserable	audible
habitable	pleasurable	credible
honorable	receivable	divisible
payable	recognizable	eligible
portable	removable	forcible
preferable	retrievable	gullible
profitable	usable	horrible
remarkable	valuable	intelligible
respectable	pliable (page 120)	legible
suitable	reliable	negligible
transferable	variable	permissible
workable	veritable	plausible
*changeable	capable	possible
manageable	hospitable	sensible
noticeable	probable	terrible
pronunceable		visible

QUESTS

1. How do the words in Able I or Ible I differ from those in Able II or Ible II?
2. How many words can you add to each column?
3. Why don't the four words at the end of Able I lose an *e* like most of the base words in Able II? See page 119 for a hint.
4. How do *regrettable* and *controllable* differ from most of their tribe?
5. Make a list of prefix opposites of Able and Ible words.
6. Write ten sentences each containing Able and Ible words. Divide the class into pairs and dictate sentences to each other.

EXERCISE

Write each Able or Ible word, filling in the *a* or *i* and any other letter needed.

1. Illeg_ble writing is not fashion__ble.
2. She is lik__ble except that she is very irrit__ble.
3. Chang____ble weather is not always agree__ble.
4. No percept__ble progress was notic____ble.
5. How can one make an unpronounc____ble word aud_ble?
6. The climber's story is too remark__ble to be plaus__ble.
7. It is permiss__ble to exchange transfer__ble tickets.
8. The Black Death was so terr__ble in 1348 as to be almost incred__ble.
9. Mother is as hospit__ble as poss__ble.
10. Judy is ador__ble; in fact, she is irresist__ble.
11. Mr. Hoodle's convert__ble was vis__ble through the trees.
12. Courage is commend__ble, cowardice contempt__ble.
13. Disagree__ble winds make the land uninhabit__ble.
14. Caution is intellig__ble if not advis__ble.
15. Father is usually sens__ble and thus quite manage__ble.

(The next special unit is Part Three, Unit 1.)

UNIT TWENTY-FIVE

FAR AND NEAR

EXPLORATIONS

What word from the list at the right goes in each blank?

The —?— are 8,000 miles apart, but the nearest —?— is many light-years away. The —?— of the highest mountain is 29,028 feet above sea level. A(n) —?— consists of a small land area surrounded by water, and the function of a(n) —?— is to provide a neck of land between two larger masses. A long journey is often called a(n) —?—. In certain parts of the world one can still find —?—s who feast on unwary travelers.

First Group
1. cannibal
2. constellation
3. delta
4. hinterland
5. isthmus

Second Group
1. oasis
2. peninsula
3. summit
4. tributary
5. vista

Third Group
1. antipodes
2. archipelago
3. declivity
4. odyssey
5. promontory

209

FAR AND NEAR—First Group

1. CANNIBAL . . . . . . beings which eat their own kind

    n Stories about cannibals gave Junior bad dreams.
    n The sufferings of the Donner party led to cannibalism.

2. CONSTELLATION . . . . a group or pattern of stars

    n Orion, the Hunter, is a familiar constellation.
    n The All-American football team is a kind of athletic constellation.

3. DELTA . . . . . flood-deposit land at the mouth of a river

    n A river delta is so called, probably because it is triangle-shaped like the Greek letter delta (Δ).
    n The Nile has a famous rice-producing delta.

4. HINTERLAND . . regions inland from the coast; back country

    n Tourists are attracted more to the coast than to the hinterland of Maine.

5. ISTHMUS . . a narrow neck or strip (of land) connecting two larger (land) areas

    n The isthmus of Panama is 31 miles wide at its narrowest.
    n The Isthmus of Corinth is in Greece.

Second Group

1. OASIS . . . . . . a fertile (watered) area in the desert

    n An American bomber crew died on the Sahara Desert trying to find an oasis.

2. PENINSULA . . . . . land projection (almost an island)

    n Florida is an important American peninsula.
    aj The Peninsular Campaign was an attack on Richmond, Virginia, by way of the peninsula formed by two rivers.

3. SUMMIT . . . . highest point, apex

    n The summit of Mt. Everest is 29,028 feet above sea level.

    n The pinnacle (high or highest point) of the temple was struck by lightning.

4. TRIBUTARY . . . that which contributes, pays, is subject to

    n The Ohio River is a tributary of the Mississippi.

    n Palestine was once a tributary of the Roman Empire.

5. VISTA . . . . a view, outlook (broad or long)

    n A vista of tree-covered mountains loomed up below.

    n Continuous westward expansion marks the vista of American history up to 1912.

Third Group

1. ANTIPODES (ăn·tĭp′ə·dēz) . . opposite point(s) (of the earth)

    n The antipodes are farther apart than the Halls of Montezuma and the shores of Tripoli.

    n The two speakers represent the antipodes (opposite extremes) of religious thought.

2. ARCHIPELAGO (är′kə·pĕl′ə·gō′) . . a group of small islands (or body of water containing them)

    n The Solomon Islands form an archipelago in the South Pacific.

3. DECLIVITY . . . . a downward slope, descent

    v There is a declivity on the other side of town.

    aj The declivitous hillsides are badly eroded.

4. ODYSSEY . . . . a long journey or wandering

    n The original *Odyssey* was the long travel story of Odysseus (also called Ulysses). Who wrote it?

5. PROMONTORY   .   .   .   .   headland, projecting cliff or rock

   n The promontory is visible far out at sea.

   n Gilbraltar is a famous promontory.

FIRST PRACTICE SET

Copy the italicized words and beside each write its meaning:

1. The aborigines of the *archipelago* were *cannibals*.
2. The *vista* of sky and sea was cut by a coastline above which loomed the rugged *hinterland*.
3. The *delta* formed by a *tributary* of the Amazon could be seen from the *promontory*.
4. From the *summit* one could see the Arctic *peninsula*.
5. A desert *odyssey* takes one from *oasis* to oasis.
6. The sea is beyond the *declivity* on the far side of the *isthmus*.
7. Viewed from one of the *constellations*, the earth's *antipodes* would seem close together.

A SUMMER ADVENTURE

Fill the blanks sensibly, using each base word once:

Our __?__ took us around a thumblike __?__ and past a __?__ that looks like a huge goat's head from below and almost eclipses the __?__ of Mont Blanc. The __?__ of the Italian __?__ that opened up before us as we approached the __?__ leading back to sea level was awe-inspiring. At length we reached the river which is the __?__ of a larger stream that waters the valley below. We followed the stream to the __?__ at its mouth near the sea. Later, on the other side of the earth, we crossed from one continent to the other by means of an __?__, which was only about a hundred yards wide in spots, and set sail for an __?__ that lies about eighty miles to the westward. There are no longer any __?__s on any of the islands, each of which is an __?__ in a wasteland of sea. It was fun thus to explore the very __?__, and we saw several __?__s which are never visible in the northern latitudes where we live.

FINAL TEST ON INDIVIDUAL UNITS

Unit 1

Write down for each blank the proper form of the word in parentheses. Watch spelling.

1. The native's __?__ (fierce) scared the two children more than the __?__ (strange) of the surroundings.
2. Live __?__ (cautious) and you have greater __?__ (happy).
3. You must sign the __?__ (agree) to obtain __?__ (employ).
4. The __?__ (govern) gave the farmers more __?__ (encourage).
5. A toothache is an __?__ (induce) to make a dental __?__ (appoint).
6. In the company's __?__ (judge) the president is __?__ (replace).
7. There was a good __?__ (argue) for __?__ (postpone) of the game.
8. Good __?__ (manage) makes a __?__ (notice) difference.
9. Breakfast in bed is a very __?__ (agree) __?__ (arrange).
10. A man who __?__ (kidnap) a little boy is __?__ (not employ).

Unit 2

Write the word from this unit that goes in each blank:

1. I __?__ (entreat) you not to __?__ (give forth) such sounds.
2. The board will __?__ (annul) its decision to __?__ (set apart) immigrants.
3. Did you __?__ (confirm) the attorney's right to __?__ (appeal to) an old law?
4. John was asked to __?__ (change somewhat) his design so that it could __?__ (be fit) for competition in the contest.
5. If the flood should __?__ (move back), it will __?__ (remove) the need for more policemen.
6. Please __?__ (refill) the washbasin so that I can __?__ (dip) the rest of the silverware.
7. By all means __?__ (praise) his reluctance to __?__ (yield to a desire) himself at the expense of others.
8. The surgeon exposed the dog's heart and watched it __?__ (throb, beat).

Unit 3

Write the word that goes in each blank.

1. A wise man is __?__ (discreet) and __?__ (industrious).
2. __?__ (quick to act) girls are sometimes more __?__ (timid) than they seem.
3. Is the man __?__ (easily deceived) as well as __?__ (easily influenced)?
4. The salesman is __?__ (pleasant), but somewhat __?__ (loud and noisy).
5. Marvin is __?__ (kindly), but somewhat __?__ (disorderly).
6. Mrs. Scott is too __?__ (proud) to admit the shortcomings of her __?__ (unruly, disobedient) and __?__ (pitiless) son.
7. Chief Rising Sun is __?__ (impassive), and very __?__ (uniform) in his behavior.

Unit 4

Write the word from this unit which goes in each blank.

1. War leaves one __?__ed (unfeeling) toward suffering and __?__ (discouraged) about the future.
2. He raised the gun, took __?__ (unhurried, calculated) aim and __?__ly (in a determined fashion) pulled the trigger.
3. A __?__ (ill-natured) father makes a __?__ (cross, complaining) child.
4. She appears to be __?__ (sadly thoughtful) about her loss, but actually she is very __?__ (indifferent) about it.
5. Martha became __?__ (feverishly excited) when she heard the __?__ (quietly cautious) footsteps in the hall.
6. John was __?__ (regretful, apologetic) for his __?__ (angry) outburst.
7. His __?__ (inactive, submissive) manner caused some people to make __?__ (smart, disrespectful) remarks.
8. The cat seemed __?__ (crazed) after eating the pain-killer.

Unit 5

Write the form of the word in parentheses which goes in each blank. Watch spelling.

1. __?__ (beauty) flowers are __?__ (plenty) in the spring.
2. The new man is __?__ (no skill) but very __?__ (duty).
3. Joe will not be alive next year unless he recognizes the __?__ (fool) and the __?__ (no sense) of reckless driving.
4. Either __?__ (willful) or __?__ (peeve) will get a person into trouble.
5. Cancer is a __?__ (dread) disease because it is so __?__ (no mercy).
6. If you ask for help __?__ (respect), no one will look at you __?__ (regret).
7. The man who is now a __?__ (trust) at Sing Sing was once one of the __?__s (trust) of a college.
8. Margaret, who dresses __?__ (style), is very __?__ (clan) at school.
9. A poet is likely to be __?__ (fancy) but not __?__ (sense of duty).

Unit 6

Write the word from this unit which goes in each blank.

1. George's __?__ (conceit) made him __?__ (declare) his superior __?__ (endurance).
2. He was small in __?__ (height) but few doubted his __?__ (superior skill).
3. Bill has only __?__ (scorn) for those who cannot endure __?__ (extreme suffering) in silence.
4. I __?__ (suppose) that he feels __?__ (regret) for the evil he has done.
5. If you __?__ (charm, ensnare) him with flattery, perhaps he will __?__ (entrust) his secret to you.
6. Do you __?__ (hint) that he should be __?__ed (praised) for his deeds?
7. The knight was __?__ed (made strong) with anger when he went forth to __?__ (oppose) his challenger.

Unit 7

Write the word from this unit that goes in each blank.

1. One of his __?__ (forefathers) was a well-known __?__ (ruthless ruler).
2. The king kept a constant __?__ (wakeful watching) over his __?__ (territory).
3. In that midnight __?__ (merrymaking), __?__ (courtesy to women) was often forgotten.
4. "We must guard the __?__ (protecting barriers) of the castle until the __?__ (turning point) is past!" the king ordered.
5. The missionary spoke with great __?__ (speaking power and skill) as he told of his __?__ (very trying experience) in India, and of the __?__ (hindrances) he had had to surmount.
6. This __?__ (piece of strategy) should bring us within sight of the __?__ (signal light) on the hill.
7. The skirts which were part of the __?__ (clothing) of the actresses looked like __?__ (waves) of surf.

Unit 8

Write the word from this unit that goes in each blank.

1. He will __?__ (approve) our brand of soap if it leaves no __?__ (remains) in the sink.
2. That was as fine a __?__ (sample) of __?__ (deer meat) as I ever tasted!
3. The general __?__ (limited) the soldiers to the barracks to teach them to __?__ (center their attention) on learning __?__ (fight) techniques.
4. If the lawyer __?__ (throws into confusion) the witness, he will __?__ (block or hinder) justice.
5. __?__ (burdened) as they were with wagons, the pioneers were nevertheless able to __?__ (pierce) the wilderness of the West.
6. Her figure __?__ (decreased) in size as it disappeared in the __?__ (whirlpool) of the tornado.
7. I cannot __?__ (observe differences) between the __?__ (copy or reproduction) and the real sculpture.

Unit 9

Write the form of the word in parentheses which goes in each blank. Watch spelling.

1. The team performed __?__ (magnificent) at a great __?__ (distant) from home.
2. The food at the hotel is __?__ (excel) and served in great __?__ (abundant).
3. __?__ (cancel) of the flight left a __?__ (vacant) to be filled.
4. The __?__ (initiate) makes you a member __?__ (permanent).
5. The __?__ (accuse) is that he cheated on an __?__ (examine).
6. __?__ (accurate) is an __?__ (admire) habit.
7. The __?__ (operate) was not very __?__ (communicate).
8. The Army demands __?__ (obey) without __?__ (explain).
9. "I came, I saw, I conquered" is a __?__ (translation) of a Latin __?__ (quote).
10. The __?__ (decorate) can charge high prices because he has no __?__ (compete) in Dudville.

Unit 10

Write the word from this unit that goes in each blank.

1. Interest __?__s (is added) at 6% annually on the __?__ (paper pledging property as security for a debt).
2. Churches are __?__ (excused) from the taxes __?__ (imposed) on real estate. After the year's taxes have been paid, a land owner may be entitled to a __?__ (return of part of the amount paid).
3. The __?__ (book recording money received and spent) shows a decrease in __?__ (income, proceeds).
4. This __?__ (prior right to buy something) on the expected __?__ (shipment) of imported goods runs out tomorrow.
5. The bank will __?__ (set a value on) the extent of your __?__ (things of value).
6. When prices __?__ (expand) your __?__ (wealth in a form to produce income) will decrease in value.
7. Payments in __?__ (amount overdue) can become a __?__ (claim) against the property.

Unit 11

Write the word from this unit that goes in each blank.

1. He ordered a __?__ (meat cut in pieces and cooked in gravy) with __?__ (cooked with onions) potatoes.
2. Would you prefer a __?__ (frozen gelatin and cream) or a __?__ (cream puff) for dessert?
3. The oil is __?__ (stale) and the water __?__ (flat, somewhat salty).
4. We had __?__ (soup containing thin strips of vegetable) to begin the meal and __?__ (small cup of black coffee) after dessert.
5. Sea water is __?__ (salty) and therefore not __?__ (fit for drinking).
6. Jim ordered a cheese __?__ (spongy baked dish) and onions __?__ (fried).
7. For Kathie the least __?__ (fit to eat) foods are potatoes __?__ (covered with bread crumbs or cheese) and pie with __?__ (covered with fluffy egg whites).

Unit 12

Write the word from this unit that goes in each blank.

1. Why __?__ (guess) about who will __?__ (take the place of) you?
2. It __?__ (happened) that the __?__ (solemn agreement) was illegal.
3. The council will __?__ (confirm) the plan to __?__ (restore to his original place) the city manager.
4. The __?__ (one sent to promote an idea) sat on the ledge that __?__s (juts out) from the building.
5. The stately old __?__ (building) was razed with a __?__ (smallest allowable amount) of effort.
6. Repeating the old __?__ (proverb) may __?__ (change, transform) the __?__ (messenger's) fear into courage.
7. Claire expects to __?__ (receive by birth) a valuable collection of old coins as a kind of __?__ (reward) for catching the thief who tried to steal it.

Unit 13

Write the form of the word in parentheses which goes in each blank. Watch spelling.

1. Jill speaks with __?__ (certain), and she has a strong __?__ (person).
2. Fried ice cream is an __?__ (absurd).
3. Almost everybody admires __?__ (sincere) and __?__ (modest).
4. Snow in May is a __?__ (possible) but not a __?__ (probable) even in Minnesota.
5. The __?__ (poisonous) of the berries led to a __?__ (fatal).
6. The boat is __?__ (electric) operated, and Bill handled it __?__ (able).
7. A __?__ (villain) boy is a __?__ (liable) to his parents.
8. There are __?__ (vary) ways to foil the enemy's __?__ (treachery).
9. __?__ (tackle) the football player __?__ (vigor) proved __?__ (advantage).
10. Members of a family should live together __?__ (harmony).

Unit 14

Write the word from this unit that goes in each blank.

1. Fear __?__ (freezes, stiffens) a person and makes him less __?__ (cheerful).
2. Flood waters that __?__ (whirl) downstream __?__ (wear away) the river bank.
3. Before you __?__ (coat with glass) the outer surface, be sure to __?__ (cut on a slant) the edges.
4. Sponge rubber is __?__ (having tiny openings) and quite __?__ (lasting).
5. The new metal is __?__ (easily drawn out) and will not __?__ (discolor).
6. We __?__ (melt together) the frames and then __?__ (toughen by heat treatment) them for extra strength.
7. The liquid used to __?__ (moisten) the meat is both __?__ (sticky), and __?__ (sharp).

Unit 15

Write the word from this unit that goes in each blank.

1. The savages were quick to __?__ (repay for) the defeat of their leader, __?__ (laying waste) everything in their path.
2. Why __?__ (curse) because the __?__ (raider, plunderer) got away?
3. A __?__ (robber, bandit) is not content merely to __?__ (steal) pennies from children.
4. After such petty __?__ (despoilments), he would not hesitate to __?__ (trespass) on the possessions of adults.
5. To __?__ (cry down) a coward is to __?__ (assail) his courage.
6. For a soldier to __?__ (feign illness) to avoid danger is to act with __?__ (dishonor) and __?__ (baseness).
7. The man who tried to __?__ (attack) the bus driver was wanted elsewhere for __?__ (theft).

Unit 16

Write the form of the word in parentheses which goes in each blank.

1. The father of an __?__ (acquaint) of mine is __?__ (not insure) because he has heart trouble.
2. It took unusual __?__ (persist) to find out why the sign __?__ed (not appear).
3. Gordon has a __?__ (grieve) which he finds __?__ (not endure).
4. What happens when an __?__ (can't be resisted) force hits an __?__ (can't be moved) object?
5. A __?__ (descend) of the richest king in Europe got out of his baby carriage __?__ (not assist).
6. This liar is an __?__ (ignore) person and his statements are __?__ (can't be relied upon).
7. Complete __?__ (adhere) to the rules is a rare __?__ (occur).
8. The __?__ (correspond) for the newspaper has great __?__ (persevere).
9. After the __?__ (transfer) of a carload of food the supply was still __?__ (not sufficient).
10. __?__ (conscience) is a good trait if not carried too far.

Unit 17

Write the word from this unit that goes in each blank.

1. The __?__ (unit of troops) held several Indians as __?__ (persons held as guarantee).
2. The __?__ (newly enlisted soldiers) were confined to their __?__ (living quarters) for three days.
3. The spy tried to __?__ (slip through) the enemy lines as their troops __?__ (spread out).
4. Can you describe the __?__ (emblems) of the __?__ (foot soldiers)?
5. The crew in the __?__ (small tower for guns) did not know that the __?__ (troops on horseback, recently motorized) was near.
6. The commandant will __?__ (assemble) the __?__ (students training to be officers) at dawn and __?__ (formally initiate) them into the armed forces.
7. He crouched behind the __?__ (mounted guns) for cover while he tried to __?__ (translate) the general's orders.

Unit 18

Write the word from this unit that goes in each blank.

1. The __?__ (petty officer in charge of rigging) inspected the __?__ (case containing the ship's compass).
2. The __?__ (flat-bottomed ship) was pumping out __?__ (dirty water).
3. They should hoist the __?__ (national flag) before the troops __?__ (go aboard).
4. By standing on the __?__ (deck railing), the sailor was able to see the __?__ (fleet of armed ships) coming.
5. The missing __?__ (instrument for measuring angular distances) was located in the __?__ (ship's kitchen).
6. The __?__ (whirling wheel) kept the ship steady enough to __?__ (operate at sea).
7. The merchant ship got separated from its __?__ (escort) in the storm, and an enemy ship forced it to __?__ (throw overboard) all its cargo.
8. In the retreat at Dunkerque, the British Navy used all the boats it could __?__ (obtain).

Unit 19

Write the word from this unit that goes in each blank.

1. An engineer will __?__ (calculate) the rate at which the space ship should __?__ (lose speed) prior to re-entry.
2. The __?__ (space traveler) did not know what the __?__ (instrument measuring height) was.
3. Gliders have __?__ (hinged wing sections for banking) but not __?__ (automatic pilots).
4. An airsick pilot suffering from __?__ (lack of oxygen) up in the __?__ (upper air 7 to 25 miles high) tried to __?__ (make steady) the plane.
5. A plane traveling at __?__ (beyond the speed of sound) will __?__ (hurl out) the pilot if an emergency arises.
6. A windmill is a kind of __?__ (engine driven by a blast) used to __?__ (drive forward) a pump or generator.
7. The __?__ (plane operating from land or water) has a __?__ (main frame) of aluminum.

Unit 20

Write the word from this unit that goes in each blank.

1. An __?__ (inflowing) of funds gave the drive new __?__ (momentum).
2. Let us __?__ (estimate the value of) the situation before we do anything that will __?__ (excite) the crowd.
3. The governor refused to __?__ (lessen) the sentence or even __?__ (deduct) a single year.
4. The __?__ (intense suffering) in her voice and the __?__ (seriousness) of her expression __?__ (make up) a very persuasive effect.
5. Watch Robert's pride __?__ (come forth) when he traces his __?__ (line of descent) back to Edmund Burke.
6. Do I __?__ (place a burden) upon you in asking you to __?__ (undertake) this cause?
7. Our relations will __?__ (grow worse) unless we can __?__ (wipe out) that bad feeling between us.

Unit 21

Write the form of the word indicated in parentheses that goes in each blank. Watch spelling.

1. To __?__ (apply wrongly) a remark is __?__ (not fair).
2. __?__ (against the British) feeling is __?__ (not justified).
3. __?__ (opposite to clockwise) motion will __?__ (opposite of wind) the rope.
4. __?__ (take arms or weapons from) the bandit before he __?__ (climbs down from) the stair.
5. A pupil is __?__ (not eligible) for the privilege if he __?__ (behaves wrongly).
6. Defeat will __?__ (give courage to) the team and make the coach __?__ (not comfortable).
7. The demands of the company are __?__ (not reasonable) and __?__ (not necessary).
8. The weight on the scales serves to __?__ (make balance opposite to) the object weighed.
9. The debaters __?__ (opposite of *agree*) about the causes of __?__ (wrong conduct) and __?__ (not social) behavior.

Unit 22

Write the word from this unit that goes in each blank.

1. The __?__ (lawyer) could not __?__ (disprove) the evidence.
2. The coroner's __?__ (representative) wanted to __?__ (bring to trial at law) us.
3. Several __?__ (major criminals) were to be __?__ (summoned for trial).
4. The prisoner decided to __?__ (forego) posting __?__ (money offered as a guarantee).
5. Will he __?__ (testify, depose) my claim to the __?__ (bequest)?
6. The jury's __?__ (decision) of "guilty" was due mainly to the __?__'s (official who determines the cause of death) testimony; however, the man may be eligible for __?__ (conditional release) later.
7. Iowa would not __?__ (transfer from another state) a person charged only with a __?__ (minor offense).

Unit 23

Write the word from this unit that goes in each blank.

1. The settings of the play are __?__ (gaudy) and the plot is __?__ (notably bad) nonsense.
2. It is not __?__ (practicable) to give out vacuum sweepers __?__ (free).
3. He who is __?__ (diligent) in his devotion may be too __?__ (tranquil) to be exciting.
4. One should be religiously __?__ (glowing) but not __?__ (sportive) during Lent.
5. Building bookcases is __?__ (difficult) labor requiring one to be __?__ (highly skillful) with tools.
6. Hardships which would prove __?__ (tormenting) for others he does not find __?__ (hateful).
7. This judge seems __?__ (positive and unreasoning), but one soon realizes that this attitude is only __?__ (outwardly apparent). Actually he is __?__ (engrossed) upon rendering just decisions.

Unit 24

Write the Able or Ible form of the word in parentheses which goes in each blank. Watch spelling.

1. The plan is __?__ (work) and doubtless __?__ (profit).
2. Water discoloration is __?__ (remove), but prompt action __?__ (advise).
3. The writing is __?__ (read) and the story __?__ (credit).
4. Be __?__ (sense) and make the books __?__ (avail).
5. A __?__ (force) answer is especially __?__ (suit).
6. The weather in April is often __?__ (change) but usually __?__ (enjoy).
7. The boy is __?__ (manage) although often __?__ (irritate).
8. His tricks are __?__ (contempt) and his intelligence __?__ (negligence).
9. The set shows no __?__ (notice) increases in the __?__ (audit) noises from static.
10. Swimming is __?__ (permit) in the lake with the __?__ (can't-be-pronounced) name.

Unit 25

Write the word from this unit that goes in each blank.

1. Notice that the __?__ (group of small islands) is like a __?__ (pattern of stars).
2. The __?__ (beings which eat their own kind) gathered at the bottom of the __?__ (downward slope).
3. The __?__ (broad view) from the __?__ (projecting cliff) includes a __?__ (river which flows into a larger) of the Nile.
4. The sportsman's __?__ (long journey) took him into the __?__s (regions away from the coast) of Burma.
5. The __?__ (highest point) of the pass is about half way between the __?__ (opposite parts of the earth).
6. The Italian __?__ (projecting stretch of land) would be a rather long __?__ (narrow neck of land) if it reached to Africa.
7. Digging a well created an __?__ (fertile area in the desert) and made it as productive as the best land in the Nile __?__ (flood-deposit land).

III

ROAD SIGNS

You will find one of four symbols beside each illustrative sentence in the regular units, thus:

> **v** to mark a *verb* form of the base word or a synonym of the base word
>
> **av** to mark an *adverb* form of the base word or a synonym of the base word
>
> **n** to mark a *noun* form of the base word or a synonym of the base word
>
> **aj** to mark an *adjective* form of the base word or a synonym of the base word

In the spelling units a number of the most troublesome words are marked with a red star, thus: *

UNIT ONE

E PLURIBUS UNUM

"My ancestors did not come over on the Mayflower," declared Will Rogers. "They went out to meet it." Will Rogers was part Indian. Even the Indians did not originate in America, however. They came over from Asia.

Where did *your* parents come from? Perhaps they were born here, in which case, where did their parents or ancestors come from? Probably from Europe, but perhaps it was from Asia or Africa. Wherever it was, they brought the old ways with them. They learned the ways of the people who were already here, and the people who were already here took over some of theirs. The same thing happened with their words.

This process of collecting hundreds of thousands of the finest people from three continents has helped make the United States a nation that can do almost anything well. The same process in words has given us a language that is exceptionally expressive because it has a wealth of words for every need. No one knows how many there really are, but the largest dictionaries contain about half a million.

Most of these words came from England. In addition, we have added thousands from other countries, discarded other thousands we didn't like or didn't need, and invented new ones by the hundred. We have also changed a great many of those we kept. For example, *colour* (British spelling) is *color* in America, *honour* is *honor, tyres* are *tires,* and the British word "wireless" is "radio" in America.

Where did the British get this language we still call English, more correctly called American English on this side of the Atlantic? It is a long story because the people of Great Britain, like those of the United States, are a blend of many elements, including Roman, Danish, French, German, and Italian, as well as Scottish, Irish, and Welsh. All of these elements contributed words to the language.

Three sources stand out, however. Most of the words in our English-American hoard came from (1) Anglo-Saxon, (2) Latin, or (3) Greek. Anglo-Saxon or Old English was the language more than a thousand years ago of what is now England. It was the language the Angles and Saxons brought with them from the forests of Germany when they invaded the island. As they took possession, they drove the Celtic people who already lived there into the hills of Wales and Scotland. In so doing they acquired Celtic words they had not used before and adapted them to their own purposes. Moreover, just by living their own lives away from their homeland they formed different attitudes and found new ways of saying things. Different climate and living conditions affected their habits, their ways, and their words.

TEN EVERYDAY WORDS IN

Modern English	Old English	Modern German	Latin
1. God	Gode	der Gott	Deus
Words we get in English:			deity
			deify
2. man	mann	der Mann	vir
	monn		homo
Words we get in English:			virile
			homicide
3. woman	wifmann	die Frau	femina
			mulier
Words we get in English:			feminine
4. father	faeder	der Vater	pater
Words we get in English:			paternal
5. mother	modor	die Mutter	mater
Words we get in English:			maternal
6. son	sunu	der Sohn	filius
Words we get in English:			filial
			affiliate
7. daughter	dohtor	die Tochter	filia
Words we get in English:			filial
8. brother	brothor	der Bruder	frater
Words we get in English:			fraternal
9. sister	sweostor	die Schwester	soror
Words we get in English:			sorority
10. friend	freond	der Freund	amicus
Words we get in English:			amicable

EIGHT DIFFERENT LANGUAGES

French	Spanish	Italian	Greek
Dieu	Dios	Dio	Θεός (theos) **theology**
homme	hombre	uomo	ἄνθρωπος (anthropos) **anthropoid**
femme	mujer femenino (adj.)	donna femmina	γυνή (gune) **gynecology**
pere	padre	padre	πατήρ, πατρός (pater, patros) **patriarch** **patriot**
mere	madre	madre	μήτηρ, μήτρός (meter, metros) **metropolis**
fils	hijo	figlio	υἱός (huios)
fille	hija	figlia	θυγάτηρ (thygater)
frere	hermano	fratello	ἀδελφός (adelphos) **Philadelphia**
sœur	hermana	sorella	ἀδελφή (adelphe)
ami **amity**	amigo	amico	φίλος (philos) **philanthropist**

When the Norman French invaded England in the year 1066 and subjugated the Anglo-Saxons (as pictured in the novel *Ivanhoe,* by Sir Walter Scott) they brought a language derived directly from Latin. Gradually, the Germanic speech of the Anglo-Saxons mixed with the Latin-derived language of the invaders. In addition, Greek words accumulated—hundreds of them—from the study of Greek and Latin by the few who were educated. Words have been accumulating ever since, and new words, especially scientific terms, are created every year from Latin and Greek roots.

In Part Three you will find words grouped largely according to their origins. The next two units, for example, contain words from Anglo-Saxon. Other units consist entirely of words from Latin or from Greek. A few units are devoted to words taken over almost unchanged from Latin-derived modern languages like French, Spanish, and Italian. There is a sampling from Germanic, Russian, and Hebrew sources in Unit 21, and Unit 22 presents words that came mostly from the Orient.

Out of many peoples we are building one nation. Out of many languages we are building one language. A language is never finished, never is final until it becomes dead; dictionaries are from five to twenty years behind. No dictionary can or should freeze the language any more than a city directory freezes the population. A language is changing and growing as long as it is alive.

The chart on page 233 shows how certain everyday words have changed as they migrated from one language to another or have in some cases been replaced.

Sources of English Words (Approximate)

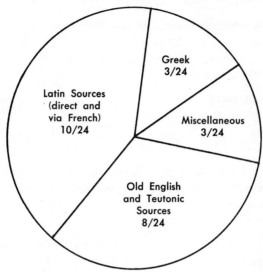

Greek
3/24

Latin Sources
(direct and
via French)
10/24

Miscellaneous
3/24

Old English
and Teutonic
Sources
8/24

THE FOUR ELEMENTS

For many centuries before science got under way, men imagined that everything on earth was made from four elements: earth, air, fire, and water. Let's see what these four words were in the two languages from which English is principally derived.

	Anglo-Saxon	*(German)*	*Latin*
1. earth	eorthe	(die Erde)	terra
	Modern words we get:		territory
2. air	lyft	(die Luft)	aer (same in Greek)
	Modern words we get:		aeroplane
3. fire	fyr	(das Feuer)	ignis, flamma (Greek *pyra*)[1]
	Modern words we get:		ignite, flame
4. water	waeter	(das Wasser)	aqua
	Modern words we get:		aquatic(s)

[1] *fire* derives from *pyra* by the operation of a strange principal or custom in the evolution of languages known as Grimm's Law.

QUESTS

1. Look up your own name in the dictionary. From what language did it come? What does it mean?
2. What light does the chart throw on the meaning of each of the following terms?

    philanthropist   anthropoid apes
    Christadelphian Church   a Russophile
    theocracy   virility
    paternity   maternity

3. How many foreign terms can you think of which include one of the words on the chart on pages 230-231? Look up the pronunciation and meaning of each unless you know it already. Here are a few, half of them French:

    Cherchez la femme   the Sierra Madre Mountains
    Fratres in urbe   the goddess Demeter
    Mon Dieu!   the Jungfrau
    "The Bonhomme Richard"   "Frère Jacques"
    Dumas père and Dumas fils   Mater Dolorosa

4. What is Sanskrit? How is it related to the English language? What is the Indo-European family of languages? How much do scholars know about a hypothetical language called Primitive Indo-European? Where was it spoken?

EXERCISE

Write the word defining the italicized word or element.

1. A Haus*frau* is the __?__ of the house.
2. To commit *homi*cide is to kill a __?__.
3. *Theo*logy is the study of the nature and ways of __?__.
4. *Donna* literally means __?__.
5. A *metro*polis is a __?__ city.
6. A *philanthropist* is literally a __?__ of __?__.
7. *Amigo* in Spanish means "__?__."
8. "*Frère* Jacques" is __?__ Jacques.
9. One's *mater*nal grandfather is one's __?__'s father.
10. A *fili*al feeling is the feeling a __?__ has toward his parents.

UNIT TWO

OLD ENGLISH HEIRLOOMS

The words which came from Old English, the language of the Angles and Saxons who settled in England more than a thousand years ago, are largely the everyday words we cannot do without. They are the words that we use most often in conversation and letter writing. Most of the words in this very paragraph, in fact, came from Old English, including *loom* in *heirloom;* but *heir* came through France from the Romans.

PROFESSOR QUIZ

How many questions can you answer?

1. Which word involves feathers?

2. Which one is a word for gardening?

3. Which one denotes laziness?

4. Which one hurts?

5. Which one attracts strongly?

6. Which ones involve sad or gloomy feeling?

Heirlooms

First Group

1. bleach
2. dole
3. hassock
4. lodestone
5. mildew
6. pall
7. seer
8. smock
9. twinge
10. wiles

Second Group

1. fledgling
2. fortnight
3. husbandry
4. sloth
5. tithe

235

OLD ENGLISH HEIRLOOMS—First Group

1. BLEACH . . . .   whitened condition, that which whitens or produces whiteness

   n The bleach of her hair is caused by the blistering sky.
   v The bones bleach (whiten) on the desert.

   See *blench* and *blanch.*

2. DOLE . . . . .   a distribution, payment to needy persons

   n Many went on the dole when the factory closed.
   v Father hates to dole out money for broken windows.

3. HASSOCK . . . . .   a stuffed object used as a footstool

   n The baby likes to roll the hassock across the room.

4. LODESTONE . .   magnetic rock, something strongly attractive

   n In ancient legend, when a ship sailed too close to a lodestone deposit, its nails were drawn out, and the ship collapsed.

5. MILDEW . . . . .   a whitish growth somewhat like mold

   n Mildew gathers on clothes left damp too long.
   v In the hot, humid summer weather the books began to mildew.

6. PALL . .   a dark covering, something gloomy which overspreads

   n A pall of fog hung over the swamp.
   n The pallbearers (from the black cloth once spread over a coffin) wore gray gloves.

7. SEER . . . .   a prophet, one who foresees

   n The seer was nearly eighty when his prophecy came true.
   n A former President becomes a kind of political seer.

8. SMOCK . . a washable outer garment to protect one's clothes

 n Barbers and internes wear white smocks.
 n Mrs. Wordlock wears a smock while doing the chores.

9. TWINGE . . . . a sharp sensation, pang

 n Arthritis causes frequent twinges in damp weather.
 n The thief suffered frequent twinges of conscience.

10. WILES . . . . deceiving, beguiling ways or tricks

 n Sam had learned to beware of his sister's wiles.
 aj The Indians were wily fighters.

Second Group

1. FLEDGLING . . . . a beginner, person ready to start out
 n A fledgling soon becomes a full-fledged scout.
 n Literally, a fledgling is a bird with feathers enough for flight.

2. FORTNIGHT . . . . a two-week period

 n The carnival lasted a fortnight.
 aj The Fortnightly Club meets every two weeks.

3. HUSBANDRY . . . . farming, wise care and management

 n By careful husbandry he built up quite a fortune.
 n Animal husbandry involves the care of domestic animals.

4. SLOTH (slōth) . . . . laziness, indolence

 n Sloth will reduce a man from riches to rags.
 aj A slothful person often dislikes slothfulness in others.

5. TITHE . . . . a tenth, small part (for religious use)

 n Many church members give a tithe of their earnings.
 n Jacob was a tither of early Bible times.

ANGLO-SAXON WORDS IN PART ONE

Words of Old English origin include: *quell* (Unit 2), *swerve* (Unit 2), *loathe* (Unit 3), *seethe* (Unit 3), *sheathe* (Unit 3), *singe* (Unit 3), *swath(e)* (Unit 3), *wane* (Unit 3), *writhe* (Unit 3), *drone* (Unit 5), *sheaf, stud* (Unit 5), *ghastly* (Unit 6), *lithe, sallow* (Unit 6), *stowaway* (Unit 8), *foster* (Unit 9), *mingle, shackle, fawn, foal, mongrel, swine, weasel, dwindle* (Unit 19), *stalk* (Unit 19), *smolder* (Unit 19), *swath(e), ember, sinew, bight* (Unit 22), *lee(ward)* (Unit 22), *cove, dell, glade, gloaming, knoll* (Unit 23), *drivel* (Unit 25).

FIRST PRACTICE SET

Copy the italicized words and beside each write its meaning in the sentence.

1. The new pilot was a *fledgling* for a *fortnight*.
2. She sat on the *hassock*, talked about *bleaches*, discussed *husbandry*, admired *sloth*, and said a *tithe* was too much to give.
3. Her *wiles* stirred *twinges* of anger in him.
4. The *seer* wore a *smock* while he fixed his car.
5. News of the *dole* cast a *pall* over the audience.
6. There was *mildew* in the container for the *lodestone*.

SECOND PRACTICE SET

Which base word in this unit fits in each of the blanks best?

1. A __?__ of jealousy.
2. A __?__ to sit on.
3. Foretold by a __?__.
4. A __?__ of darkness.
5. A __?__ for the unemployed.
6. A __?__ to wear at work.
7. A __?__ fighter's first prize.
8. The __?__ of a turtle.
9. Some church members give a __?__.
10. Her __?__s draw him like a __?__.
11. The course in __?__ lasted a __?__.
12. Chemists discuss __?__es.
13. __?__ collects on damp wallpaper.

UNIT THREE

MORE HEIRLOOMS

All of the words in this unit, like those in Unit Two, come from the language of the Angles, Saxons, and Jutes, who settled in England before and during the Dark Ages. The majority of these words came to us from Germany by way of England.

A ROUGH TRIP

Fill each of the blanks appropriately, using words from the column at right.

Air pockets and up-currents made the plane ride above the mountains very bumpy that day, but the pretty and —?— stewardess did much to —?— our fear and —?— our courage by her —?— manner. The view did much to —?— for our discomfort; in fact, it made us —?— for wings like a bird.

More Heirlooms

First Group
1. atone
2. bolster
3. forbear
4. spurn
5. yearn

Second Group
1. blithe
2. comely
3. listless
4. stalwart
5. uncouth
6. winsome

Third Group
1. allay
2. enthrall
3. sunder
4. winnow

239

MORE HEIRLOOMS—First Group

1. **ATONE** . . . . to make amends (for)

   v Leon tried to atone for his mistake.
   n Buying the candy was an act of atonement.

2. **BOLSTER** . . . . to support, sustain, reinforce

   v Jim whistled in the dark to bolster his courage.
   n A pillow is a gentle bolster.

3. **FORBEAR** . . . . to restrain oneself, hold back, be patient

   v "Good friend, for Jesus' sake forbear
      To dig the dust enclosed here." (Shakespeare's epitaph)
   n Forbearance sometimes wins one's enemies over.

4. **SPURN** . . . . to reject or push aside scornfully

   v Why did Kathi spurn the woman's offer of assistance?
   n Spurns do not discourage a door-to-door salesman.

5. **YEARN** . . . . to long for, desire earnestly

   v Uncle Herbert yearns for the good old days.
   aj There was a yearning look in Mary's eyes.

Second Group

1. **BLITHE** . . . . light-hearted, gay, cheerful

   aj "Hail to thee, blithe spirit!" is addressed to a skylark.
   av The teachers greet us blithely every morning.

2. **COMELY** . . . . attractive in form and features

   aj Ruth plays the role of a comely country girl.
   n Susan's comeliness won her many friends.

3. **LISTLESS** . . . . spiritless, indifferent

   aj Rainy weather makes one listless.
   n We lost the game because of the team's listlessness.

4. **STALWART** . . . . strong and upstanding, brave

   aj The stalwart defenders of the castle never wavered.
   n Their stalwartness gave them the victory.

5. **UNCOUTH** . . . . rude, rough, unrefined

   aj Daniel Boone and Davy Crockett were somewhat uncouth.
   n The sailor's uncouthness kept him from making friends.

6. **WINSOME** . . . . . . pleasant, charming, captivating

   aj Trudie's winsome ways are most appealing.
   n The little clerk's winsomeness won her many friends.

Third Group

1. **ALLAY** . . . . to put at rest, to quiet, to relieve

   v The news that he survived will allay her fears.
   v Music proved powerless to allay the tension Nora felt.

2. **ENTHRALL** . . . . to captivate, hold spellbound

   v That lecturer knows how to enthrall an audience.
   aj Some girls find baseball games enthralling.

3. **SUNDER** . . . . to sever, cut apart, separate

   v War sunders all normal ties with the enemy country.
   av The tent was torn asunder by the wind.

4. **WINNOW** . . . . to blow chaff from (grain), sift

   v It was once the custom to winnow wheat by hand.
   v The wind was winnowing the leaves in the trees.

ANGLO-SAXON WORDS IN PART TWO

Words of Old English derivation presented as base words in the regular units of Part Two include: *ruthless* (page 127), *beguile* (page 136), *anneal* (page 168), *boatswain* (page 184), *wale* in *gunwale* (page 185). *Wield, fickle, uncouth, truce* and, *callow* are other words of Old English origin.

FIRST PRACTICE SET

Copy the italicized words and beside each write its meaning:

1. Nothing will *allay* his grief or *atone* for the crime.
2. You may want to *spurn* the offer, but please *forbear*.
3. The bride is *blithe*. She *yearns* for a new car.
4. The rider is *comely* and *winsome*.
5. At the wedding the best man had to *bolster* the groom's courage; now nothing can *sunder* him from his bride.
6. The bride's brother is rather *uncouth* and somewhat *listless*.
7. *Winnowing* the beans is not an *enthralling* task.
8. He had the reputation of being a good-natured, *stalwart* leader.

SECOND PRACTICE SET

Using a different one of the base words of this unit for each blank, what is the best thing to do with each of the following?

1. Angry words? __?__.
2. Good intentions? __?__ them. How? __?__ly and with zest.
3. Temptations? __?__ them in a __?__ manner.
4. A degrading friendship? __?__ it.
5. Lofty ambitions? __?__ to achieve them and then go to work.
6. Serious mistakes? __?__ for them, if possible.
7. Unfounded suspicions? __?__ them. Regard them as __?__.
8. An assortment of good and bad friends? __?__ them.
9. People you meet while selling cars? Be __?__ and __?__ them. Even if they are __?__, you may captivate them.
10. Sickly, underfed girls? Good food and outdoor sports may make them __?__ in time.

UNIT FOUR

DOUBLE TROUBLE

When a doubled letter appears in a word there is usually a reason. The reason may be a prefix, or it may be a well-established principle of pronunciation, or it may be a custom of the word family or its root ancestors.

I. A Prefix Did It

Often a prefix is attached to a word or root that begins with the same letter that the prefix ends with. Thus, "misspell" has a prefix ending in *s* attached to a word that begins with *s*. If a person remembers this fact, he will never misspell "misspell." There are quite a few such words:

To *ab*breviate   To *trans*ship the goods
A drug *ad*dict   *Un*natural behavior
To *con*nect a wire   *Over*ripe tomatoes
To *dis*sect a frog   *Over*ride a veto
A *non*negotiable check

243

Several prefixes change their last letter to agree with the first letter of the root or word to which they are attached. This trait causes most of the double letters that occur because of prefixes. Note carefully what happens in each of the following words using prefixes.

ad-:

*accept	*af*flict	*ap*ply	*at*tack
*ac*cess	*ag*gressive	*appoint	*at*tention
*accident	(*pushing forward*)	*ar*rest	*at*tempt
*ac*climate	*exa*ggerate	*ar*rive	*at*test (PART
*ac*cord	*al*liance	*as*sault	TWO, UNIT 22)
*af*fect	*al*low	*as*semble	*at*tract
*af*firm	*an*nounce	*as*sert	

con-:

*col*lapse	*com*mand	*co*operate	*cor*rect
*col*lect	*com*mence	*co*ordinate (*place*	*cor*relate
*col*lege	*com*mit	*in the same rank*)	*cor*respond
*col*lide	*com*mercial		*cor*rupt (PART ONE,
			UNIT 1)

ex-:

*ec*centric (*queer,*	*ef*face (*wipe out*)	*ef*ficient
off-center)	*ef*fect	*ef*fort
*ec*clesiastical (*pertaining*		
to the church)		

in-:

*il*legal	*im*mense (lit. not	*im*mune
*illegible	measurable)	*ir*regular
*il*literate (*unable to*	*im*merse (PART TWO,	*ir*responsible
read or write)	UNIT 2)	*ir*religious
*il*logical	*im*modest	*ir*reverent
*il*lustrate	*im*mortal	*ir*rigate
	*im*movable	

sub-:

*success	*suf*fer	*sum*mon	*sur*render
*suc*cumb	*suf*ficient	*sup*ply	*sur*reptitious
(*yield, die*)	*suf*fix	*sup*port	(*sly, secret*)
*suc*cinct	*suf*focate	*sup*pose	*sur*round
(*brief, terse*)	*sug*gest	*sup*press	

ob-:

*occasion	*of*fend	*op*ponent
*oc*cupy	*of*fense	*opportunity
*oc*cupation	*of*fer(ing)	*opposite
*occurrence		*op*press

II. Words Ending in *-ing* and *-ed*
(Review Part One, Unit 4)

Double letter:	Compare:	Double letter:	Compare:
bellowing	(ceiling)	borrowed	(stored)
calling	(failing)	omitted	(recited)
filling	(filing)	planned	(planed)
killing	(piling)	referred	(impeded, hindered)
sorrowing	(boring)	wedded	(ceded)

III. *-ly* Words

These words add *-ly* to a word that ends in *-al* or *-ful*.

*finally	actually	accidentally	faithfully
generally	continually	confidentially	hopefully
really	electrically	intentionally	gracefully
*usually	manually	internally	truthfully

IV. It Happens at the End of a Word

Certain words liks *bailiff* (Part Two, Unit 22), *tariff*, and *plaintiff* end in *-ff*. Quite a few words end in *-ss: careless(ness)*, *compass*, **trespass*, **harass*. List others.

V. It Happens in the Middle of a Word

carrot	fission	battalion (PART	dollar
(cf. caret)	issue	TWO, UNIT 27)	(cf. dolor)
error	tissue	comma	glitter
terror	mission	(cf. coma)	(cf. glider)
(cf. tedious)	(cf. miser)	*dessert	latter
sorrow	*necessary	gossip	(cf. later)
(cf. soda)	possible	happen	written
*tomorrow	(cf. postal)	*parallel	(cf. writer)

Explain the principle illustrated in the last column. Do any of the words violate the principle as stated in Part One, Unit 4?

VI. Some Words Contain a Double Double

*accidentally	address	*committee
*accommodate	coffee	commission
*annually	assess	*occurrence
*embarrass	*misspell	*unnecessary

VII. Vowels Are Often Doubled

choose (chose)	buccaneer (PART	mountaineer	cooperate
*loose (lose)	ONE, UNIT 8)	volunteer	coordinate
	engineer		

A Problem

Read aloud the words in the list below, separating the syllables to help fix double letters in mind. Then, arrange them in groups like the groups above according to prefixes, endings, and middle letters. If a word fits in two different sets, list it in each group. Here are the words:

*accident, *accidentally, *accommodate, accompany, accompanying, accent, accordance, according, accomplish, accounts, *accurate, accuse, accustom, addressed, affair, afford, allotment, ammunition, anniversary, annual, *annually, apparatus, apparent, appeal, appe-

tite, approach, appropriate, approximately, assume, attack, attempt, attitude, balloon, battalion, * beginning, blizzard, bookkeeping, cannon, cannot, career, carrot, cartoon, challenge, chauffeur, collapse, comment, commission, 'commit, committed, corrupt, cunning, degree(s), * disappoint, disapprove, dissatisfied, * dropped; embarrass, engineer, especially, essay, exceptionally, follow, forgotten, generally, gossip, gradually, hopped, * immediate, immense, incidentally, mastiff, * misspell, molasses, naturally, necessity, * occasion, occasionally, occupy, occur, * occurred, opportunity, opposite, * parallel, personally, pioneer, plaintiff, pontiff, * possess, practically, really, * recommend, referring, remittance, sheriff, staff, * stopped, struggle, stubborn, * success, suggest, summon, supposition, surrender, surround, * syllable, tariff, tennis, terrible, territory, * tobacco, tomorrow, traffic, tunnel, * unnecessary, * usually, vessel, volunteer, warrant, wholly, * written.

SENTENCES FOR PRACTICE

Write some or all of the following from dictation.

1. Gossips occasionally possess accurate information.
2. The chauffeur avoided an accident by running over the mastiff.
3. The sheriff appointed a committee to study traffic.
4. The danger does not warrant our possessing ammunition.
5. A commission will assess the property and make recommendations.
6. The balloon gradually ascended to a height of approximately 16,000 feet.
7. By dividing words into syllables, you may avoid the embarrassment of misspelling them.
8. A volunteer usually drives the apparatus.
9. Family allotments made much bookkeeping necessary.
10. The battalion stubbornly refused to surrender.
11. The collapse of the tunnel occurred during a blizzard.
12. The tariff on tobacco seems wholly unwarranted.
13. The plaintiff occasionally challenged our statements.
14. The anniversary speech was an appeal for peace.
15. The editor disapproved of the cartoon about pioneers.

SECOND PRACTICE SET

Write for each blank the double-lettered word that is indicated, using the list below to prompt you if necessary:

1. You must not __?__ (permit) such tension to increase.
2. Do not __?__ (make larger) and do not __?__ (make shorter) the story of the fight.
3. The auto __?__ (mishap, wreck) __?__ (drew toward it) much attention.
4. The huge rock is __?__ (not movable), but perhaps we can __?__ (ride over) it.
5. There is __?__ (as a rule) some ice cream for those who __?__ (operate together) with the leaders.
6. The __?__ (court official) was much __?__ (upset, ashamed) when he found that the prisoner had escaped.
7. Income taxes must be paid __?__ (each year). The Government is very willing to __?__ (receive) the tax money.
8. The man was __?__ (not guilty) of the crime for which he had to __?__ (undergo anguish).
9. If we __?__ (encircle) the building, the criminals inside will have to __?__ (yield, give themselves up).
10. The __?__ (large body of troops) fought on a battle line __?__ (running always at same distance) to the railroad.

UNIT FIVE

LATIN WEAVINGS

Each of the base words in this unit may be traced to a word in Latin. Some of the words came directly to English with little change. Others came by way of French or Old French, with changes that give the word a French appearance.

SISTER SUE

Fill the blanks appropriately, using words from the column at the right.

She likes to —?— her cheeks and go "poof"! She is not old enough to —?— her face with lipstick, and she will not —?— the process of eating her meals no matter how much Mother —?—s with her. She likes the —?— of the living room drapes and sometimes she tries to climb them. She seldom goes to bed of her own —?—. She is only three.

Latin Weavings

First Group

1. rudiment
2. simile
3. suffrage
4. tenant

Second Group

1. texture
2. valor
3. vestige
4. volition

Third Group

1. dishevel
2. distend
3. edify
4. desecrate
5. embellish
6. expedite
7. expostulate

LATIN WEAVINGS—First Group

1. **RUDIMENT** . . . . basic element or principle

    n A grade school often teaches the rudiments of music.
    aj Rudimentary (very crude) drawings are found in the cave.

2. **SIMILE** . . . . a comparison using *like* or *as*

    n "Proud as a peacock" is a too-familiar simile.
    n Similes in literature are usually fresher than those in everyday conversation.

3. **SUFFRAGE** . . . . the right to vote (in political matters)

    n The campaign for women's suffrage was a long one.
    n Should suffrage be extended to the colonists?

4. **TENANT** . . occupant, especially a person who pays rent to
    occupy a house or some land

    n The tenant does not want to leave.
    n The election extends Governor Grover's tenure (act or right of holding a position) for two more years.

    Words containing **-ten-** include **tenable, tenant, tenacious, tenacity.** See **-tain- -ten-** in Part Three, Unit 14.

Second Group

1. **TEXTURE** . . structure, composition, characteristics, especially
    of a fabric

    n A blind man recognized canvas by its rough texture.
    n From its texture, the music sounds like Mozart's.

    Cf. **textile.** Both **texture** and **textile** derive from the Latin.

2. **VALOR** . . . . courage, bravery

    n Mr. Clinton showed great valor in fighting the forest fire.
    aj Tales of the Trojan War tell of many valorous deeds.

3. **VESTIGE** . . . . a trace, remnant

n Not a vestige of the food remains.
aj Are human toes really vestigial (věs·tij′ĭ·əl) claws?

4. **VOLITION** . . . . act of will, desire, or choice

n Robert went of his own volition.
n For free men, volition takes the place of compulsion.

Third Group

1. **DISHEVEL** . . . . to muss up, disorder

v Do not dishevel my hair.
aj The boy had a dishevelled appearance after the fight.

2. **DISTEND** . . . . to stretch, enlarge, swell

v Overeating will distend one's stomach.
n Excess helium caused distention of the balloon.

3. **EDIFY** . . . . to make (one) better, improve

v Prejudices do not edify a person.
n One reads books for edification as well as amusement.

4. **DESECRATE** . . . . to violate the sacredness of, to profane

v Soldiers desecrated the church by keeping their horses in it.
n Trampling on the flag is an act of desecration.

5. **EMBELLISH** . . . . to decorate, adorn

v Illustrations embellish the entire manuscript.
n Father's signature has no embellishments.

6. **EXPEDITE** . . . . to hasten, speed up, accelerate

v How can we expedite the shipment?
n A Government expediter was appointed.

7. **EXPOSTULATE** . . . . to scold, entreat a person

   v Did you expostulate with him about his tardiness?

FIRST PRACTICE SET

Write the meaning in the sentence of each italicized word.

1. Does universal *suffrage* involve a man if he is only a *tenant*?
2. Randolph does not know the *rudiments* of politeness, he lacks every *vestige* of good manners, and he will never of his own *volition* say, "Thank you." His influence is not *edifying*.
3. "Soft as rabbit's fur" is a *simile* describing *texture*.
4. She *desecrated* the flag by trying to *embellish* it.
5. Why *expostulate*? There is no way to *expedite* the project. Its cost will be *distended* by politics and graft.
6. The wind gave her a *dishevelled* appearance.
7. He showed great *valor* in his first battle.

TOO MUCH AND TOO LITTLE

What is the result, in terms of the first group of base words, of too much:

1. Food? It __?__s one.
2. Nonsense? Teachers __?__.
3. Delay? You must __?__.
4. Slang? It does not __?__.
5. Roughhouse? It __?__s one.
6. Loud noise? It __?__s a church.
7. Too plain a costume? You try to __?__ it.

Which of the base words of the second group goes in each blank for the results of too little?

1. Wisdom? Not even the __?__s.
2. Imagination? Can't think of a __?__.
3. Freedom? Citizens are denied __?__.
4. Evidences of a crime? No __?__s could be found.
5. Skill? He did not recognize the __?__ of the black sand.
6. Restraint? She went of her own __?__ without consent.
7. Luck? They could not find a __?__ to live on the farm.
8. Courage? She had no __?__.

UNIT SIX

ROMANIFIC ADJECTIVES

All of the adjectives in this unit are derived directly or indirectly from Latin words.

APPLICATIONS

Which word from the list at the right may best be applied to:

First Group
1. colossal
2. consecutive
3. eminent
4. eternal
5. eventual
6. excessive
7. imminent
8. insurgent
9. mutual
10. prevalent

1. The Great Pyramid? —?—

2. A profit-sharing company? —?—

3. A band of rebels? —?—

4. A hobo? —?—

5. An event about to happen? —?—

6. A free-will offering? —?—

7. A birthmark? —?—

Second Group
1. congenital
2. itinerant
3. momentous
4. proficient
5. voluntary

253

ROMANIFIC ADJECTIVES—First Group

1. **COLOSSAL** . . . . huge, immense, enormous
   - aj The national debt is colossal.
   - n The Colossus of Rhodes was a huge statue of Apollo at the harbor's entrance.

2. **CONSECUTIVE** . . . following one another (in numerical or regular order)
   - aj The cards are arranged in consecutive order.
   - av Arrange the papers consecutively according to scores.

3. **EMINENT** . . . . outstanding, lofty, distinguished
   - aj An eminent doctor died yesterday.
   - n The Bok Tower stands on an eminence in Florida.
   - n The class discussed Mark Twain's eminence as a writer.
   - av Both candidates are eminently qualified for the Presidency.

4. **ETERNAL** . . . . . . timeless, everlasting, never ending
   - aj What to wear is a girl's eternal problem.
   - av Joe said he would be eternally grateful.
   - n The waiting period seemed an eternity.

5. **EVENTUAL** . . . . final, ultimate
   - aj What is the eventual solution of unemployment?
   - n One must be prepared for all eventualities (outcomes).

6. **EXCESSIVE** . . . . . having more than enough, too much
   - aj Excessive speed is a major cause of auto accidents.
   - av He was not excessively eager to leave home.

7. **IMMINENT** . . . about to happen, threatening, impending
   - aj Death was imminent for 20,000 men.
   - n Because of the imminence of the storm, we did not start.

8. **INSURGENT** . . . . . . rising in opposition, rebellious

    aj An insurgent group arose within the Democratic party.
    n Insurgents won control of a Latin-American country.

9. **MUTUAL** . . . . shared, benefiting each (party)

    aj There was a mutual fondness between teacher and pupil.
    av The earlier date proved mutually satisfactory to both teams.
    n Between citizens and their government a high degree of mutuality should exist.

    Cf. *reciprocal.*

10. **PREVALENT** . . . . . widespread, widely occurring, rife

    aj Malaria was prevalent in swampy areas of Africa.
    n The prevalence of honesty makes national credit cards feasible.

Second Group

1. **CONGENITAL** . . . . existing or beginning at birth, inborn

    aj The deformity on his hand is congenital.
    aj The boy's heart has a congenital defect.

2. **ITINERANT** . . . . traveling from place to place

    aj A company of itinerant musicians came to town.
    n What will your itinerary (route of travel) be in Europe?

3. **MOMENTOUS** . . . . very important, of great consequence

    aj Launching the first space ship will be a momentous event.
    n The momentousness of Easter must not be forgotten.

4. **PROFICIENT** . . . . skillful, adept, well versed

    aj A store manager needs to be proficient in arithmetic.
    n Mr. Gopple's proficiency in bowling won him a prize.
    av Doris makes candy proficiently.

5. VOLUNTARY . . . . done by one's own choice

   aj All school sports are voluntary.
   av The thief confessed voluntarily.

FIRST PRACTICE SET

Copy the italicized words and beside each write its meaning.

1. An attack by the *insurgents* appeared *imminent*.
2. The dinosaurs were *colossal;* their disappearance was not *voluntary*.
3. The man with *itinerant* habits often has a *congenital* distaste for work.
4. Three *consecutive* holidays give everyone *mutual* happiness.
5. A *proficient* golfer does not use an *excessive* number of strokes.
6. According to an *eminent* authority, disease is *prevalent* in India.
7. Is *eternal* joy the *eventual* lot of everyone?
8. The senator made a *momentous* announcement.

THE DAM

Which of the base words of this unit best fits in each blank? Use each word only once.

Building the dam would be a __?__ task, one that seemed at times almost __?__, even though it was expected to take only twenty years—provided war did not at any time become __?__. It took a group of five __?__ engineers a year or more to plan it. No one could devote more than five __?__ days to it at a time because each traveled quite a bit and thus lived a rather __?__ life. Each engineer was very __?__, though not inclined to do an __?__ amount of work, and they had __?__ confidence in each other. One proved very __?__ in thinking up ideas to solve practical problems, one was a kind of __?__ who wanted to try new ways of doing things, and one had always been a __?__ doubter. Good will and confidence were __?__ among them, and they believed the dam was a __?__ project of great __?__ importance.

UNIT SEVEN

GREEK GIFTS

Each of the base words in this unit may be traced to the ancient Greek language. As a group, Greek-derived words are mostly technical terms pertaining to the theater, to geography, to philosophy, to religion, and to the sciences, especially medicine.

AT CHURCH

Can you fill the blanks correctly?

The minister gave a —?— of the life of Moses and the —?— of the children of Israel from Egypt. The anthem was a —?— about the beauty of holiness, and the choir sang it with real —?—. The director had a —?— for waving his arms, however.

Base Words

First Group

1. canopy
2. elegy
3. exodus
4. fantasy
5. lyric
6. martyr
7. parable
8. phenomenon
9. synopsis
10. titan

Second Group

1. ecstasy
2. genesis
3. mania
4. ostracism
5. phobia

257

GREEK GIFTS—First Group

1. **CANOPY** . . . . a tentlike covering or shelter

   n The queen sat under a canopy.
   n The sky is often thought of as a canopy.

2. **ELEGY** . . . . a poetic lament, for someone who has died

   n The poet offered to write an elegy.
   n Thomas Gray wrote a mock elegy about a cat which drowned in a bowl of goldfishes.

3. **EXODUS** . . . . . a large-scale departure or migration

   n The exodus from the burning building was orderly.
   n What happens in the Book of Exodus?

4. **FANTASY** . . . . something unreal or imagined

   n The side-hill gopher is a creature of fantasy.
   n The play *Outward Bound* is a fantasy about the hereafter.
   aj The story that the girl is a witch is fantastic (fanciful).

   A *phantasm* is a fantasy or a specter.

5. **LYRIC** . . . . a poem of strong feeling

   n Wordsworth wrote many lyrics.
   aj Marcia has a fine (musical or song-like) lyrical voice.

6. **MARTYR** . . . . one killed or harmed for holding a belief
   or principle

   n St. Peter was an early Christian martyr.
   n What American president suffered martyrdom?

7. **PARABLE** . . . . . a brief story which illustrates a truth

   n The parable of the Good Samaritan was an answer to the question, "Who is my neighbor?"

8. PHENOMENON . . . . . . (unusual) fact or occurrence

   n A new star is a scientific phenomenon.
   aj Henry Ford's efficiency was phenomenal (extraordinary).

9. SYNOPSIS . . . . . . a summary, condensed statement

   n Could you give a synopsis of the play?
   aj Matthew is one of the "Synoptic Gospels."

10. TITAN . . . . a person of gigantic size or power

   n The Titans were supermen of ancient Greek mythology.
   n John D. Rockefeller Sr. became a titan of the oil industry.
   aj Sunspots are caused by titanic explosions.
   n Why was the *Titanic*, which sank in 1912, so named?
   n Antitrust laws exist to limit titanism in industry.

Second Group

1. ECSTASY . . . . . wild delight, or other strong feeling

   n The sight of the diamond filled Jane with ecstasy.
   n Mr. Simmons writhed in an ecstasy of rage.

2. GENESIS . . . . beginning

   n The feud had its genesis in a minor disagreement.
   n Why is the Book of Genesis so called?

3. MANIA . . . . a craze or passion, madness

   n Aunt Sarah has a mania for antiques.
   n A maniac is a madman, frenzied and disordered.

4. OSTRACISM . . . . exclusion, banishment

   n People who are different are often victims of social ostracism.
   v The people of the village tried to ostracize the stranger.

5. PHOBIA . . . .   a deep-seated, unreasoning fear

    n Why do some people have a phobia about snakes?

    n A Russophobe is a person who fears or hates Russia.

FIRST PRACTICE SET

Copy the italicized words, and beside each write its meaning in the sentence.

1. A poet wrote an *elegy* about the scientist who had studied atomic *phenomena.*
2. A *fantasy* is much different from a *lyric.*
3. The author wrote a *synopsis* of his book on *phobias.*
4. There was an *exodus* of all those who hated the foreign *titan.*
5. The *parable* was about a king sitting under a silken *canopy.*
6. With near *ecstasy* he described the *genesis* of his housing plan.
7. *Martyrs* have a *mania* for being right.
8. It is not pleasant to suffer *ostracism.*

SECOND PRACTICE SET

Which of the base words of this unit fits best in each blank?

1. *Alice in Wonderland* is a __?__.
2. Bad-mannered persons may well expect __?__.
3. Patriotism calls for __?__ (poem), especially in the case of a man who was a __?__ for freedom.
4. The United Nations had its __?__ in 1945.
5. A busy man appreciates a __?__ of a long novel.
6. The week-end __?__ from the city calls for careful driving.
7. A victory by our team would create __?__ in the student body.
8. A __?__ is a story to teach a lesson.
9. A Colonial bed needs a __?__ to look right.
10. Distrust of others can become a __?__.
11. Nervousness about snakes can become a __?__.
12. Goliath was a __?__.
13. A calf with two heads is a rare __?__.
14. A tribute to a dead hero can become an __?__.

UNIT EIGHT

THE LATIN-GREEK FLAVOR

Quite a few familiar words contain a *y*, not at the end in an *-ly* ending, but in the interior of the word. Here are twenty, all of Greek or partly Greek origin except those in the first column and *gypsy:*

Group I

crying	analysis	dynasty	mystify	symbol
dying	analyze	encyclopedia	myth(ical)	sympathy
(*expire*)	*crystal	gymnasium	oyster	symphony
lying (*all*	cycle	gypsy	*psychology	*synonym
meanings)	cylinder	gyroscope	rhyme	system
*dyeing	dynamite	(PART TWO,	*rhythm	typewriter
(*coloring*)	dynamo	UNIT 18)	style	typhoid
trying		myriad	*syllable	typical
		*mystery		

Study them. Pronounce them. Write down other words that could be added to the list.

261

QUESTS

1. What does *dyn-* mean? List other *dyn-* words.
2. Write down the adjective form of fifteen of the words in the second, third, fourth, and fifth columns.
3. List ten words not on the list above (or forms of them that are not listed) which begin with *sym-* or *syn-* and their definitions.

Group II

In several word-building units you have practiced making adverb forms by adding *-ly* to an adjective form thus, *without dropping* the final *e* or anything else:

absolutely	intensely	merely	rapidly
definitely	largely	precisely	safely
extremely	likely	positively	scarcely
*immediately	lively	properly	strictly

Able and *Ible* words (Part Two, Unit 24) and a few others do drop the *e* at the end and replace it with *y*.

admirable	admirably	*true	truly
inseparable	inseparably	due	duly

Words which end in *y* usually change the *y* to *i* before they add *-ly*:

hastily	readily	tastily
ordinarily	satisfactorily	warily

Note: the three-letter words *dry*, *shy*, and *wry* keep the *y*: *dryly*, *shyly*, *wryly*; but *drily* is permissible.

QUESTS

1. Write the *-ly* form of each base word in Part Two, Unit 23, except *gratis*.
2. Write sentences using ten of the words above.

Group III: *Ph* Words

Most of the words which use *ph* for the sound of *f* are of Greek origin. Study the following:

*sphere	autograph	phone	nephew
atmosphere	photograph	phonograph	orphan
hemisphere	(page 271)	symphony	triumph
stratosphere	stenographer	telephone	typhoid

What is the literal or root meaning of each word?

Group IV: Plurals

A few dozen words from Latin still keep the plurals they had in their own language two thousand years ago.

-us (Latin)		*-is* or *-es* (Latin)	
alumnus	alumni	analysis	analyses
fungus	fungi	crisis	crises
radius	radii	synopsis	synopses (page 257)
		thesis	theses

-um (Latin)

erratum	errata
stadium	stadia
medium	media
minimum	minima (page 160)
phenomenon	phenomena (page 257)

QUESTS

1. Write the plural of *terminus, addendum, bacterium, curriculum, stratum, datum, axis, hypothesis, ellipsis.*
2. Look up the origin of words in Quest No. 1 you do not know.

FIRST PRACTICE SET

Write the following sentences from dictation.

1. The man tried to solve the mystery of the upper atmosphere.
2. A gypsy saw the telephone in the gymnasium.
3. An ellipse invariably has two foci.
4. Her nephew answered the telephone warily.
5. That orphan is the victim of typhoid bacteria.
6. A stenographer wrote down every syllable of the dying man's analysis.
7. This dynamo performs reliably in the car's electrical system.
8. Myriads of ice crystals dance in rhythm.
9. The class is studying the rock strata in the desert.
10. Tears are a symbol of sympathy and a synonym for sorrow.

SECOND PRACTICE SET

Write down the word which goes in each blank:

1. A chemist will a__?__ (find what is in) the blood stains that m__?__ (puzzle) the police.
2. Two a__?__ (graduates) of State College wrote a poem on the c__?__ (moving through stages) of the seasons.
3. Come im__?__ (at once) if you want to see the ph__?__ (happenings) known as the Northern Lights.
4. A s__?__ orchestra (large, well-proportioned orchestra) performed __?__ (admirable).
5. This en__?__a (set of informative books) refers to newspapers and magazines as "mass __?__" (plural of *medium*).
6. The last member of the d__?__ (series of rulers) died of t__?__ fever.
7. The c__?__er (long round object) contains cr__?__ls (bright angular pieces) of glass-like rock.
8. The plane flies through the at__?__ (air) of the Western hem__?__ (half of the globe).
9. Handle d__?__te (explosive) very war__?__y (cautiously).
10. Our __?__ogy (mind science) class must meet in the g__?__m (place for athletic exercise).

UNIT NINE

LEARNING TO COUNT IN LATIN AND GREEK

Each of the classical languages had a set of numbers which survives today as a set of prefixes. The object of this unit is to find out what they are and how they are used.

NUMBER PLEASE!

What number goes in each blank?

1. —?— dance in a *quad*rille.

2. A *tri*logy is a series of —?— books.

3. A *bi*ped has —?— feet.

4. The *penta*thlon is an athletic meet having —?— events.

5. The *octo*pus has —?— tentacles.

6. A *hepta*gon has —?— sides.

7. A *centi*pede has —?— feet.

8. A *mille*nium lasts —?— years.

Number Prefixes

Latin	Greek
First Group	
1. uni-	mono-
2. du(o)-	bi-
3. tri-	tri-
4. quad(ri)-	tetra-
Second Group	
5. quin(que)-	pent(a)-
6. sex-	hex(a)-
7. sept-	hept(a)-
8. octo-	octa-
Third Group	
9. non(a)- nov-	ennea-
10. dec(im)-	deca-
11. cent(i)-	hect(o)- hec(a)-
12. mill(e)- mill(i)-	kilo-
13. semi-	hemi- demi-

LEARNING TO COUNT—Study Guide

1. UNI-, MONO- . . . . one

    n A *uni*cycle has only *one* wheel.
    aj The class studied *uni*cellular (*one*-celled) animals.
    n The count raised his *mono*cle (*single* eyeglass).
    n The *mono*logue (*one* person talking) continued.

    Cf. **units, unify** (to make *one*), **monopoly** (*one* person in control), **monoplane** (*one*-winged plane).

2. DU(O)-, BI- . . . . two

    aj The car has *du*al (*two*) controls.
    aj *Du*plicate (*two*fold) prizes were given.
    aj *Bi*weekly (every-*two*-weeks) payments are expected.

    Note: **di-** means **two** in words like **dicotyledon**, a plant having two seed leaves. Do not confuse with **dia-** (through, between, or across) in words like *dialect, diameter, diaper, diocese, dielectric*.

3. TRI-, TRI- . . . . three

    n *Tri*plets were born.
    n Type in *tri*plicate (*three*fold).
    aj The *tri*ennial (every-*three*-years) election took place in January.

4. QUAD(RI)-, TETRA- . . . . four

    n *Quad*ruplets (*four* babies at one birth) are rare.
    n A *quadr*ant is one-*fourth* of a circle.
    n A *quadr*angle is a *four*-cornered court, usually found in a college.
    n A *tetr*arch (tē'trärk) ruled one-*fourth* of a province.
    aj A square is a *tetra*gonal figure which has *four* sides or angles.

    Note: **Quar-** as in **quarter** and **quart** is a familiar variant of the Latin word for **four**.

PRACTICE SET

Write the meaning of each italicized prefix.

1. A *quadri*lateral has __?__ sides.
2. *Triune* means __?__ in one.
3. A *bi*polar battery has __?__ poles.
4. A *mono*tonous voice stays on __?__ tone most of the time.
5. A *duodecimal* number system has __?__ plus __?__, or twelve as a base.
6. *Tetra*meter has __?__ feet or measures per line.
7. The *Uni*on is a gathering of the states as __?__ nation.
8. *Tri*meter is a verse having __?__ measures per line.

Second Group

5. QUIN (QUE)-, PENT(A)- . . . . **five**

   n One of the Dionne QUIN-tu-plets died. (Note accent.)
   n Our basketball *quin*tet played well.
   n A *penta*gram is a five-pointed star.
   n *Pente*cost is the fiftieth day (after the Passover).

6. SEX-, HEX(A)- . . . . **six**

   n A *sex*tet is a group of *six* (singers, usually).
   n A *sex*agenarian is a person in his *sixties*.
   n A *hex*agon is a *six*-sided figure.
   n A *hex*archy is a group of *six* states or rulers.

7. SEPT-, HEPT(A)- . . . . **seven**

   n In Roman times *Sept*ember was the *seventh* month.
   n A *sept*uagenarian is a person in his *seventies*.
   n A *hepta*gon has *seven* sides.
   aj It is *hept*angular.

8. OCTO-, OCTA- . . . . **eight**

   n An *octa*ve includes the *eight* tones of a musical scale.
   n *Octo*ber was once the *eighth* month.

PRACTICE SET

Write the meaning of each italicized prefix.

1. An *octo*syllable is a word with __?__ syllables.
2. To *quin*tuple a figure, multiply it by __?__.
3. A *sex*tuplet is one of __?__ children born at the same time.
4. An *octa*gon has __?__ sides.
5. A *sept*ennial event occurs every __?__ years.
6. A *penta*hedron has __?__ sides.
7. *Hept*archy is a rule by __?__ people.
8. A *hexa*gonal figure has __?__ angles.

Third Group

9. NON(A)-, NOV-, ENNEA- . . . . nine

    n A *nona*gon is a *nine*-sided figure.
    n A *nona*genarian is in his *nineties*.
    n A *nov*ena is a Catholic act of worship lasting *nine* days.
    n An *ennea*d is a group of *nine* (gods, usually).

    Note: ***Nov***(a)- and ***novo***- mean ***new,*** as in ***novelty***.

10. DEC(IM)-, DECA- . . . . ten

    n A *deca*de is a *ten*-year period.
    n The Ten Commandments are known as the *Deca*log.
    v To *decim*ate an army is to destroy every *tenth* man.

11. CENT(I), HECT(O)-, HEC(A)- . . . . one hundred

    n A *centi*pede has *one hundred* legs.
    n A *cent*ury is *one hundred* years.
    n A *hecto*meter (hĕk′tə·mē·tər) is *one hundred* meters or 328.1 feet.
    n A *heca*tomb was the mass sacrifice of *one hundred* oxen.

12. MILL(E)-, MILL(I)-, KILO- . . . . one thousand

    n A *milli*on is a *thousand* thousand.
    n A *milli*gram is *one-thousandth* of a gram.
    n A *kilo*gram is *one thousand* grams.

13.   SEMI-, HEMI-, DEMI- . . . .   half

   aj A *semi*annual event comes every *half* year.
   n A *hemi*sphere is *half* a sphere.
   n A *demi*god is *half* god and half man.

PRACTICE SET

Write the meaning of each italicized prefix.

1. A *nona*gon has __?__ sides.
2. A *hecto*gram is a weight of __?__ grams.
3. A *semi*annual event occurs every __?__ year.
4. A *milli*pede should, from its name, have __?__ feet.
5. A *deca*pod (such as a lobster) has __?__ legs.
6. A *kilo*watt hour is __?__ watts used in an hour.
7. A *centi*grade thermometer has __?__ degrees on the scale.
8. A *demi*tasse is a small or __?__ cup.
9. A *demi*volt in horsemanship is a __?__ leap.

QUESTS

1. *Unilateral* means *one-sided.* Continue the series through four.
2. Continue the series beginning *baby, twins, triplets* through eight.
3. List the singer series—*solo, duet, trio*—through eight.
4. How many can you add to the series beginning *double, triple, quadruple?*

UNIT TEN

FAMILIAR PREFIX PAIRS

(Latin and Greek)

Both Latin and Greek prefixes are given here to show their similar meanings. Review Unit 21 in Part Two before you start on this unit.

Write the prefixes which explain the italicized words.

1. A —?—syllablic word has *many* syllables.

2. —?—lithic behavior is the kind one would expect from a man of the *"new"* Stone Age.

3. An —?—present person would seemingly be *everywhere* at once.

4. —?—locution is talking all *around* a subject without getting anywhere.

5. The —?—cardium is a membrane *around* the heart.

Prefix Pairs

Latin	Greek
First Group	
1. circum-	peri-
2. con-, com-, co-,	sym-, syn-
3. lux-, luc(i)-	photo-
4. magn(i)-	mega-
Second Group	
5. multi-	poly-
6. nov-	neo-
7. omni-	pan(to)-
8. prim-	proto-
Third Group	
9. sui-	auto-
10. super- ultra-	hyper-
11. sur-	epi-
12. tele-	

FAMILIAR PREFIX PAIRS—First Group

1. **CIRCUM-, PERI-** . . . . around
   v Who was the first to *circum*navigate (sail *around*) the world?
   n The *peri*meter is the measure (*-meter*) *around* a body or figure.

   Cf. **periscope, period**.

2. **CON-, COM-, CO-, SYM-, SYN-** . . . . . together, with
   n A *con*vention is a coming (*-vent-*) *together*.
   n *Com*pression is a pressing *together*.
   n *Co*operation is working *together*.
   n *Sym*pathy is feeling (*-pathy*) sad—or happy—*with* someone.
   n A *syn*thesis is a placing *together* of elements or ideas to make something new.

   Query: What does **synopsis** on page 259 mean literally?

3. **LUX-, LUC(I)-, PHOTO-** . . . . light
   n *Luci*fer means *light* bearer (*-fer*).
   v Please *eluci*date (en*light*en).
   aj A *photo*electric cell responds electrically to *light*.

4. **MAGN(I)-, MEGA-** . . . . (very) large or great
   v Why *magn*ify (make *large*) the dangers or discuss their
   n *magn*itude (*large*ness)?
   n A *mega*phone produces a very *large* sound.

PRACTICE SET

Write the meaning of the italicized prefix for each blank.

1. A *photo*meter measures the intensity of ___?___.
2. To *circum*vent a plot is to thwart it or get ___?___ it.

3. A *peri*scope is a device to be used to look above or __?__ something.
4. A *magna*nimous person is one with a __?__ soul (*anima*).
5. A *sym*posium is pulling __?__ the ideas on a given subject.
6. A trans*luc*ent substance permits __?__ to pass through it.
7. To *col*laborate is to work (or labor) __?__.

Second Group

5. MULTI-, POLY- . . . . many

   n A *multi*graph makes *many* copies.
   n A *poly*glot can speak or write *many* languages.

   Cf. **multi**lateral, **poly**phonic.

6. NOV-, NEO- . . . . new

   n A *nov*ice is one who is new at something.
   n A *nov*a is a star *new* at least in brightness.
   n *Neo*n was the *new* gas when discovered.

   Cf. **nov**el, **neo**phyte.

7. OMNI-, PAN(TO)- . . . . all

   aj An *omni*scient person is an *all*-knowing one.
   aj *Pan*chromatic film responds to *all* colors.
   n A *panto*mime is *all* dumb show—no speaking.

8. PRIM-, PROTO- . . . . first

   aj A *prim*e minister is the *first* minister in importance.
   n A *proto*type is a *first* or original model or pattern.

   Cf. **prim**ary, **prim**itive, **prim**eval, **prim**ate, **prim**er, **proto**col.

PRACTICE SET

Write the meaning of the italicized prefix in each sentence.

1. *Poly*technical training involves __?__ skills.
2. An *omni*potent person is __?__-powerful (potent).
3. *Proto*col has to do with who gets __?__ or preferred places.
4. *Mega*lomania is an overwhelming sense of one's own __?__ness.
5. An in*nov*ator is one who starts something that is __?__.
6. A *prima* donna is the __?__ lady singer in an opera.
7. *Pan*-Americanism is the cooperation of __?__ the republics of North and South America.

Third Group

9. SUI-, AUTO- . . . . self

   aj An *auto*matic machine is *self*-operating.
   n One's *auto*graph is one's *self* writing (*-graph-*).
   n *Sui*cide is the killing or cutting off of one*self*.

   A person who is **sui generis** is of his own (*self's*) kind and therefore unique.

10. SUPER-, ULTRA-, HYPER- . . . over, above, beyond (normal), excessive(ly)

    aj *Super*sonic speeds are *beyond* the speed of sound.
    aj An *ultra*modern person is *beyond* what is normally modern.
    aj A *hyper*critical person is *excessively* critical.

11. SUR-, EPI- . . . . on, upon, to, above

    n A *sur*tax is a tax *upon* or *on top of* a tax.
    n The *epi*dermis is *upon* or *on top of* the dermis.
    n An *epi*taph is an inscription *upon* a tombstone.

12. TELE- . . . . far off, at a distance

    n *Tele*vision is seeing (*-vision*) *at a distance*.
    n A *tele*scope is another instrument for *far-off* seeing.

PRACTICE SET

Show the meaning of the italicized prefix in the following sentences by filling in the blanks properly.

1. An *epi*cycle is a cycle __?__ a cycle.
2. An *auto*mobile is so called because it is __?__ moving.
3. *Hyper*acidity is __?__ acidity.
4. *Tele*type machines typewrite news from a __?__.
5. To *sur*mount an obstacle is to go __?__ it.
6. The *super*intendent is __?__ the men in his department.
7. *Ultra*violet rays are __?__ the violet rays in the light spectrum.

UNIT ELEVEN

LATIN ROOTS AND PREFIXES

Write for each blank a definition of the italicized prefix.

Prefixes

First Group
1. ad-
2. inter-
3. post-
4. pre-, ante-

Second Group
5. pro-
6. re-
7. sub-
8. trans-

Roots

First Group
1. -cede-, -ceed-, -cess-, -gress-, -grad-
2. -cur(r)-, -curs-
3. -duc(t)-
4. -fer-, -lat(e)- -port-, -portat-

Second Group
5. -flect-, -flex-
6. -fus(d)-
7. -pel-, -puls-
8. -spec(t)-, -spic- -vide-, -vis-

1. To *pro*mote someone is to move him __?__.

2. A *trans*oceanic flight takes one __?__ the ocean.

3. A *suspic*ious person usually wants to __?__ __?__ the surface of things.

4. A *previs*ion is a __?__ __?__ what is going to happen.

5. To *repel* an invader is to __?__ him __?__.

A LATIN BREAKDOWN—PREFIXES

1. **AD-** . . . . **to, toward**

   (Note: The *d* frequently changes to the first letter of the root to which it is joined. Sometimes the *d* is dropped altogether before *s*, as in *aspect*. Cf. **allocate, allot, allure, append, ascribe, addict, adjoining, astringent,** and others.

   v To *ad*here to the original plan is to stick (*-here-*) *to* it.
   aj *Ad*hesive tape sticks *to* something.
   v To *ap*pease is to give peace *to* or pacify.

2. **INTER-** . . . . **between or among**

   v To *inter*cept a pass is to take (*-cept-*) or seize it *between* the passer and receiver.
   aj *Inter*scholastic contests involve events that take place *between* schools.

   Cf. **inter***change,* **inter***cede,* **inter***communicate,* **inter***fere* (strike between), **inter***lude,* **inter***marriage,* **inter***national,* **inter***penetrate.*

3. **POST-** . . . . **after, behind**

   v What does it mean to *post*date a check?
   n A *post*script comes *after* the main part of the letter as an afterthought.

   Cf. **post***lude,* **post***graduate,* **post***pone.*

4. **PRE-, ANTE-** . . . . . **before, ahead of time, in front of**

   n A *pre*monition is a warning *before*hand.
   aj Murder is *pre*meditated (planned-*ahead-of-time*) killing.
   n *Ante*meridian (A.M.) means occurring *before* noon.

   Cf. **pre***lude,* **pre***plan,* **pre***pay,* **pre***heat,* **ante***room,* **ante***chamber,* **ante***cipate.*

PRACTICE SET

Fill the blanks in the following sentences with a word or words that explain the italicized prefixes.

1. *Pre*mature effort is expended __?__ it is needed.
2. A *post*humous book appears __?__ the author's death.
3. An *inter*lude is a period of time __?__ the acts.
4. An *ad*junct is something joined __?__ an arrangement.
5. The invention of printing *ante*dated, or came __?__, the time of Columbus.

Second Group

5. PRO-. . . . . forward, favoring, before

   v To *pro*mote a plan is to move or push it *forward*.
   n *Pro*crastination is *favoring* (putting *forward* until) tomorrow.

   Cf. **pro**-Russian, **pro**pose *(place before)*, **pro**spect, **pro**tect, **pro**test.

6. RE- . . . . back(ward), again

   v To *re*act is to act *back*.
   v To *re*cognize is to know *again*.
   v When a condition *re*curs, it happens *again*.

   Cf. **re**adjust, **re**born, **re**form, **re**fresh, **re**gain.

7. SUB-. . . . . under, beneath

   n A *sub*cellar is *under* a cellar, a *sub*agent works *under* an agent, and apartments are sometimes aj *sub*let.

   Note: The *b* often changes to agree with the first letter of the root, as in **suf**fer, **suf**fuse, **suc**ceed, **suc**cumb, **sug**gest.

8. TRANS- . . . . across

   aj *Trans*verse lines cut *across* each other.
   v To *trans*cend is to climb *across* or beyond.

   Cf. **trans**port, **trans**atlantic, **trans**figure, **trans**ient, **trans**it(ion), **trans**mit, **trans**oceanic, **trans**parent.

PRACTICE SET

Write the word or words that explain the italicized prefixes.

1. A *pro*-British policy is one __?__ the British.
2. One who *trans*gresses the law literally "walks" __?__ it.
3. To *re*habilitate men is to make them useful __?__.
4. A *sub*marine sails __?__ the surface of the sea.
5. A *pro*spect is what you see as you look __?__.

ROOTS

1. -CEDE-, -CEED-, -CESS- . . . . **go**
   -GRAD-, -GRESS- . . . . **go or walk**

   v To pro*gress* or to pro*ceed* is to *go* forward.
   aj An ag*gress*ive man is a *going*-toward (*ad-*) or pushing man.
   aj An ante*ced*ent is the noun which *goes* before a noun or pronoun and thus identifies it.
   n A di*gress*ion is a *going* away from or a wandering, especially in a speech.

   Cf. **ingress, egress, regression, recede, precede, proceed.**

2. -CUR(R), -CURS- . . . . **run(ning)**

   aj *Curr*ent literally means *running*. So does *course*.
   v To in*cur* dislike means to *run* into it. A *courier* is a *runner*.
   n An ex*curs*ion is a *running* out from (the place where one lives).

   Cf. **concourse,** a running together; **recur,** to run back, that is, happen again.

3. -DUC(T)- . . . . **lead**

   v To ab*duct* is to kidnap or *lead* away a person.

   What do in**duce**, in**duct**, de**duce**, de**duct**, **duct**ile (Part Two, Unit 14), con**duct**, pro**duct**, noncon**duct**or, aque**duct**, intro**duce**, and **duct** mean? List other **-duct-** words.

4. -FER-, -LAT(E)- . . . .
   -PORT-, -PORTAT- . . . . carry, bear, bring

   v To col*late* is to *bring* together data for critical study.
   aj A sopori*ferous* drug is sleep-*bringing*.
   aj An odori*ferous* article is odor-*carrying*.

   > Cf. con*fer*, re*fer*, de*fer*, inter*fere*, trans*fer*, trans*late*, super-*lative*, re*late*, and many others.
   > Re*port*, ex*port*, im*port*, pur*port*, por*ter*, and sup*port* are a few of the commonest from -*port*-.
   > Cf. *portage*, a canoe *carry*; de*portment*, one's behavior.

   ### PRACTICE SET

   Write a word or words to explain the italicized roots or prefixes.

   1. The in*curs*ion of the barbarians means their __?__ in.
   2. To im*port* something is to __?__ it into the country.
   3. To in*duct* officers is to __?__ them into office.
   4. Coni*ferous* trees are cone-__?__ trees.
   5. A de*grad*ing action is one which __?__ down below standards.
   6. The re*curr*ence of an illness means that it __?__ __?__.

   ## Second Group

5. -FLECT-, -FLEX- . . . . bend

   v To de*flect* a blow is to *bend* it away from one.
   aj An in*flex*ible person is one who is un*bending*.

6. -FUS(E)- . . . . pour

   v To inter*fuse* good feeling is to *pour* it *among* people.
   v A spring tonic will in*fuse* (*pour in*) new life.

7. -PEL-, -PULS- . . . . drive or push

   v Bad manners re*pel* (*drive* back) a person.
   n Jet pro*pulsion* (*driving* forward) attains terrific speed.

   > Cf. *pulsate*, throb; *dispel*, drive away; *propel* (page 189); im-*pulse*, a *pushing* (toward action).

8.   -SPEC(T)-, -SPIC-   . . . . to look (at)
     -VIDE-, -VIS- . . . . to see

aj A *suspicious* person is always *looking* (*-spic-*) or *peeking*
   under (*sus-*) what appears on the surface.

n *Introspection* is *looking within* oneself.

n The *prospect* (*forward look*) appears good.

Cf. *expect, inspect, respect, conspicuous*, and their kin; also,
spectator, spectacle, spectacular, specter(ghost), *spectrum*, and
speculate.

aj A *provident* person *looks forward* or *foresees* his needs.

n A *visor* has to do with *seeing*, and a *vista* (page 211) is a *sight*
   or *view*.

PRACTICE SET

Write the word or words that explain the italicized roots and
prefixes in the following sentences.

1. A *spect*er, or a ghost, is something startling to __?__.
2. To ex*pel* someone is to __?__ him out.
3. When you in*flect* a verb, you __?__ it into its various forms.
4. An in*fus*ion of new life is a __?__ in of vigor and a fresh outlook.
5. He who is im*puls*ive __?__s toward, or does, something without thought.
6. *Revis*ion of a piece of work means, literally, to __?__ it __?__.

UNIT TWELVE

LATINSTRUCTION

In the language of the ancient Romans, *-struct-* was a root meaning *build,* and it means the same today. To *instruct* is literally to *build in* facts, ideas, or attitudes. To *construct* is to *build together* a mass of materials. A *destructive* person is one who *un-builds* or *builds down.*

This unit is an activity in building up words from Latin prefixes and roots, many of which you have had in previous units or will encounter soon.

Write the words that go in the blanks below.

Group I

Base Form		Noun Form -ion	Adjective Form -ive
1. accede	(*comply*)	__?__	
2. __?__	(*plead, go between*)	intercession	
3. __?__	(*go back*)	__?__	recessive
4. concede	(*grant or yield*)	__?__	__?__
5. __?__	(*withdraw*)	__?__	secessive
6. __?__	(*go before*)	precedence[1]	

---

[1] Look up *precession,* an astronomical term, if possible.

281

Group II

1. proceed   (*go forward*)   __?__ or __?__
2. __?__   (*go beyond*)   excess   __?__
3. __?__   (*accomplish   __?__ or __?__   successive
              one's pur-
              pose*)

Group III

1. __?__   (*go forward*)   progression   __?__
2. __?__   (*wander from   __?__   digressive
              topic*)
3. transgress (*do wrong*)   __?__

What body of men in Washington is named by a noun that belongs to the Gress Family? What noun belonging to the same family means *an outgoing?*

FURTHER ACTIVITY

1. For each of the following groups of guide words, build a set similar to those above. There are a few irregularities.

   compel, expulsion, repulsive
   abduct (no -*ive* form), *induct, deduction, conductive*
   produce, reduction, introductory
   **recur, occurrence* (-*ent* form rare), *concurrent*
   respect (watch spelling), *inspector, prospective*
   reflect, inflection, deflective
   import, transporter, deportation
   report (be careful!), *supporter, exportation*
   translate, dilation, relatable
   construct, destruction, instructive

2. Write the verb for each word in the groups below. Then change it to past tense. If the word is starred (*), write an -*ive* form beside the verb. Study the meaning of each word. Note that the word root is given before each group.

   *SCEND, SCENT (climb): *ascent, descent*
   CLINE (lean or lie): *inclination, declension, reclining*
   SERT (join together): *assertion*, desertion, insertion*
   TORT (twist): *contortion, distortion, extortion, tortuous*
   STINGU, STINCT (prick): *distinction*, extinction**

3. Write the *-tion* form for each of the words below. If a word is starred (*), write its *-al* or *-ive* form beside the *-tion* form.

> *institute*, constitute*, destitute*
> *exhibit, inhibit*, prohibit**
> *attend*, contend, distend, extend*, intend, pretend*
> *repute, compute, dispute, impute*

WORD-BUILDING EXERCISE

Write the correct form of the word in parentheses.

1. His fondness for candy is __?__ (excess).
2. The man was convicted on charges of __?__ (extort).
3. The cost of materials is __?__ (prohibit).
4. Do you have a __?__ (retain well) memory?
5. The case against her is entirely __?__ (suppose).
6. Criticism should be partly __?__ (construct).
7. The new rule is not __?__ (apply) to this case.
8. Is __?__ (inquisitive) a sign of intelligence?
9. Political leaders expect __?__ (oppose).
10. An eclipse is a rather uncommon __?__ (occur).

CHALLENGE SET

Copy the italicized words, and beside each write its meaning in the sentence:

1. He *contends* that *importation* of cotton is not necessary.
2. The doctors *concur* in stating that malaria is *recurrent*.
3. We will *accede* to the demand for their *deportation*.
4. Her eyes *dilated* when she saw the *repulsive* creature.
5. He will *intercede* for the *transgressors*.
6. Watch the clouds *recede* under the *compulsion* of the wind.
7. *Deduct* the time spent on *digressions*.
8. A *reflector* helps shut out *excessive* sunlight.
9. The leaders will *confer* regarding tax *deductions*.
10. The musicians will *secede* from the union unless granted *precedence*.

UNIT THIRTEEN

FIFTEEN LATIN ROOTS

If you set them out in your garden and water them carefully, they will produce a useful and varied harvest for you.

INFORMATION, PLEASE

1. The an*nunci*ation to Mary was a
   —?— to her that she would bear
   a son.

2. To re*vert* to a bad habit is to —?—
   back to it again.

3. To *eject* a person is to —?— him
   —?—.

4. A con*fid*ant is someone you —?—
   very much.

5. A *fact*otum is a —?—-it-all.

Roots

First Group
1. -clude-, -clus-
2. -dic-, -dict-, -dica-
3. -fact-, -fect-, -fic(t)-
4. -fid(e)-
5. -flu(en)-, -flux-

Second Group
1. -fract-
2. -ject-
3. -mit(t)-, -miss-
4. -nounc(e)-, -nunci-
5. -pli(c)-, -plex-

Third Group
1. -serv-
2. -sist-
3. -solv-, -solut-
4. -ven(i)-, -vent-
5. -vert-, -vers-

LATIN ROOTS—First Group

1. **-CLUDE-, -CLUS** . . . . **shut**

   v n *include, inclusion . . . shut(ting)* in
   v n *exclude, exclusion . . . shut(ting)* out
   v n *seclude, seclusion . . . shut(ting)* a part

2. **-DIC(T)(A)-** . . . . **say, command**

   n A *dicta*tor is one who has "the say." He *commands*.
   n The king issued an *edict* (command, a speaking out).
   n A *dicta*phone is a mechanical ear that records what one *says*.

   Cf. pre**dict,** in**dic**ate, ad**dict, dict**ate, **dict**ation, **dict**atorial.

3. **-FACT-, -FECT-, FIC(T)-** . . . . **make or do**

   n A clothing *fact*ory exists to *make* clothes.
   v Literally, to manu*fact*ure is to *make* by hand (*manu-*).
   n *Fict*ion is *make*-believe.
   n Af*fect*ion is a "making" toward (*ad-*), or pretending to be what one is not.

4. **-FID(E)-** . . . . **faith, trust**

   n *fid*elity . . . *faith*fulness, loyalty
   n in*fid*el . . . lacking *faith* or trust in God
   n per*fid*y . . . breach of *faith*, disloyalty

5. **-FLU(EN)-, -FLUX-** . . . . **flow(ing)**

   n con*flu*ence . . . *flowing* together (of the two rivers or lives)
   n ef*flu*ence . . . an out*flowing*
   aj super*flu*ous . . . *flowing* above or beyond

PRACTICE SET

Write the definition for each italicized root.

1. To con*fide* in a person is to ___?___ that person with your secrets.
2. It is impolite to contra*dict*, or ___?___ the opposite.
3. A *fluid* is so called because it ___?___.
4. Arti*facts* are objects ___?___ by men of early times.
5. The evidence does not pre*clude*, or ___?___ beforehand, the possibility of arson.

Second Group

1. **-FRACT-** . . . . **break, bend**

   aj A *fract*ured (*broken*) leg resulted from the fall.
   n In*fract*ion (*breaking*) the rules will result in punishment.

   Cf. *fraction, refract, diffraction.*

2. **-JECT-** . . . . **cast or hurl**

   n A pro*ject*ile is an object *hurled* forward or forth.
   aj Ab*ject* means cast down or *downcast.*

   Cf. *interjection, projection, injection, dejection, objection.*

3. **-MIT(T)-, -MISS-** . . . . **send, sent**

   v e*mit* . . . *send* forth . . . e*miss*ion, e*miss*ive
   v dis*miss* . . . *send* away . . . dis*miss*al
   v trans*mit* . . . *send* across . . . trans*miss*ion, trans*mit*ter

   Cf. *mission* (a sending), *missionary* (one sent), *commission* (a sending, or group sent), *committee.*

4. **-NOUNC(E)-, -NUNCI-** . . . . **declare**

   v De*nounc*ing graft is (literally) *declar*ing it down (*de-*).
   n An an*nunci*ator *declares* a call and tells where it came from.

   Cf. *announce, ennunciate, nuncio.*

5.   -PLI(C)-, -PLEX- . . . .   fold

   v To im*pli*cate one in a crime is literally to *fold* him into it.
   aj A com*pli*cated situation is literally *fold*ed together (*com-*).
   aj Quadru*plex* operation is four*fold* operation.

   Cf. *duplicate, triplicate, quadruplicate, multiplication, multi-*
   plex, application.

PRACTICE SET

   In the blanks provided write a definition for the word with
the root in italics.

1.   To re*mit* a sum of money is to __?__ back payment on request.
2.   Ap*pli*cation of a rule means to __?__ it to fit the situation.
3.   A __?__ in a bone is called a *fract*ure.
4.   To pro*nounce* a word means to __?__ it correctly.

Third Group

1.   -SERV-. . . . .   keep, save

   v Why pre*serv*e this picture any longer?
   v Did he re*serv*e (*keep* back) the tickets for you?

   Cf. *conserve, conservation, reservation, preservation.* What is
   a conservative?

2.   -SIST- . . . .   (to make to) stand

   v Will you as*sist* (*stand* to, help) me?
   v She in*sist*s (*makes a stand*) that I was there.

   Cf. *consist, desist,* ***exist,*** *persist, resist, subsist.*

3.   -SOLV-, -SOLUT- . . . .   loosen

   v *solv*e . . . *"loosen"* a problem
   v dis*solv*e . . . *"loosen"* a solid substance
   v ab*solv*e . . . *"loosen"* a person from (guilt)

   Cf. *solut*ion, ***soluble, solvent.***

4.   -VEN(I)-, -VENT- . . . . **come, coming**

   n A conv*en*tion (*coming* together) takes place soon.
   v Will the government inter*ven*e (*come* between) in the dispute?

   Cf. *convene, intervention, prevention, invention, circumvent.*

5.   -VERT-, -VERS- . . . . **turn**

   v To a*vert* a disaster is to turn it away (*ab-*).
   n A*vers*ion is a dislike (*turning* away from) something.
   v To con*vert* a garage into a rumpus room is to *turn* it to a new plan.
   v To di*vert* attention is to *turn* it away from something.
   n A di*vers*ion is a pastime which *turns* one away from a job or other occupation.

   Cf. *averse, conversion, diverse* (varied), *advertise.*

PRACTICE SET

   In the blanks provided write a definition for the word with the root in italics.

1. To con*serve* means to __?__ (together) that which is left.
2. To pre*vent* is to stop something from __?__ing ahead of time.
3. To re*vert* to type is to __?__ back to one's original way of being.
4. When the Elks con*vene*, they __?__ together.
5. To *solve* a problem is, literally, to __?__ it, or understand it.

QUESTS

1. For each of the roots in this lesson, make a verb by adding to it one of the prefixes you studied in Part II, Unit 21, and in Part III, Units 10 and 11.
2. For the fifteen words you made in Quest number 1, set up tables that show if they have verb, noun, and adjective forms.

UNIT FOURTEEN

FIFTEEN MORE—MOSTLY LATIN

ROOT MEANINGS

Supply for each blank an appropriate word from one of the roots in the lists at the right.

1. In a voice scarcely a——?—— (capable of being heard), she begged the clerk to ——?—— (make right) the error.

2. The d——?—— (ruling) reason for requesting an ——?—— (fair, even) adjustment was fear of the con——?——s (results that would follow).

3. S——?—— (tight) requirements make medicine a difficult v——?—— (calling) to enter.

Roots

First Group
1. -aud(i)-, -audit-
2. -domin-
3. -equ(i)-, -par(i)-
4. -jur(e)-, -juri(s)-
5. -merge-, -mers-

Second Group
1. -micro-
2. -mort-
3. -pend-, -pense-
4. -rect-, -ortho-
5. -sequ-, -secut-

Third Group
1. -string-, -strict-
2. -tain-, -ten(t)-
3. -tort-
4. -voc-, -vocat-
5. -volve-, -volu(t)-

MORE LATIN ROOTS—First Group

1. **-AUD(I)-, -AUDIT-** . . . . hear, listen to

    n An *audi*ence is a group of *hearers* or listeners.
    n An *audi*torium is a place for *hearing* programs. An *audi*tion is a *hearing*.

    Note: ***Phon(e)*** means sound as in *tele**phone**, **phon**etics, antip**hon**al, dicta**phone*** (Part Three, Unit 13), *eu**phon**y, mega**phone*** (Part Three, Unit 10), *caco**phon**y*.

2. **-DOMIN-** . . . . to rule, ruling

    aj A *domin*ant trait is a *ruling* trait.
    v To *domin*ate is to *rule*.

    Cf. ***domin**ation, **domin**ion, **domin**eer, Anno **Domin**i*.

3. **-EQU(I)-, -PAR(I)-** . . . . equal(ly)

    aj The two hills are *equi*distant from the village.
    n *Equa*nimity is *equa*lness, *even*ness, or *calm*ness of mind (-*anim*-).
    aj An *equa*ble climate is an *equal* or *even* climate.
    n The two teams seem almost on a *pari*ty (equal terms) in performance.

    Cf. ***equi**lateral, **equa**tion, **equi**poise, **equi**librium, com**pare**, dis**pari**ty, com**par**ative, dis**par**age, **par***.

4. **-JUR(E)-, -JURI(S)-** . . . . right, law, justice

    n An in*jur*y is literally something not according to the *law*.
    n *Juris*prudence is the study of *law* or *justice*.

    Cf. *ab**jure**, ad**jure**, con**jure**, per**jure***.

5. **-MERGE-, -MERS-** . . . . dip

    v e*merge*, *dip* forth or out of   **n** e*merge*nce
    v sub*merge*, *dip* under . . .   **n** sub*mers*ion
    v im*mers*e, *dip* into . . .   **n** im*mers*ion

PRACTICE SET

Write the words that describe the italicized roots.

1. *Equi*poise involves __?__ weights.
2. An *aud*itor in a course is a l__?__ and not a doer.
3. A *jury* determines the __?__ of a case.
4. *Domin*ation is the process of __?__.
5. *Par*ity is a condition of __?__ity.

Second Group

1. **-MICRO-** . . . . **very small, tiny**

   n *Micro*be means *small* life (*bios*).
   n A *micro*meter measures *very small* distances.
   n A *micro*phone handles *very small* sounds.

2. **-MORT-** . . . . **death**

   aj A *mort*al wound is a *deadly* one.
   aj The *mort*ality rate is the *death* rate.
   n What is a post *mortem*?

3. **-PEND-, -PENSE-** . . . . **hang or weigh**

   v To ex*pend* money is literally to *weigh* it out.
   aj An inde*pend*ent person is literally one who is not (*in-*) *hanging* (*-pend-*) down from (*de-*) anything. What is an ap*pend*age?

4. **-RECT-, -ORTHO-** . . . . **(make) right, correct**

   v Can you *rect*ify (make *right*) your mistake?
   aj He belongs to an *ortho*dox (teaching *right*) group.

5. **-SEQU-, -SECUT-** . . . . **follow**

   n A *sequ*ence is a series of events or facts *following* each other.
   n Con*sequ*ences are what *follow* one's actions.

PRACTICE SET

Write the words that describe the italicized roots.

1. To *execute* an order is to __?__ it out.
2. "La *Morte* d'Arthur" means "The __?__ of Arthur."
3. The *sequel* to an event is the incident which __?__.
4. *Micro*chemistry is the chemistry of __?__ quantities.
5. An *ortho*phonic speaker produces the __?__ sound.

Third Group

1. **-STRING-, -STRICT-** . . . . draw together, tighten

   v To re*strict* one's privileges is to *draw* back or *tighten* them.
   aj *String*ent laws are tight laws.   **n** An a*string*ent *contracts* bodily tissues to stop bleeding or for some other reason.

   Note: -TRACT- means *draw* in a slightly different sense: at*tract* (draw toward), con*tract* (draw together) the opening, ex*tract* (draw out) the poison, re*tract* (draw back or withdraw) a statement.

2. **-TAIN-, -TEN(T)-** . . . . hold

   v To de*tain* a person is to *hold* him from going.
   aj A re*ten*tive memory *holds* facts well.
   n A bulldog has great *ten*acity or *holding* power.

   Cf. con*tain*, re*tain*, main*tain*, per*tain*, *ten*able, *ten*ets, de*tention*.

3. **-TORT-** . . . . twist, wrest

   n Ex*tort*ion is *wresting* money or information from someone.
   v To con*tort* one's face is to *twist* it out of shape.

   Review dis*tort*, dis*tort*ion in Part One, Unit 16. **Torque** in mechanics is the *twisting* which produces rotation. **Torsion** bars in a car absorb the *twisting* of the frame or wheels on rough road.

4. **-VOC-, -VOCAT-** . . . . call

   n One's *vocat*ion is his *calling* or occupation.
   n A con*vocat*ion is a *calling* together or assembly.

   Cf. *revoke* (*call* back or cancel), *provoke* (*call* forth), *invoke* (*call* into action).

5. **-VOLVE-, -VOLU(T)-** . . . . roll

   n In*volut*ions are *rollings* in or folds.
   n A re*volut*ion is a *rolling* over—or back—in human affairs.

   Cf. *revolve, involve, evolve, evolution, volume, voluble.*

PRACTICE SET

Write the words that describe the italicized roots.

1. A *ten*able belief is one to which a person can __?__ .
2. Dis*tort*ion of the truth is a __?__ing of it.
3. A task which de*volves* upon a person is one which literally __?__s down upon him.
4. A *voc*abulary consists of the words one can __?__ to mind.
5. A per*tin*ent remark is one which per*tains*, i.e., __?__s to the topic being discussed.

ROOTSOME PAIRS

In this unit there are 15 pairs of Latin and Greek roots often seen in print. Consider yourself well informed if you can answer the following questions.

CAN YOU?

1. What is a *bene*factor?

   A —?— doer.

2. Eo*hipp*us was a kind of —?—.

3. *Manu*al labor is —?— labor.

4. *Psycho*therapy is the cure or treatment of disorders of the —?—.

5. A *podi*atrist is a —?— doctor.

6. A *chrono*graph measures and records —?—.

	Latin	*Greek*
First Group		
1.	-ami(c)-	-phil-
2.	-aqua- -aque-	-hydro-
3.	-bene-	-eu-
4.	-civi(s)- -urb(s)-	-polit- -poli(s)-
5.	-equ(es)-	-hipp(o)-
Second Group		
1.	-hal(e)-	-spir(e)-
2.	-man(u)-	-chiro-
3.	-ment-	-psych(o)
4.	-nat(e)- -nasc-	-gen(e)-
5.	-nomen- -nomin-	-onym-
Third Group		
1.	-ped-	-p(o)us- -pod-
2.	-scribe- -script-	-graph- -gram-
3.	-stell(a)-	-astra(a)-
4.	-temp(o)-	-chron(o)-
5.	-vita-	-bio-

ROOTSOME PAIRS—First Group

1. **-AMI(C)-, -PHIL-** . . . . friend(ship), love(r)

    n A *philanthropist* (*friend* of mankind) is often very generous.
    aj *Amicable* (*friendly*) relations exist with England.
    n An Anglo*phile* loves or is *friendly* to the British.

    Cf. *inimical*, *philately* (fĭ·lăt′ĕ·lĭ), *philosophy*, *philharmonic*.

2. **-AQUA-, -AQUE-, -HYDRO-** . . . . water

    n *Aqua*planing is great fun. What is an *aque*duct?
    n *Hydro*dynamics, or *water* dynamics, is a branch of engineering.
    n *Hydro*therapy is treatment by *water*, i.e., baths.

    Cf. *aquatic(s)*, *aquarium*, *aqueous* (watery), *aquamarine*, *hydraulic(s)*, *hydroplane*, *hydroelectric*.

3. **-BENE-, -EU-** . . . . well

    n What is a *bene*factor? What does *Bene*dict mean, literally?
    aj *Eu*phonious music sounds *well*, i.e., is harmonious.

    Cf. *benefit*, *benediction*, *eugenics*, *eulogy*.

4. **-CIVI(S)-, -POLIT-** . . . . citizen
    -URB(S)-, -POLI(S)- . . . . city

    aj *Civic* pride is a *citizen's* pride; n *politics* is the expression of *citizen*ship.
    n Metro*polis* is literally a "mother" *city*.
    aj Sub*urb*an areas are "under" a *city* in a geographic sense.

    Cf. *civility*, *civilian*, *uncivil*, *police*, *geopolitics* (world politics).

5. **-EQU(ES)-, -HIPP(O)-** . . . . horse

    aj An *eques*trian statue is one of a person on *horse*back.
    aj An *equi*ne manner is *horse*like.
    n A *hippo*potamus, literally, is a river *horse*.
    n A *hippo*drome was an arena for *horse* races or shows.

PRACTICE SET

Write as many words as you can without looking back. On the second try you should be able to fill them all without going back.

1. *Amity,* or __?__ship, should prevail in Philadelphia, the city of brotherly __?__.
2. A *hippo*drome was an arena for __?__s and thus a place devoted to *equine* (__?__) achievements.
3. An aquamarine (color of sea __?__) hydroplane (landing on __?__) would be hard to see.
4. The company gave three cheers for their *bene*volent (__?__-wishing) host.
5. The mayor read a *eu*logy (a speaking __?__) of the dead publisher.

Second Group

1. **-HAL(E)-, -SPIR(E)-** . . . . breath(e)

   v To in*hale* is to *breathe* in; ex*hale,* to *breathe* out.
   n An a*spir*ant *breathes* or *strives* toward something.

   Cf. *per**spir**e, in**hal**ation, re**spir**ation, **spir**it, in**spir**it, di**spir**ited.*

2. **-MAN(U)-, -CHIRO-** . . . . (by) hand

   n *Mani*cure is care (*-cure-*) of the *hands* and fingernails.
   n A *chiro*practor is one who treats by use of the *hands.*

   Cf. **man***euver* (Part Two, Unit 7, **mani***pulate,* **manu***facture* (Part Three, Unit 13), **chiro***graphy* (handwriting). Note: **manu** sometimes becomes **mani.**

3. **-MENT-, -PSYCH(O)-** . . . . mind

   aj A de*ment*ed person has lost some of his powers of *mind.*
   n *Psych*ology is the study of the *mind.*

   Cf. **ment***al,* de**ment***ia* (madness), **Psych***e,* **psycho***analyze.*

4. **-NAT(E)-, -NASC-, -GEN(E)-** . . **born, (giving) birth, producing**

n A *native* of Philadelphia was *born* there.
aj *Nascent* energy is fresh, *new-born* energy.
n Eu*gen*ics is the science pertaining to well-*born* children.

> Cf. **native*ity, nat**al*, in*nate*, **progeny**,* **gen**esis (Part Three, Unit 7), *con**gen**ital (Part Three, Unit 6).

5. **-NOMEN-, -NOMIN-, -ONYM-** . . . . **name**

v To *nomin*ate a person is to *name* him for election to an office.
n An ant*onym* is a word or *name* with an opposite meaning.

> Cf. *cog**nomen**, de**nomin**ation, syn**onym**, hom**onym**, acr**onym**.*

PRACTICE SET

Fill in the blanks without looking back.

1. To ex*pire* is to __?__ one's last. Ex*hal*ations are out-__?__ings.
2. Those in the *psycho*pathic ward are suffering (*-path-*) from disorders of the __?__.
3. The cog*nomen* Swift became the family __?__.
4. *Mane*uver means, literally, __?__ work.
5. In*nate* ideas are ideas within a person's mind when he is __?__.

Third Group

1. **-PED-, -P(O)US-, -POD-** . . . . **foot**

n A *ped*estrian is one who travels by *foot*.
v One who im*ped*es another's progress puts his *foot* against it.

> Cf. **ped**al, **ped**estal, im**ped**iment, **pod**iatrist.* Ex*ped*ite, to speed up something, means literally to free someone caught by the foot.

2. **-SCRIBE-, -SCRIPT-, -GRAPH-, -GRAM-** . . . . **write, writing**

v To sub*scribe* to a magazine is to under*write* it.
n A *script* is *writing*, and a *graph* is a kind of *writing*.

3.   -STELL(A)-, -ASTR(A)- . . . . star

   aj He played a *stellar* game of basketball.
   n *Astro*nomy is the science of the *stars*.

   Cf. **Stella, constellation** (Part Two, Unit 25), *interstellar,*
   astrology, astral, disaster.

4.   -TEMP(O)-, -CHRON(O)- . . . . time

   aj That which is *tempo*rary exists for a short *time* only.
   aj The *chron*ological order of events is their *time* order.

   Cf. **tempo, temporize, chronicle, chronology, synchronous.**

5.   -VITA-, -BIO- . . . . life

   aj Literally, a *vital* issue is one involving *life* itself.
   n *Bio*chemistry is the chemistry of plant and animal *life*.

   Note: **Vivi,** alive, appears in **vivify** (to make alive), **vivid.**
   Cf. **microbe** (Part Two, Unit 14), **biology, antibiotics.**

PRACTICE SET

Fill in the blanks without looking back.

1. A *chrono*meter measures __?__; a *pedo*meter measures the
    distance traveled on __?__.
2. The *tempo* of the music is the __?__ rate at which it is played.
3. To de*vita*lize a substance is to take out its __?__-giving
    properties.
4. *Bio*physics is the study of plant and animal __?__.
5. *Astra*l light comes from the __?__s.

QUESTS

1. Write a noun form of *lucid, elucidate, magnify, magnificent,*
    nominate, impede, amiable, and *beneficent.*

UNIT SIXTEEN

VERB-MAKER ROOTS

Most of the roots in this unit come from Latin verbs. Most of them produce verbs in English and quite a few other words as well.

Find a word that will define the italicized root.

1. A *loqu*acious pal —?—s too much.

2. She does not know when to *termin*ate (put an —?— to) her visits.

3. A *mut*able shape is —?—able.

4. Inconsiderate people im*pose* their wishes and desires (—?— them against yours).

5. A re*sent*ful person —?—s an injury far too long.

6. He inter*rupts* me (—?— in among my words) when I am talking.

First Group
1. -fini, -termin-
2. -grati-, -gratu-
3. -her(e)-, -hes-
4. -jug(a)-, -junc(t)-
5. -loc(u)-, -loqui-, -log(ue)-

Second Group
1. -mand-, -mend-
2. -mot(e)-, -mob-
3. -mut(e)-
4. -plen(t)-
5. -pos(e)-, -posit-, -pon-

Third Group
1. -rog(a)-
2. -rupt-
3. -sect-, -cid(e)-, -cis-
4. -sent(i)-, -path-
5. -therm-

299

VERB-MAKER ROOTS—First Group

1. **-FIN(I)-, -TERMIN-** . . . . **end, limit**

   v To *fin*ish a job is to put an *end* to it.
   aj If the universe is *fin*ite, it has an *end* or boundary.
   v To *termin*ate a contract is to *end* it.
   aj An in*termin*able speech seems *end*less.

   Cf. *confine, define, final, exterminate, terminal, determine.*

2. **-GRATI-, -GRATU-** . . . . **please, delight**

   v Peanuts *grat*ify the monkeys in the zoo.
   v To cong*ratu*late a winner is to join him in *delight*.
   n You give the waitress or porter a *gratu*ity because you find the service pleasing.

   Cf. **grateful, gratitude, gratuitous.** What does *persona non grata* mean? **Gratis** (free) comes from the Latin word *gratia*, a favor. (See Part Two, Unit 22.)

3. **-HER(E)-, -HES-** . . . . **stick or cling**

   v Gum will ad*here* or *stick* to a desk.
   aj Ad*hes*ive tape *clings* to an injured finger.
   aj In*her*ent selfishness *clings* because it is inborn.

   Cf. *cohere, cohesive. Inherit, heritage* (Part Two, Unit 12), and **heredity** come from a closely related root.

4. **-JUG(A)-, -JUNC(T)-** . . . . **yoke, join**

   v To sub*juga*te an enemy is to put him under a *yoke* (of bondage).
   n The con*junct*ion of two stars, two lives, or two words is their meeting or *joining*.

   Cf. *junction, juncture, conjugal* (Part Three, Unit 6), *conjugate, conjunctive, subjunctive, injunction.* Two related roots are involved, **jugum** (yoke) and **jungere** (to join).

5.   -LOC(U)-, -LOQU-, -LOG(UE)   . . .   talk, speak(ing), speech

    n A *locut*ion is a way of *speaking*.
    aj A *loqu*acious person is very *talk*ative.
    n A *dialog*(ue) consists of two persons *talking*.
    n Geo*logy* is the study of the earth (*geo-*) literally talking about itself.

        Log comes from the Greek (ὁ λογος, **ho logos**). It is the root of all the **-ology**.words. List a dozen or two.

PRACTICE SET

Write for each blank a suitable word containing the root in parentheses following the blank.

1. Applause will always __?__ (*-grati-*) an artist.
2. The speech seemed to last for hours; it was in__?__(*-term-*).
3. The judge issued an in__?__ (*-junc-*) to stop the strike.
4. She is very __?__ (*-loqu-*).
5. Pebbles will not __?__ (*-here-*) unless they are sticky.

Second Group

1.   -MAND-, -MEND-   . . . .   order, command, entrust, commit

    v To counter*mand* a decree is to *order* it not to be carried out.
    n Palestine was once a *mand*ate *entrust*ed to the British.

        To *commend* (from the same root) is to entrust, praise, give over to another's keeping.

2.   -MOT(E)-, -MOB- . . . .   move, moving

    v To de*mote* a man is to *move* him down to a lower rank.
    n E*mot*ion is a *moving* out or forth of feeling.
    v To *mob*ilize an army is to *move* it together for action.

        Cf. **motive, motion, mobility, immobile**.

3. **-MUT(E)-** . . . . change

   v Alchemists tried to trans*mute* base metals into gold.
   aj An im*mut*able decree cannot be *changed*.
   n A biological *mut*ation is an unexpected *change* in the progeny.

   Cf. com***mute*** (Part Two, Unit 20), com***mut***ation, ***mut***ability.

4. **-PLEN(T)-** . . . . fill, full(ness)

   v To re*plen*ish the freezer is to *fill* it again.
   aj A *plent*eous or *plent*iful supply is a *full* supply.
   n A *plen*itude of delights is a *fullness* or completeness.

   Cf. ***plen***ary, ***plen***ipotentiary (*full* power to act), ***plen***um.

5. **-POS(E)-, -POSIT-, -PON-** . . . . put or place

   v To de*pose* a king is to *put* him down from the throne.
   n A com*posit*ion is words or music *put* together, the latter by a com*pos*er.
   n An op*pon*ent is one who *places* himself against you.

   The **-pose-** words and the **-pon-** words come from two different Latin roots of similar meaning and confused derivations. Cf. **-sert-** in such words as *insert*(*ion*), *assert*(*ion*), and *desert*(*ion*).

PRACTICE SET

Write for each blank a suitable word containing the root in parentheses following the blank.

1. Thousands of people wrote to beg that the governor com__?__ (*-mute-*) the boy's sentence.
2. There seemed to be no __?__ (*-mot-*) for the crime.
3. The coach ought to com__?__ (*-mend-*) his team for their spirit.
4. The two young com__?__s (*-pos(e)-*) were op__?__s (*-pon-*) in a contest.
5. Each Congressman has a __?__ (*-mand-*) from the people who elected him.

Third Group

1. **-ROG(A)-** . . . . ask, say, declare

    v to inter*rog*ate a suspect is to *ask* him questions.
    aj A de*rog*atory remark *says* something unfavorable.

    Look up *ab**rog**ate, pre**rog**ative,* and ***arrog**ant.*

2. **-RUPT-** . . . . break, burst

    v To dis*rupt* a meeting is to *break* it up.
    n An inter*rupt*ion is a *breaking* into what one is doing.
    n A *rupt*ure is a *breaking* or *bursting* of some kind.

    Cf. ***abrupt**(ness),* ***corrupt**(ion)* (Part One, Unit 11), ***erupt**(ion).*
    Review ***-fract-*** in Unit 13, on page 284.

3. **-SECT-, -CID(E)-, -CIS-** . . . . cut

    v To dis*sect* a frog is to *cut* it apart.
    v To de*cide* a matter is to *cut* it off from further thought.
    n The surgeon made an in*cis*ion (a *cut*) in the patient's abdomen.

    Cf. ***re*sect*ion, *vivi*sect*ion, *sui**cide*** (self-killing), ***fratri**cide*** (brother killing), ***de**cis**ion, ex**cis**ion.*

4. **-SENT(I)-, -PATH-** . . . . feel(ing)

    v To dis*sent* is to *feel* differently from others about an issue.
    n *Sent*iment is *feeling.*
    n *Path*os is a condition which arouses *feelings* of pity.
    n Anti*path*y is a strong *feeling* against something.

    Cf. ***senti*ment*(ality),* ***a**path**y,* ***em**path**y,* ***sym**path**y.* In **path*ology,*** **path*ologist,*** and other words of the same family, ***-path-*** means suffering or disease. The root is Greek.

5. **-THERM-** . . . . heat

    aj A *therm*al reaction involves *heat.*
    n A *therm*ometer gauges the *heat* that is present.
    aj A *therm*os bottle imprisons *heat.*

    Other heat words: ***therm*ite, *therm*onuclear, *therm*odynamics.**

PRACTICE SET

Write for each blank a suitable word containing the root in parentheses following the blank.

1. The passing of a fire engine did not in__?__ (-*rupt*-) the meeting.
2. The edges of the in__?__ (-*cis*) must be sewed together to insure healing.
3. Charity appeals to our more generous __?__s (-*senti*-).
4. Mr. Grey does not like to have his wife in__?__ (-*rog*-) him.
5. We could tell from my __?__ (-*therm*-) that the freezing point had been reached.

UNIT SEVENTEEN

PARLEZ-VOUS FRANÇAIS?

(Do you speak French?)

All words in this unit came from French and in most cases retain their French pronunciation. Some are used regularly in English, such as *corps* and *denouement*. Others such as *guerre* are used in familiar phrases like *croix de guerre* but have never become naturalized citizens of the American language. Some have accent marks in French which they have gradually lost in English usage.

Find appropriate words for the blanks, using the words that you find in the two groups of French words at the right.

THEATER PROJECT

The actors formed a —?— and began to build up a —?— of plays they could present. Each selected the —?— he thought he could play best. At first they had no actresses and the men were awkward in scenes such as a —?—-a-—?— between ladies. In May each year they held a —?— for their wives and lady friends.

A Famous French Proverb

"Cherchez la femme."
("Look for the woman.")

Base Words

First Group

1. carte
2. chateau
3. corps
4. coup
5. denouement
6. enfant
7. fait
8. fete

Second Group

1. guerre
2. jour
3. pièce
4. repertoire
5. reveille
6. role
7. tête

305

PARLEZ-VOUS FRANÇAIS?—First Group

1. **CARTE** . . . . card, bill of fare
   - n The count's *carte de visite* (visiting card) was black with white letters.
   - n The manager gave the foreman *carte blanche* (literally, "white card," thus freedom to do what he thought best) in the machine shop.

2. **CHATEAU** (shă·tō′) . . . large French country home, castle
   - n Voltaire owned a chateau in Switzerland.
   - n Fire destroyed numerous chateaux in France.

3. **CORPS** (kōr) . . organized body or group, especially military
   - n Joe wanted to join the Marine Corps.
   - n A corps of volunteers fought the forest fire.

4. **COUP** (koo) . . . . a blow or stroke
   - n A *coup d'etat* is a military or political "stroke" that overthrows or upsets a government.

5. **DENOUEMENT** (dā·noo′män) . . the outcome or "untying" of a plot or situation, especially in literature
   - n The denouement of the affair was the execution of the spy.
   - n Death brought a denouement to a long and baffling illness.

6. **ENFANT** (än·fän′) . . . . child, infant
   - n An *enfant terrible* says shocking things.
   - n *Enfants perdus* (literally, "lost children") is a term applied to troops cut off or otherwise doomed.

7. **FAIT** (fĕt) . . . . an act or deed
   - n Charlotte was confronted by a *fait accompli* (an act already accomplished) when she tried to aid her sister.

8. **FETE** (fāt) . . . . . outdoor party, festival, social affair

   n The ladies held a lawn fete.

   aj The much-feted (much-entertained) explorer is now in Texas.

Second Group

1. **GUERRE** (gâr) . . . . war

   n *"C'est la guerre"* (It's the war) is a common explanation for wartime inconveniences and dislocations.

2. **JOUR** (zhŏŏr) . . . . day

   n *"Bonjour,* Madame" (Good day, Madam) is a common French greeting.

   n The *plat du jour* in a restaurant is the special plate of the day.

   Cf. *journal, adjourn, journey,* also from the Latin, *diurnus,* daily.

3. **PIECE** (pyĕs) . . . . article, item, short play

   n The *piece de resistance* at a dinner is the main item or dish.

4. **REPERTOIRE** (rĕp'ər·twär') . . list of plays or parts a person or troupe can perform; store of material

   n The violinist played every number in his repertoire.

   aj What is a repertory theater?

5. **REVEILLE** (rev'ə·lǐ) . . . . morning call to get up

   n A bugle sounds reveille each morning at 6:00 a.m.

   n "Till Reveille" was a popular song during World War II.

6. **ROLE** . . . . . a part one plays or function one assumes

   n Her role in the play is that of a waitress.

   n The once-rich heiress began her new role as a working girl.

7. **TÊTE** . . . . head

    n A tête-à-tête is a private, heads-together conversation.
    av They sat tête-à-tête (face to face).

FIRST PRACTICE SET

    Practice reading the following sentences, with the teacher's help. Copy the italicized words or phrases and beside each write its meaning in the sentence.

1. A brilliant sales *coup* saved the company from failure.
2. How would you like the *role* of bugler for *reveille?*
3. He was awarded the *croix de guerre* for bravery.
4. The story about the old *chateau* soon became a legend.
5. The *soupe de jour* was cold and the *pièce de resistance* tough.
6. While they drank their tea, the ladies had a *tête-à-tête*.
7. The transfer of the drum *corps* soon became a *fait accompli*.
8. She exhausted her *repertoire* of songs at the village *fete*.
9. The little boy eventually became an *enfant gâté* (spoiled).
10. Giving the director *carte blanche* led to a tragic *denouement*.

SECOND PRACTICE SET

    Which of the base words goes in each blank? Use each word once—where it fits best.

1. __?__ comes at dawn in every army __?__.
2. This little play is a __?__ that we added to our __?__ recently when we gave it at a May Day __?__.
3. The __?__ of a heart-broken father at the __?__ of a story is hard to act.
4. Women's secrets are often transmitted __?__-à-__?__.
5. The word *tou*__?__ means *every day*, or *always*.
6. The *croix de* __?__ is a war decoration.
7. The dinner was a __?__ *accompli* before our __?__ *terrible* got home to disrupt it.
8. The enemy seized the __?__ by a well-planned __?__.
9. Ordering *à la* __?__ can be expensive.

UNIT EIGHTEEN

ENCORE

PROBLÈMES

1. Who are the elite?

2. What are belles-lettres?

3. What is a première?

4. How soon is *tout de suite?*

5. What are hors d'oeuvres?

6. Who are the *nouveaux riches?*

7. Which girl in the class is the most

   petite?

Les Mots (The Words)

First Group

1. beau, belle
2. bien
3. bon, bonne
4. elite
5. entrée
6. gauche
7. hors
8. jeune

Second Group

1. née
2. nouveau
3. passé
4. petit, petite
5. premier, première
6. sans
7. tout, toute

French motto: "Tout bien ou rien."
("[Do] everything well or not at all.")

309

ENCORE—STUDY GUIDE

1. **BEAU** (bō, masc.), **BELLE** (bĕl, fem.) . . . . . . beautiful

   aj *"Le beau pays de la France"* is "the beautiful country of France."

   n She was the *belle* (beautiful one) of the Popcorn Party.

2. **BIEN** (byăN) . . . . well (as adverb)

   av *"Eh bien"* is like our "Oh well . . ."

   aj *Bienvenue* means *welcome.*

3. **BON** (bôn, masc.), **BONNE** (bŭn, fem.) . . . . . . good

   aj *Bon ami* or *bonne amie* means *good friend.* A *bon mot* is a *good word.*

   aj *Bonne foi* is *good faith.*

4. **ELITE** (ĭ·lēt′) . . . . select, superior

   n All of the socially elite of Hoodville were at the party.

   aj Elite type is smaller than pica type on a typewriter.

5. **ENTRÉE** (än·trā′) . . . . . . main course, right of entry

   n The entrée consisted of turkey croquettes.

   n Only two persons had entrée to the banker's home.

6. **GAUCHE** (gōsh) . . . . left, awkward, clumsy

   aj Bert's social behavior is gauche.

   n It was sheer gaucherie (awkwardness, bungling) to get into an argument with his hostess.

7. **HORS** (ôr) . . . . outside, without

   av To be *hors de combat* is to be out of the fight, disabled or no longer in the running.

   n The *hors d'oeuvres* consist of appetizers or relishes at the beginning of a dinner before the regular meal.

8. **JEUNE** (zhûn) . . . . **young**

   aj *Une jeune fille* is *a young girl.*
   n *Auberges pour jeunesse* are French youth hostels.

Second Group

1. **NÉ(E)** (nā) . . . . **born** *(né is masc., née, fem.)*

   aj Mrs. Frank Perry (née Mae Wilkins) was killed in a crash.

2. **NOUVEAU** (nōō·vō') . . . . **new**

   aj The *nouveaux riches* are the newly rich, who sometimes make a gaudy display of their wealth.

3. **PASSÉ** (pă·sā') . . . . **out of date, outmoded**

   aj Long skirts are sometimes passé, sometimes in style.

4. **PETIT** (pĕ'tĭ, masc.), **PETITE** (pə·tēt', fem.) . . **little, small, tiny, insignificant**

   aj Frances is playful and petite.
   aj Petit larceny is a small or petty theft.

5. **PREMIER** (prĭ·mĭr'), **PREMIÈRE** (prē'mĭər) . . . . . **first**

   n A premier is the first minister of a state.
   n The première (first showing) will be held in Salt Lake City.

6. **SANS** (sän) . . . . **lacking, without**

   aj *Sans foi* means *without faith* or *faithless.*
   aj To be *sans peur* is to be *without fear.*

7. **TOUT** (tōō, masc.), **TOUTE** (tōōt, fem.) . . . **all, everybody, everything**

   n *Toute le monde* means *all the world* (monde).
   n *Tout de suite* means *at once, immediately.*

FIRST PRACTICE SET

Write the meaning in the sentence of the italicized words.

1. The "*Bon*homme Richard" means __?__man (*homme*) Richard.
2. The *Elite* Guard was presumably composed of __?__ persons.
3. "*Tout bien* ou rien" means "__?__ __?__ or not at all."
4. The *entree* (__?__) was pickled pigs feet.
5. A *petit* jury is a __?__ jury as compared with a grand jury.
6. The British *première* (__?__ showing) was held in Stratford.
7. Madame Beauchamps, *née* (__?__) Susan Turtleby, is now very much *passée* (__?__).
8. No longer a *belle* (__?__), she is *hors de combat* (__?__) as regards society.
9. The *nouveau* (__?__) *riches* are often *gauche* (__?__) in manner.
10. "*Sans culottes*" (__?__ breeches) was a term used to describe leaders of the French Revolution, who wore long trousers instead of breeches.
11. Madame Beauchamps, though still *petite* (__?__), is no longer *une jeune fille* (__?__).
12. "*Tout* comprende, c'est *tout* pardonner" is a French proverb meaning "To understand __?__ is to forgive __?__."

A DATE

Which base word in this unit belongs in each blank?

1. At the door he said, "__?__ soir!" (*Soir*, evening, is masc.) Hers was one of the few homes to which he had __?__.
2. "Shall we dance?" he asked. "Très __?__ (very well), she replied.
3. She was young (__?__), beautiful (__?__), and small (__?__).
4. At forty-three he was really __?__ and rather __?__ because he weighed 211 pounds.
5. She was a cute __?__ *d'oeuvre*, but he was __?__ *de combat*.
6. His father had been __?__ of Monaco, and her mother belonged among the __?__, for she was an Arbleberry, __?__ Teresa Wentworth. Neither belong to the __?__ *riches*.
7. In __?__ *honnêteté* (*honesty*, fem.), it was for her an affair __?__ *l'amour*.

UNIT NINETEEN

IN ITALIAN

The language of Italy came directly from Latin. It has contributed many words and phrases to the English language. A majority of these pertain to one of the fine arts. Can you discover what it is?

PRESTO

Can you find in the list at the right a word to answer each of the questions?

Group One
1. adagio
2. allegro
3. andante
4. crescendo
5. largo
6. pianissimo
7. pizzicato
8. presto

1. Which one could you hide in?

2. Which displays delight?

3. Which one has increasing volume?

4. Which pertains to plucked strings?

Group Two
1. grotto
2. gusto
3. impresario
4. intermezzo
5. libretto
6. stiletto
7. tirade

5. Which is the most solemn?

6. Which is the fastest?

7. Which one is likely to prove fatal?

IN ITALIAN—MUSICAL MODES

1. **ADAGIO** (ə·dä′jō) . . . . **slow and graceful**

    aj The adagio movement is very restful.
    n She played an adagio (composition in adagio rhythm).

2. **ALLEGRO** (ə·lā′grō) . . . . **brisk, lively**

    aj Play the allegro part a little faster.
    n Milton's poem, "L'Allegro," concerns the joyous or lively man, who likes to go places and do things.

    Allegretto time is a trifle slower than **allegro,** but faster than *andante.*

3. **ANDANTE** (än·dän′tĭ) . . . . **moderately slow**

    aj The andante section was written first.
    n Tschaikowsky's "Andante Cantabile" has a flowing quality that is especially delightful.

4. **CRESCENDO** (krə·shĕn′dō) . . . . **(with) increasing volume**

    aj The crescendo measures come after the pause.
    n The crescendo (increasing volume) of production rose to new heights after the war.

5. **LARGO** (lär′gō) . . . . **very slow and stately**

    n Are you familiar with the "Largo" from Dvořák's *New World Symphony?*
    aj *Larghetto* is faster than **largo** but not so fast as *andante.*

6. **PIANISSIMO** (pē′ə·nĭs′ə·mō) . . . . . . **very, very softly**

    av The part representing the lover's reply should be played pianissimo.

7. **PIZZICATO** (pĭt·sə·kä′tō) . . . . . . **twanged or plucked**

    aj The pizzicato effect portrays sudden alarm.

8. PRESTO . . . . quickly, rapidly

   av It takes nimble fingers to play well a passage marked presto, or prestissimo (very, very rapidly).

MUSICAL OR DRAMATIC

1. GROTTO . . . . a cave or imitation of one

   n The boys hid in a grotto on the hillside.
   n The friars lived in grottoes near Naples.

2. GUSTO . . . . great zest or relish

   n Uncle Joshua eats lobster with great gusto.
   aj Delicate flavors appeal to one's gustatory (tasting) sensitiveness.
   The word **gusto** in Italian means *taste*.

3. IMPRESARIO (ĭm'prə·sär'ĭ·ō) . . . manager or director of a theatrical enterprise

   n The impresario arranged for a benefit performance.
   n The plane crash killed two impresarios of television.

4. INTERMEZZO (ĭn·tər·mĕt'zō) . short, sparkling piece (between acts of a major work)

   n The violinist played an intermezzo entr'acte.
   n Each composer wrote an intermezzo.

5. LIBRETTO (lĭ·brĕt'ō) . text or book (giving the words of an opera)

   n We bought a copy of the libretto before going to the opera.
   n The critic wrote librettos for Italian operas.

6. STILETTO . . . . . a kind of dagger (slender and pointed)

   n The murderer used a stiletto.
   n The treasure chest contains several rusty stilettos.

   Stiletto may be traced to the same Latin word as *stylus* and *style*.

7. **TIRADE** . . . . . violent, prolonged speech or outburst

   ⁿ The coach treated the squad to a tirade about teamwork.
   ⁿ Hitler's tirades once electrified the world.

FIRST PRACTICE SET

Copy the italicized words and beside each write its meaning.

1. The *adagio* section is harder to play than the *andante* part.
2. A *crescendo* of wails went up from the *grotto*.
3. The *impresario* announced this show with *gusto*.
4. According to the *libretto*, the theme is played *pizzicato*.
5. Children like the *presto* and *allegro* sections best.
6. The *largo* movement comes last and begins *pianissimo*.
7. The maniac waved a *stiletto* as he continued his *tirade*.
8. The *intermezzo* was unusually brief.

SECOND PRACTICE SET

Can you answer each question appropriately?

1. What musical pace would you recommend for:
     A square dance? __?__ or __?__
     A wedding procession? __?__ or __?__
     A stately funeral? __?__
2. How would you describe a love song being played as to loudness? __?__ A song requiring plucked strings? __?__ Music to represent a rising storm? __?__
3. What would each of the following be looking for, most likely?
     A fleeing bandit? __?__
     An operagoer? __?__ A would-be murderer? __?__
4. How would a boy describe his circus adventure? with __?__.
5. Who presents the show? __?__
6. What comes between the acts? __?__
7. What would you expect from an angry orator? A __?__.

SPANISH CONTRIBUTIONS

Like France and Italy, the Iberian peninsula (Spain and Portugal) has its modern stake in our language. Many of its words have come into the American language, especially during the past century, and especially in the Southwest.

What is the nature of the Spanish contribution? The words in this unit offer at least a hint of an answer.

A COWBOY

How many questions can you answer sensibly, using a word from the list at the right?

1. What is his chief trait? —?—.

2. What does he ride on? A —?—.

3. Where could you see him perform? At

   a —?—.

4. Where are the cows and horses kept?

   In the —?—.

5. When does he rest? During a —?—.

6. When does he have the most fun? At a

   —?—.

Base Words

First Group

1. adios
2. bolero
3. bravado
4. caballero
5. calaboose
6. corral
7. crusade
8. desperado

Second Group

1. fiesta
2. mesa
3. patio
4. pinto
5. rodeo
6. siesta
7. toreador

SPANISH CONTRIBUTIONS—First Group

1. ADIOS (ä·dyôs') . . . . good-by, farewell

    n The Spaniards say *adios*, the French say *adieu(x)*—from
    the Latin *ad Deum*—"to God" or "God be with you."

2. BOLERO (bō·lâr'ō) . . . a short, loose jacket, usually open-
                                          fronted; a kind of gay Spanish dance

    n Kay was wearing a red bolero.
    n Maria especially likes to do the bolero.

3. BRAVADO (bra·vä'dō) . . boastful or defiant show of courage

    n Jose's claim that he could outshoot the outlaw was sheer
    bravado.

4. CABALLERO (kăb'əl·yâr'ō) . . Spanish gentleman or cavalier

    n There was once a young caballero who danced a bolero.

5. CALABOOSE . . . . prison, jail

    n A caballero found himself in the calaboose.

6. CORRAL (kə·răl') . . . . . large enclosure for livestock

    n The cowboys drove the herd into the corral.
    v It took several hours to corral all of the animals.

7. CRUSADE (kroo·sād') . zealous, concerted action for a cause
                                                                    or idea

    n The Revolutionary War became a crusade for freedom.
    n Bill Hutchinson will be remembered as a labor crusader.

8. **DESPERADO** (dĕs′pə·rā′dō) . . . . **a desperate lawbreaker**

   n Jesse James was a notorious desperado. Name others.
   n Desperadoes have a tendency to die young.

Second Group

1. **FIESTA** (fĭ·ĕs′tə) . . . . . . **holiday, saint's day, festival**

   n "For it was fiesta, and we were so gay,
       South of the border, down Mexico way."

2. **MESA** (mā′sə) . . . . **small, elevated tableland**

   n A mesa is usually rock, with steep, clifflike sides.
   n Mesa Verde in Colorado is the green or verdant mesa.

3. **PATIO** (pä′tĭ·ō′) . . . . **a courtyard**

   n The serenaders gathered in the patio.
   n Many modern homes have patios.

4. **PINTO** . . . . **a varicolored horse or pony**

   n The boys were riding their pintos.

5. **RODEO** (rō′dĭ·o) . . . . . **horse and cattle-roping show**

   n Rodeos are like medieval tournaments with cowboys instead
     of knights showing their skill.

6. **SIESTA** (sĭ·ĕs′tə) . . . . **rest period at midday**

   n The rain brought an unexpected siesta.
   aj The siesta custom prevails widely in hot climates.

7. **TOREADOR** (tôr′ĭ·ə·dôr′) . . . **a bullfighter, usually mounted**

   n "Toreador, make ready!"
   n The toreador was injured fatally.

   Other bullfight words: *picadores*, horsemen who prod the bull;
   banderilleros footmen who distract the bull; the *matador*, who
   kills the bull.

PRACTICE SET

Copy the italicized words and beside each write its meaning.

1. *"Adios!"* the *desperado* shouted as he went to the *calaboose*.
2. Wearing a *bolero,* she stayed on the *mesa* during the *siesta*.
3. Garcia rode his *pinto* to the *fiesta*.
4. A *patio* is not large enough for a *rodeo*.
5. The *caballero* joined a *crusade* against higher taxes.
6. The *toreador* rode over from the *corral,* trying to show his *bravado*.

A MODERN __?__

Can you fill each blank sensibly, using each base word once? Fill first the blanks you are sure about. Rearrange the words if necessary.

1. He lives on a hillside, not on a __?__ like Indians.
2. He dances the __?__.
3. He was a __?__ in many bullfights.
4. He enjoys a __?__ after the midday meal.
5. Because of his wealth he fears every __?__ who is not already in the __?__.
6. He went on a __?__ against bullfights.
7. Sitting on the __?__ fence he tells with great __?__ about his adventures.
8. He looks forward each year to the gala __?__.
9. He rides on a __?__.
10. His home has a large __?__.
11. He competes in many a __?__.
12. His last word is always, "__?__"!

WHAT HAPPENED TO HIM?

Can you finish the story about the gay Spanish gentleman? Make it serious or humorous—but no longer than a page.

UNIT TWENTY-ONE

NORTHWARD AND EASTWARD

German words in the English language are far more numerous than this book seems to indicate. The great majority, however, have been in the language for a thousand years. Our Scandinavian word heritage came, like the German, largely by way of Old English.

INTERROGATION

Can you answer the following questions from the lists at right and below?

1. Which one is a story?

2. Which is icy?

3. Which one is a teakettle?

4. Which one is not the real thing?

5. Which is angelic?

German
1. blitzkrieg
2. ersatz
3. fraulein

Dutch
1. bruin
2. maelstrom
3. trek

Scandinavian
1. berserk
2. saga
3. swain
4. thwart

Hebrew
1. kosher
2. seraph
3. shibboleth

Russian
1. samovar
2. tundra
3. ukase

NORTHWARD AND EASTWARD

GERMAN

1. **BLITZKRIEG** . . . . lightning war, sudden attack

   n Atomic bombs led the enemy to launch a blitzkrieg.
   n A two-day political blitzkrieg won the election.

2. **ERSATZ** (ĕr·zäts') . . . . . a substitute, usually inferior

   aj The material was ersatz—some kind of coarse cloth.
   aj The natives eat a kind of ersatz meat made from nuts.

3. **FRAULEIN** (froi'līn) . . . . unmarried girl

   n My sister corresponds with a German fraulein.
   aj Fraulein Schmidt is her name.
   n A *hausfrau* is a housewife.

DUTCH

1. **BRUIN** (broō'ĭn) . . . . a bear

   n The three little bruins lived in the forest.
   n What are The Chicago Bruins?

2. **MAELSTROM** . . . . whirlpool

   n Poe's "Descent Into the Maelstrom" is a hair-raising tale.

3. **TREK** . . . . a journey (originally by oxcart)

   n The long trek over the prairie began in April.
   n The trekkers returned from an all-day hike.

SCANDINAVIAN

1. **BERSERK** . . . . frenzied, crazed, violent

   aj College students sometimes go berserk after a big game.
   aj The man went berserk after his wife died.

2. SAGA (sä′gə) . . . . . . a heroic (Norse) legend or tale

   n The book contains sea sagas of the Vikings.

   n The *Forsyte Saga* is the tale of a modern family.

3. SWAIN . . . . a country youth (in love)

   n "Who is Sylvia that all our swains commend her?"

4. THWART . . . . to prevent, frustrate, defeat

   v Is there no way to thwart the villain?

RUSSIAN

1. SAMOVAR . . . . urn for making tea in Russia

   n A samovar is a tall, stately urn, like the urns our grandparents had.

2. TUNDRA . . . . icy, treeless Arctic plains

   n Will the polar tundras ever be inhabited?

   n The prairies become a kind of tundra in winter.

3. UKASE (ū′kās) . . . . an official decree

   n A Tennis Association by its ukase put the new rule into effect.

   n A School Board ukase makes work permits obtainable.

HEBREW

1. KOSHER (kō′shər) . sanctioned or clean (according to Jewish law)

   aj This new market sells kosher meat.

2. SERAPH . . . . heavenly being, angel

   n Cherubim (angelic beings, beautiful children) and the seraphim (plural, higher angelic order) are familiar figures in Hebrew and Christian literature.

   aj Laura has a cherubic (babylike and beautiful) face, and Connie has a seraphic (angelic) smile.

3.   SHIBBOLETH . . . .   a password, test word

n "Thank you" is a shibboleth of politeness.

NOTE: For Shibboleth story, see Judges 12: 1-16.

PRACTICE SET

Copy the italicized words and write the meaning of each.

1. The *fraulein* went *berserk* when the *blitzkrieg* began.
2. In the Danish *saga* a *swain* fell in love with a *seraph*.
3. The Jewish scouts took only *kosher* food on their long *trek*.
4. A venturesome *bruin* got drowned in a *maelstrom*.
5. There was no way to *thwart* Father's *ukase*.
6. The *samovar* was lost somewhere on the *tundra*.
7. What *shibboleth* can detect *ersatz* courage?

WHERE FIND?

In terms of the base words of this unit, where would you be most likely to find:

1. Driftwood? In a __?__.
2. The swiftest action? In a __?__.
3. Cheap materials? In __?__ carpeting.
4. Ice? On a __?__.
5. A __?__? In a story about angels.
6. Tea? In a __?__.
7. A love affair? Between a __?__ and her __?__.
8. Approval for a new soccer rule? In an official __?__.
9. Insanity? In a person gone __?__.
10. Meat properly killed? In a __?__ market.
11. A good story? In a __?__.
12. Fur? On a __?__.
13. An ox cart? On a cross country __?__ in 1840.
14. Safety from spies? In the use of a __?__.
15. What would you do about an evil plot? __?__ it.

UNIT TWENTY-TWO

A FEW FROM THE ORIENT

Several units could be built from Oriental borrowings, but a sampling must suffice. These include one Eskimo and three Amerindian (American Indian) words. Can you suggest a reason for grouping these with the words from Asia?

ASIATIC TOUR

Can you fill the blanks, using words from the lists at the right and below?

The most important city we visited

was a —?— for tourists. The wealthiest

person we saw was a —?—, and the most

mysterious was a —?—. We saw a —?—

moving across the desert, and we bought

souvenirs in a —?—. We crossed Bering

Strait in a —?— and had quite a —?—

with customs officials.

Japan and China
1. banzai
2. jujitsu
3. kowtow
4. kumquat

Persia
1. bazaar
2. caravan

India
1. juggernaut
2. maharaja(h)
3. swami

Arabia
1. mecca
2. salaam

Eskimo
1. kayak

Amerindian
1. powwow
2. sachem
3. tepee

325

A FEW FROM THE ORIENT

JAPANESE

1. BANZAI . . . . . Japanese greeting, battle cry meaning
"(May you live) ten thousand years."

   n A chorus of banzais filled the air.

   aj A banzai charge in World War II was a suicidal charge by
   Japanese troops.

2. JUJITSU . . . . Japanese art of wrestling

   n Jujitsu uses skill and knowledge to put mere weight at a
   disadvantage.

   aj "Judo" is a term for simple jujitsu tactics taught in the
   armed forces.

3. KOWTOW (rhymes with powwow) . . bow of slavish deference

   n A Chinese kowtow consisted of kneeling and touching one's
   forehead to the ground.

   v The man thinks he must kowtow to his boss.

   Cf. *grovel, obsequious, abject.*

4. KUMQUAT . . . . small orangelike fruit or tree

   n Kumquats are used in preserves and candy.

   n Sometimes they are called cumquats.

PERSIAN

1. BAZAAR . . . . a market place, a fair

   n She bought the Persian rug in a bazaar near Damascus.

   n The ladies are planning a church bazaar.

   Note: Do not confuse **bazaar** with **bizarre** (strange, queer—
   from a Spanish-Basque word meaning *beard*).

2. CARAVAN . . . . . a company or procession (of travelers)

n The caravan moved slowly eastward across the desert.
n A caravan of covered wagons crossed the Mississippi.

INDIAN

1. JUGGERNAUT . . any object of blind, self-destroying devotion

n The Juggernaut was a huge car carrying the idol of the
Hindu god Krishna in yearly processions. Sometimes worshipers threw themselves under the wheels.
n A vastly superior army is often called a juggernaut.

2. MAHARAJA(H) . . . . . . major Hindu prince or ruler

n The English did not depose all the Maharajas in India.
n One of the Wise Men may have been a maharajah.

Raja means ruler and **maha** means great or chief. Cf. *maharani,
mahatma, yoga, Brahma, Brahamin, Vedas, Vedanta, avatar.*

3. SWAMI (swä′mĭ) . . . . a Hindu mystic or seer

n The king consulted a swami about going to war.
n The editor of a newspaper is a kind of swami.

The word **swami** originally meant lord or teacher and was a
term of respect.

Cf. *pundit,* a wise or learned man, and *mahatma.* Both are
Hindu, the latter being derived from Sanskrit.
Other Hindu words: *fakir* (fə·kĭr′), *yoga, yogi, maharajah.* The
word *bungalow* came from Bengal.

ARABIC

1. MECCA . . . much visited (religious or trade) center; goal

n Mecca is the holy city of the Moslems, hence its attractiveness for pilgrims.
n Chicago is the mecca of the American Midwest.

2. SALAAM (sə·läm') . . . . a very low bow

n The salaam is a very ceremonious greeting, less abject than a kowtow.

v Be sure to salaam when you enter the room.

Note: Do not confuse **salaam** with *salami* (Italian), a kind of sausage meat.
Other Arab-obtained words: *caliph, simoom, amber, saffron.*

AMERINDIAN

1. POWWOW . . . . a festive ceremony, talkfest

n The scouts gathered for a powwow around the campfire.
n The party leaders held a powwow in Cleveland.

2. SACHEM (sā'chəm) . . . . Indian chief

n The sachem favored friendship with the British.
n Mr. Biggs is the sachem of Pugville politics.

3. TEPEE (tē'pē) . . . . Indian tent

n Many Indians once lived in tepees.
n In summer boys like to sleep in backyard tepees.

Cf. *wigwam, totem* (emblem).

ESKIMO

1. KAYAK (kī'ăk) . . . . . . a small, light, canoelike boat

n The Eskimos covered their kayaks with sealskins.
n Joe got a canvas-covered kayak for Christmas.

Miscellaneous: From Australia came *boomerang;* from Egypt, *ebony;* from Africa *voodoo* and *hoodoo.*

FIRST PRACTICE SET

Write the meaning of the italicized words in the sentences.

1. With loud *banzais* a Japanese platoon rescued the general who had refused to *kowtow* to the British.
2. A *swami* pretended to call up the spirit of a *sachem*.
3. The Indians held their *powwow* in a *tepee*.
4. A *kayak* is no place for a *salaam*.
5. The *caravan* carried goods to be sold in Persian *bazaars*.
6. Hollywood is the *mecca* of movie worshipers. It is sometimes their *juggernaut*.
7. The *maharaja* chewed *kumquats* while taking lessons in *jujitsu*.

AMERICANS ABROAD

Find a base word in the unit for each of the blanks.

1. Asia is quite a __?__ for wealthy American __?__s.
2. They travel in modern __?__s of buses and gather for nightly __?__s in expensive hotels.
3. They do many a __?__, so to speak, before great paintings.
4. Mr. Beebop likes to buy souvenirs at Oriental __?__s and to consult Hindu __?__s about his future.
5. He seldom __?__s to native customs, but he will eat __?__.
6. His knowledge of __?__ is quite a protection at night.
7. In Japan he watched crowds shouting __?__s to the emperor.
8. He thinks any foreign army is a good example of a __?__.
9. His grandson, who likes Algonquin lore, has a __?__ in his back yard and likes to pretend he is an old, wise __?__.
10. Last summer he gave the boy a __?__ to take to camp.

UNIT TWENTY-THREE

AT THE HOSPITAL

The words in this unit are Latin-derived except *hemorrhage*, which came from Greek by way of French, and *cauterize* and *diagnose* came from Greek by way of Latin.

HEALING WORDS

Fill the blanks correctly with words chosen from the right-hand column.

First Group
1. abrasion
2. contusion
3. hemorrhage
4. incision
5. lesion
6. suture
7. tincture

1. The doctor made an —?—; later he closed it with a —?—

2. To keep the wound clean, he applied a —?— of iodine.

Second Group
1. amputate
2. diagnose
3. fumigate
4. pollute

3. It is often necessary to —?— a room where contagious disease has been.

Third Group
1. cauterize
2. coagulate
3. lacerate
4. succumb

4. To —?— an arm or a leg is a serious operation.

AT THE HOSPITAL—First Group

1. ABRASION . . . . surface or skin injury, a wearing away

   n Floor burns are a form of abrasion.
   n Sandpaper is an abrasive; it wears away a surface.

2. CONTUSION . . . . bruise type of injury

   n A contusion does not break the skin but is an injury underneath, as from a blow.
   n A concussion is an injured condition (of the brain, for example) caused by a heavy blow.

3. HEMORRHAGE . . . . bleeding, usually extensive

   n His accident caused an internal hemorrhage.
   n Bleeding from a pinprick is not usually considered a hemorrhage.

4. INCISION . . . . . cut or gash (especially by a surgeon)

   n The surgeon made a two-inch-long incision.
   aj Incisive remarks are very penetrating.
   n An incisor is a tooth for cutting or biting.

5. LESION . any hurt, injury, or change in an organ from disease

   n The doctor studied the effects of brain lesions.

6. SUTURE . . . . surgical stitches or stitching

   n The sutures were removed after a few days.
   n Suturing requires skillful fingers.

7. TINCTURE . . . . . medicine in solution (usually alcohol)

   n Tincture of iodine is iodine dissolved in alcohol.

   The more basic meaning of **tincture** is a *slight trace* or (as a verb) *to color* or *tinge* something slightly.

Second Group

1. **AMPUTATE** . . . . to cut off (as a leg or arm)

    v The surgeon had to amputate the patient's leg at the knee.
    n The amputation was performed by Dr. Smeed.

    > A surgeon *excises* (cuts out, removes) a tumor. He *severs* (cuts) a nerve in some cases.

2. **DIAGNOSE** . . . . . to identify, discover what is wrong

    v The boy's inability to talk made his illness difficult to diagnose.
    n The doctors did not agree in their diagnoses.
    aj Greek doctors had considerable diagnostic skill.

3. **FUMIGATE** . . . . . to destroy germs with a gas or vapor

    v Doctors decided to fumigate the entire house.
    n Fumigation is often used to destroy vermin.

4. **POLLUTE** . . . . make foul or unclean

    v In some cities, smoke has polluted the atmosphere.
    n Water pollution is often a danger at camp sites.

Third Group

1. **CAUTERIZE** . . . . to sear or burn

    v It is sometimes necessary to cauterize a wound.
    n The surgeon used cautery to stop the bleeding.

2. **COAGULATE** . . . . to thicken or harden

    v Blood will coagulate when exposed to the air.
    v The white of an egg coagulates when it is cooked.

3. **LACERATE** . . . . to tear, mangle, cut severely

    v Ted's arm was badly lacerated by the collision.
    n Lacerations are more serious than abrasions.

4.   SUCCUMB   .   .   .   .   to yield, give up (one's life)

   ᵥ Joe did not succumb to his sister's flattery.
   ᵥ The uncle who had heart trouble finally succumbed.

PRACTICE SET

Copy the italicized words and beside each write its meaning.

1. The nurse will treat *abrasions* but not *contusions.*
2. The *incision* was closed with *sutures.*
3. A *hemorrhage* was caused by the abdominal *lesion.*
4. The *tincture* dried up and the benzoin *coagulated.*
5. The injured hand requires that we *amputate* it.
6. The doctor decided to *cauterize* the *lacerated* leg.
7. Vermin will *pollute* the house if you do not *fumigate* it.
8. The injury, which was *diagnosed* as a fractured skull, was so severe that the patient *succumbed.*

MAN HURT IN ACCIDENT

Write the word that goes in each blank, using each base word only once. Rearrange if necessary to make each one fit.

1. Mr. Grizzleby had an accident when he went to __?__ a dairy because its milk had become __?__ed.
2. There were __?__s where his shoulder hit the door frame and possible internal __?__s which the doctor could not __?__ at once.
3. There were __?__s on the man's left arm which the doctor treated with __?__ of iodine.
4. The other arm was so severely __?__d by flying glass that it was necessary to __?__ it at the hospital.
5. The man almost __?__ed because the doctor could not stop the __?__ quickly enough.
6. The doctor had to __?__ a deep cut on the man's leg to stop bleeding because the blood would not __?__ normally.
7. This leg cut was almost as straight as a surgeon's __?__; the doctor closed it with __?__s.

UNIT TWENTY-FOUR

THE SUMMIT IN SPELLING

This book presents most of the principles and most of the problems of English spelling. It covers most of the words commonly misspelled and most of the words usually included in spelling books. The purpose of this summit unit is to review the principles, the problems, and the words most often misspelled. It will close with a list of familiar words that have proved to be the hardest words in the English language to spell.

I. Can-Cane

An amazing number of words, especially one- and two-syllable words end in a *long* vowel, a single consonant, and an *e*. Or there is a *short* vowel and a single consonant without an *e*.

pan	pane	not	note	human	humane
wan	wane	dot	dote	envelop	envelope

| *cloth(s) | clothe(s) | | couplet |
| wreath(s) | wreathe(s) | | complete |

334

II. Pinning and Pining

In -*ing* forms with a *single* consonant in front of the -*ing*, the vowel in front of the single consonant is nearly *always* long. If this vowel in front of the -*ing* is short, you double the consonant.

aquaplaning	————	taping	*dining
planning	*beginning	tapping	dinning
lining	biting	*writing	combining
wrapping	sitting	sinning	*occurring

The same principle applies quite generally—a doubled consonant if the vowel in front of it is short, a single consonant if the vowel is long.

*latter	plodder	concussion	cannot	sitter
*later	exploder	fusion	demote	spider

III. Plurals

Add -*es* to form the plural when the pronunciation indicates an extra syllable.

class	church	fish	bridge
classes	churches	fishes	bridges

Add *s* to most musical words ending in -*o*, to the number words *two* and *zero*, and to words ending in -*o* with a vowel in front. Add -*es* to most of the other words to form the plural:

alto	solo	Negro	hero
altos	solos	Negroes	heroes

Change final *y* to *i* and add *es* when a consonant precedes the final *y* of a word:

baby	enemy	monkey	turkey
babies	*enemies	monkeys	turkeys

IV. Pestiferous Pairs

Careful pronunciation and attention to meaning will keep one from confusing pairs of words that sound alike but are really quite different. Distinguish between the pairs below. Review Part One, Unit 10 for others.

also sorry	all so sorry	adapt	adopt
almost happy	all most happy	angle	angel
already here	all ready here	dairy	diary
	*all right	quite	quiet
maybe there	may be there	loose	lose
*coarse	course	*altar	alter
*dessert	desert	*capitol	capital
*later	latter	*cease	seize
*principal	principle	suit	suite
*stationery	stationary	*who's	whose

V. -ar(y), -or(y), -er(y)

Common words ending in *-ar* are likely to have a *g, d,* or *l(i)* in front of the *-ar. I* is a favorite letter in front of *-or* words, with *v(i), n(i),* and *r(i)* often occurring with it. Words ending in *-er* are normal and therefore numerous. If these give trouble, review the material that is in Part One, Unit 12.

beggar	actor	inferior	doer
*calendar	doctor	interior	learner
cellar	emperor	junior	loser
*grammar	error	senior	shirker
similar	*scissor(s)	superior	worker
dictionary	history	*mystery	
honorary	memory	slippery	
military	victory	*stationery (*paper*)	
salary	celery	trickery	

VI. -al, -el, -il-, -ol

Pronounce these words to fix them in mind.

*accidental(ly)	barrel	civil	carol
equal(ly)	label	devil	control
general(ly)	model	evil	patrol
local(ly)	novel	pencil	pistol
*principal(ly)	travel	stencil	

VII. Pronounce the Spelling

Accurate pronouncing will help fix these in mind.

a words:

*because	servant	surface	standard
*Niagara	vacant	comrade	image
liable	human	message	candidate
*Satan	musician	accurate	celebrate
*separate	usual(ly)	chocolate	lemonade

e words:

atheist	*tragedy	dependent	elm
hundred	remedy	different	film
hurried	society	recent	*athletics
*quiet	variety	student	lightning

i words:

*definite	ancient	horrid	splendid
family	bulletin	timid	victim
*privilege	spirit	*prejudice	sacrifice

o words:

harmony	ballot	perilous	among
victory	champion	*humorous	glamour
period	opinion	*grievous	

Miscellaneous words:

environment	library	*secretary	across
government	recognize	surprise	*college
*Wednesday	sandwich	whether	drowned
			partner

VIII.   Silent Letters

A silent letter is likely to be overlooked because it is not pronounced. What other spelling problems are there?

silent a:

heard	cease	sweat	loan
beacon	disease	measure	hoard
deaf	stream	captain	boast
health	increase	* villain	marriage
	season		

silent b, c, d, e:

debt	scene	pledge	vengeance
plumb	* conscious	bridge	* forfeit
tomb	discipline	lodge	height
	fascinate	grudge	surgeon

silent g, h, i:

campaign	ghoul	bought	pier
* sovereign	shepherd	naughty	frontier
gnome	character	* freight	business
feign (*pretend*)	chasm	straight	pursuit

silent k, n, p, t, u:

knowledge	autumn	mortgage	* guarantee
knife	hymn	listen	disguise
knoll	psalm	often	circuit
knave	pneumonia	hustle	resource

IX.   I Before E

It's *i* before *e* except after *c* when the sound is *ee*. When the sound is not *ee*, the spelling is usually *-ei*, except for one-syllable words like *die* and words like *friend* and *sieve*.

words pronounced ee				words not pronounced ee	
grief	relieve	thief	weird	sleigh	friend
shriek	receive	seize	deceive	sieve	heir
receipt	believe	priest	pierce	vein	stein
piece	leisure	siege	seize	weight	

X. Word-Built Words

ence — ance

convenience	penitence	*perseverance	confidence
obedience	difference	remembrance	excellence
patience	*grievance	appearance	

able — ible

credible	acceptable	*noticeable	visible
durable	reliable	advisable	manageable
honorable	*resistible	explainable	pronounceable
horrible	variable	gullible	*permissible
		perceptible	

other words

fierceness	skillful	*certain
*judgment	dreadful	curious
descendant	defenseless	*probably
arrangement	peevish	humility

★ ★ ★ ★ ★ ★ ★ **XI. Fifty Toppers** ★ ★ ★ ★ ★ ★ ★

1. accidentally
2. accommodate
3. beginning
4. believe
5. calendar
6. college
7. committee
8. conscience
9. conscious
10. definite
11. deity
12. disappear
13. disappoint
14. embarrass
15. existence
16. February
17. foreign
18. forfeit
19. grammar
20. grievance
21. harass
22. judgment
23. misspell
24. mischievous
25. neighbor
26. niece
27. ninety
28. occasion
29. occurrence
30. omitted
31. parallel
32. perseverance
33. picnicking
34. prejudice
35. privilege
36. psychology
37. quiet
38. receive
39. rhythm
40. scissors
41. secretary
42. separate
43. sovereign
44. stationary
45. stationery
46. tragedy
47. until
48. villain
49. Wednesday
50. writing (written)

SENTENCES FOR PRACTICE

Write the following sentences from dictation.

1. He is planning the writing of an article about dining in Rome.
2. Negroes sing solos in churches.
3. The men have already made the water pipes function all right.
4. We approached the altar that stood in the desert.
5. We found a calendar and a grammar book in the cellar.
6. Her uncanny memory of history is a mystery.
7. A novel about the Civil War was burned accidentally.
8. They usually travel in separate cars to Niagara Falls.
9. Lightning scared a hundred quiet students.
10. The family is the victim of an ancient prejudice.
11. The college library across the street is open on Wednesday.
12. The captain was the villain in the fraud.
13. The surgeon's discipline kept him from seeking vengeance.
14. The shepherd's pursuit ended at the chasm.
15. The debtor's disguise did not guarantee his escape.
16. The siege brought grief to the priest.
17. My friend used his leisure to seize the thief.
18. The new arrangement shows good judgment and adds noticeably to our convenience.
19. Sincerity and perseverance make quite a difference.
20. It is incredible that anyone could be so gullible.

PRACTICE SET

1. In the begin___ing.
2. Six hero___(plu.).
3. The princip___ sum.
4. Station___ry Sphinx.
5. Pair of scis___rs.
6. A vac___nt house.
7. A news bul___t_n.
8. Counterf___t money.
9. American front___r.
10. Six pies ap___ce.
11. Prayer of pen___t___nce.
12. Many des___nd___nts.
13. Permis___ble profit.
14. Curious n___ghbors.
15. Study of p___chology.
16. Dis___pointing outcome.
17. His n___ce in Naples.
18. For___n travel.
19. Pricks of cons___nce.
20. Lessons in gram___r.

UNIT TWENTY-FIVE

ON BECOMING A NAME

''I AM BECOME A NAME.''—Tennyson's *Ulysses*

A surprising number of our words are living memorials to the name of a person who did something unusual or acquired a reputation which has lasted for fifty years—or five thousand years.

The words in the list at the right have been used so widely as *words* that they have almost ceased to be *names*. There is an interesting story back of each one.

STRANGE FELLOW

Which of the words from the column at right fill each blank sensibly?

1. What did he wear? —?—

2. What weapon does he carry? —?—

3. What laughable errors does he sometimes make in speaking? —?—

4. How does he walk? Aimlessly. He —?—s.

5. What does he write? —?—s.

6. How will he be executed? —?—

7. What will be his place of burial? —?—

First Group
1. czar
2. guillotine
3. limerick
4. martinet
5. mausoleum
6. spoonerism

Second Group
1. havelock
2. hooligan
3. nimrod
4. shillelagh
5. solon

Third Group
1. boycott
2. lynch
3. meander
4. mesmerize

341

ON BECOMING A NAME—First Group

1. **CZAR**   .   king, ruler, dictator *(from Caesar, via Russia. It was the emperor's title.)*

    ∎ Does the motion picture industry have a czar?
    ∎ The president of the largest union is a labor czar.

2. **GUILLOTINE** (gĭl'ə·tēn)   .   .   a beheading machine *(from Dr. J. I. Guillotin, 1738–1814, who first proposed its use.)*

    ∎ The guillotine claimed hundreds of victims during the French Revolution, including the man whose name it bears. It is still used in France.

3. **LIMERICK** .   .   .   .   a kind of nonsense poem *(from a town in Ireland.)*

    ∎ A limerick has five lines, with rhythm and rhyme. Thus:

    > "There was a young lady from Niger,
    > Who smiled as she rode on a tiger.
    >   They came back from the ride
    >   With the lady inside,
    > And the smile on the face of the tiger."

4. **MARTINET**   .   .   a strict drillmaster or disciplinarian *(from the name of a French army drillmaster.)*

    ∎ The sergeant is more of a martinet with the men than the major.
    ∎ The father is a martinet with his sons.

5. **MAUSOLEUM** (mô·sə·lē'əm)   .   .   a splendid tomb or sepulchre *(from Mausolus. His tomb was one of the Seven Wonders of the Ancient World.)*

    ∎ Les Invalides (where Napoleon is buried) is a famous mausoleum.
    ∎ The Jefferson Memorial in Washington, D. C., is not a mausoleum.

6. **SPOONERISM** . . a transposing of sounds by mistake *(from a famous Oxford don, Rev. William A. Spooner, noted for making such slips.)*

   ◫ Example: "The boy rode down the street on a well-boiled icicle." Usually it is the initial sounds of words that are transposed, especially the consonants, in committing a spoonerism.

Second Group

1. **HAVELOCK** . . . . hat covering which protects the neck *(from the name of an English general, Sir Henry Havelock.)*

   ◫ The WAVES wear havelocks when it rains.
   ◫ Sir Henry wore a havelock as a protection against the sun.

2. **HOOLIGAN** . . a shiftless person or ruffian *(said to be from a Hooligan family which lived in London.)*

   ◫ Only hooligans would harass a widow that way.
   ◫ Hooliganism is often a problem at Hallowe'en.

3. **NIMROD** . . a hunter, one fond of hunting *(from Nimrod, a mighty hunter. See Genesis 10:8-10.)*

   ◫ Hundreds of nimrods will be out the day the season opens.
   ◫ Juvenile nimrods perform in make-believe.

4. **SHILLELAGH, SHILLALAH** (shə·lā′lə) . . a cudgel or club *(from a town in Ireland famous for its oak trees.)*

   ◫ Men once found it wise to carry a shillelagh at night.
   ◫ The coach's rebuke is a verbal shillelagh.

5. **SOLON** . . wise man, legislator *(from Solon, a wise Athenian lawgiver, 639?–559 B.C.)*

   ◫ "Local Solons Kill Tax," the headline read.
   ◫ Why is *solon* often used in headlines?

Third Group

1. **BOYCOTT** . . to refuse to patronize, purchase or use *(from a Captain Boycott in Ireland, who was thus treated in 1880.)*

    v The pickets urged travelers to boycott the new hotel.
    n The boycott covered all the hotels in Ridgeville.

2. **LYNCH** . . to execute a person without trial *(probably from Charles Lynch, a Virginia planter, 1736–1796, who, as justice of the peace, took into his own hands the punishment of disorderly persons.)*

    v A mob gathered to lynch the murderer.
    n Lynchings were fairly common in the old West.

3. **MEANDER** . . to wander aimlessly or listlessly *(from a Greek name for a river famous for its winding course.)*

    v The dog meandered across the fields.
    v Cows meander through the meadows.

4. **MESMERIZE** . . . . to put under one's charm or power, to hypnotize *(from F. A. Mesmer, who pioneered in hypnotism about 1775.)*

    v A skillful orator can mesmerize an audience.
    n Experiments in mesmerism aided the science of psychology.

FIRST PRACTICE SET

Copy the italicized word and write the meaning of each.

1. A *hooligan* wanted to *lynch* the *czar* of gangland.
2. The French aristocrats could not successfully *boycott* the *guillotine*.
3. The *limerick* contained a *spoonerism*.
4. Unskillful *nimrods* meander all through the woods.
5. A distinguished *solon* deserves a *mausoleum*.
6. The *martinet* was fond of swinging a *shillelagh*.
7. The nurse wearing a *havelock* can *mesmerize* her patients.

J O E

Write the words that will fill each blank correctly, using each base word only once. Some words may need to be altered slightly before they will fit.

1. As a boy Joe Wobblewood's destructiveness earned him a reputation as a __?__ and he carried a __?__ made from a maple branch.
2. He was the __?__ of his little gang because he could __?__ the other boys into obeying him.
3. In the Army, Joe became a real __?__ with the best-drilled platoon, but his men were often angry enough to __?__ him on the nearest tree.
4. Fond of guns, he later became a __?__ who liked to __?__ through the woods shooting rabbits.
5. At length, elected mayor, he became one of Bugville's __?__s and built a __?__ over the grave of its founder.
6. He was fond of __?__s and other kinds of humorous poetry; he had a collection of __?__s and other slips of the tongue.
7. Because of his interest in the French Revolution, he kept a model of a __?__ on his dresser, using a razor blade for a knife.
8. He called a __?__ a "neck curtain" and believed men should __?__ such devices.

FINAL TESTS ON INDIVIDUAL UNITS

Unit 1

Write the word from this unit which belongs in each blank:

1. Most English-American words come from the __?__, __?__, or Greek language.
2. A dictionary is likely to be out of date __?__ years after the day it is published because_____.
3. French is one of the European languages derived from __?__. Sanskrit was the ancient language of __?__.
4. Children usually display a __?__ (befitting a son or daughter) fondness for their parents and a __?__ (brotherly-sisterly) feeling for each other.
5. A father is expected to be __?__ (manly) and a mother __?__ (motherly).
6. "God" is our everyday word for the D__?__. The study of that which pertains to God is called __?__.
7. A __?__ is a group of girls or women who call themselves sisters and are very __?__ (womanly) in their behavior.
8. Citizens of the city of __?__ (Brotherly Love) should be __?__ (friendly).
9. The __?__ (land) was occupied by __?__ (manlike) apes.
10. The __?__ (friend of mankind) is fond of __?__ (water) sports.

Unit 2

What form of the base word from this unit goes in each blank?

1. It will __?__ (turn white) in the sun or gather __?__ (whitish growth like mold) in the cellar.
2. Can he give a __?__ (tenth) without a __?__ (pang)?
3. The __?__ (one who foresees) despises __?__ (laziness).
4. The __?__ (stuffed object used as footstool) lasted only a __?__ (two-week period).
5. He is a __?__ (beginner) at animal __?__ (care).
6. The __?__ (kind of magnetic rock) had magnetic __?__ (ways of beguiling).
7. A __?__ (washable outer garment) is a kind of __?__ (dark covering) for one who is living on a __?__ (grant to needy persons).

Unit 3

Write the form of the base word from the unit which goes in each blank.

1. Carol __?__s (desires earnestly) to __?__ (make amends).
2. Joyce makes a __?__ (light-hearted) and __?__ (charming) wife.
3. Fun will __?__ (put at rest) your fears and __?__ (blow chaff from) your cares.
4. John is __?__ (strong, brave) enough to __?__ (push aside scornfully) a bribe.
5. Money alone will not __?__ (reinforce) a __?__ (spiritless) campaign or __?__ (captivate) the voters.
6. Let him __?__ (restrain himself) to __?__ (sever) a well-established friendship.
7. Mollie was __?__ (attractive) but unfortunately rather __?__ (unrefined) in manners.

Unit 4

Write the word from this unit which belongs in each blank:

1. Do not __?__ (shorten, using *ab-*) words in a formal invitation or employ __?__ (unreadable—with *il-*) handwriting.
2. The ac__?__ (mishap) did not cause the lady to col__?__ (fall together).
3. You cannot dis__?__ (cut apart) a frog without hurting it.
4. __?__(*write*—past part.) instructions tell how to operate the machine __?__ (by hand: *-manu-*).
5. The plaint__?__ (one who brings court action) accused him of being a tres__?__ (intruder) on our land.
6. The word "deed" general__?__ refer__?__ (past tense) to a legal document.
7. Don't let the mast__?__ (dog) get __?__ (untied).
8. The space will __?__ (have room for) only ten without emb__?__ment (feelings of shame or annoyance).
9. Write the ad__?__ (street and town) down and do not mis-__?__ (get letters wrong) it.
10. The com__?__ (group appointed) us__?__ (ordinarily) meets on Tuesday.

Unit 5

Write the base word from this unit which belongs in each blank:

1. She __?__ (remonstrated) with her husband for opposing woman's __?__ (right to vote).
2. On his own __?__ (act of will) he will __?__ (speed up) the work.
3. The __?__ (comparison using "like" or "as") compared her __?__ (bravery) to that of a rabbit.
4. Hardly a __?__ (trace) of the __?__ (occupant's) fear remained.
5. Any attempt to __?__ (decorate) the grave will only __?__ (violate the sacredness of) it.
6. Wind will __?__ (mess up) the room and rain will damage the __?__ (structure, composition) of wall covering by staining and __?__ (stretching) it.
7. Training in the __?__ (basic elements) of music will certainly __?__ (improve) anyone.

Unit 6

Write the base word from this unit which belongs in each blank:

1. __?__ (existing at birth) defects often appear in __?__ (following a series) generations.
2. The project will be either an __?__ (outstanding) success or a __?__ (enormous) failure.
3. Arrival of an __?__ (traveling) singer was not a __?__ (very important) event.
4. The danger from __?__ (rebellious) elements is not only __?__ (threatening) but is __?__ (ultimate) as well.
5. There is __?__ (common to both) respect between the two because they are both __?__ (skillful, adept) at mathematics.
6. Is __?__ (too much) fondness for candy __?__ (widespread) in America?
7. Religion is __?__ (everlasting), and it is also __?__ (taken up by one's own choice).

Unit 7

Write the base word from this unit which belongs in each blank:

1. Trees formed a __?__ (tentlike covering) for his recital of the __?__ (poetic lament).
2. News of the __?__ (large-scale departure) interrupted the __?__ (something imaginary).
3. The __?__ (deep-seated fear) had its __?__ (beginning) in an accident during childhood.
4. The football __?__ (huge person) had a __?__ (craze) for fried chicken.
5. __?__ (wild delight) is a __?__ (occurrence) of happiness.
6. The __?__ (poem of strong feeling) celebrates a famous __?__ (one killed for holding to a principle) who was subjected to __?__ (banishment from society).
7. The __?__ (brief story illustrating a truth) is a __?__ (summary) of a much longer story.

Unit 8

Write the words which are indicated below, filling the blanks with the required words or letters:

1. It is easy to find s_non_ms for words of one s__lable.
2. Sue likes the r__thm of g_psy dances.
3. Ancient dy_ing (coloring) is quite a m_st__y.
4. The g_roscope is a __?__ (true+ly) remarkable device.
5. "Come im__d__ly (at once)," was the message on the c_l_nder.
6. Two __?__ (alumnus–plu.) discussed the role of "mass m_____ (medium–plu.)" in national elections.
7. A s_____ (globe) has many __?__ (radius–plu.).
8. Rock str_____ (plu. of stratum) provide many geological phen_____ (plu.–phenomenon).
9. Anal__is of the crash d_____ (plu. of datum) began at once.
10. A g__mnas__um is not a place for __?__ (lie–present participle) down.

Unit 9

Write the number that goes in each blank:

1. A *milli*pede supposedly has __?__ feet and a *centi*pede supposedly has __?__.
2. An *octo*pus has __?__ feet or tentacles; there are __?__ children in a set of *quin*tuplets.
3. A *penta*gon has __?__ sides and a *nona*gon __?__.
4. The *tri*umvirs, __?__ rulers, ruled most of the *hemi*sphere, i.e.,
   __?__.
5. There are __?__ performers in a *sex*tet, and a *semi*-annual
   concert comes __?__ a year.
6. A *hexa*gonal building has __?__ sides and a *hecta*gonal one
   would have __?__.
7. *Tetra*meter verse has __?__ beats per line and *hepta*meter has
   __?__.
8. A college *quadr*angle has __?__ angles or sides, and *du*al control is control by __?__ persons.
9. A *deca*de is __?__ years and a *septe*nnial celebration comes
   once in __?__ years.
10. *Demi*tasse is a __?__ cup, and an *octa*ve is a cycle of __?__
    musical tones.

Unit 10

Finish the definition by supplying the word or words that go
in each blank:

1. A *multi*million-dollar business involves __?__ millions and a
   heavy *sur*tax is levied __?__ the regular tax.
2. The *Magna* Charta was the __?__ Charter of 1215 A.D., and
   *mega*lomania is an abnormal sense of __?__ness.
3. *Neo*lithic tastes belong to the __?__ Stone Age; and an *innova*-
   tion is something __?__.
4. To *circum*scribe one's efforts is to put (i.e., write) barriers __?__
   them, and *poly*phonic music would have __?__ sounds or
   voices.
5. *Super*human exertions are __?__ a man's normal ability; and
   a *hyper*sensitive person is __?__sensitive.

6. Trans*luc*ent material lets __?__ through it, and a *peri*scope enables one to look __?__ an obstacle.

7. The *epi*logue of a play is a speaking __?__ at the end, and a *sym*phony consists of sounds __?__.

8. *Com*passion is the act of feeling __?__ someone, and a *tele*phone brings sound __?__.

9. An *omni*potent person has __?__ power, and *prim*acy is the condition of having __?__ place or position.

10. A *pan*-Asian conference would involve __?__ the countries of Asia, and an *auto*mobile is a __?__-moving vehicle.

Unit 11

Write the word that goes in each blank:

1. The *prospect* of success is literally a __?__ __?__ to it.
2. To *transport* a person to Africa is to __?__ him __?__.
3. When an act *recurs,* it __?__ __?__.
4. To *induct* a new member is to __?__ him __?__ the group.
5. To *reduce* one's weight is to __?__ it __?__ to what it ought to be.
6. A friend who *intercedes* is one who __?__ __?__.
7. To *propel* a boat is to __?__ it __?__.
8. A *post*script is written __?__ a letter, and a *pre*scription is something written __?__ it is necessary to act.
9. A fluid which *suffuses* something is one you literally __?__ __?__ its surface.
10. An *aspect* of a problem is literally a __?__ or __?__-__?__ it.

Unit 12

Write an appropriate form of each word in parentheses:

1. She had no __?__ (incline) to watch the __?__ (proceed).
2. He is a self-__?__ (assert) person and has a very __?__ __?__ (decide) manner.
3. Two high school students got a __?__ (concede) to sell soft drinks during the __?__ (convene).
4. A foreign-born __?__ (transport) of stolen goods faces __?__ (deport).

5. An old man wrote his __?__ (recollect) of the __?__ (secede) of South Carolina.
6. Unmarried men take __?__ (precede) in the __?__ (select) of draftees.
7. Monopoly is an __?__ (instruct) game for __?__ (construct) minds.
8. Can you __?__ (distinct) the name on the __?__ (advertise)?
9. Each __?__ (apply) must pass a test; there will be no __?__ (except).
10. Treachery is a __?__ (despise) kind of __?__ (transgress).

Unit 13

Write the defining word which goes in each blank:

1. *Flu*ids are liquids which __?__.
2. To re*vert* to a habit is to __?__ back to it.
3. Con*fid*ence is __?__ in or with someone.
4. A con*serv*ative person wants to __?__ what he already knows or inherits.
5. To contra*dict* a statement is to __?__ the opposite.
6. To dif*fract* light rays is to __?__ them apart.
7. To e*ject* a person is to __?__ him out.
8. Living in se*clus*ion is living __?__ apart from others.
9. A *miss*ionary is a person __?__ somewhere.
10. When Congress con*ven*es, it __?__ together.
11. When a thing is com*plic*ated it is very much __?__ together.
12. To pro*nounc*e a word is to __?__ it forth.
13. To per*sist* is to __?__ through until one succeeds.
14. A *solv*ent __?__s a solid substance so it becomes part of a liquid.
15. Dirt in*fect*s a wound by __?__ its way into it.

Unit 14

Write the defining word or words that go in each blank:

1. The task of cleaning the cellar de*volves* (it __?__ down) upon me.
2. When a ship sub*merges*, it __?__ under the surface.
3. *Rect*itude is __?__ conduct.
4. The *sequel* of a story is what __?__.
5. Dis*tort*ion is __?__ing the facts.
6. In an *equi*lateral triangle, the sides are __?__.
7. To *domin*eer over a person is to __?__ him.
8. To *audit* a course is to __?__ it.
9. A *mort*ician deals with victims of __?__.
10. A *micro*scope offers a view of very __?__ objects.
11. An *ortho*dontist makes one's teeth __?__.
12. To pro*voke* an attack is to __?__ one forth.
13. A re*tain*ing wall __?__s the earth back.
14. *String*ent laws are __?__ laws.
15. When disasters im*pend*, they __?__ over one.

Unit 15

Write the defining word which goes in each blank.

1. An *ami*able person is __?__ly.
2. *Civic* duties are those of a __?__.
3. In*nate* ability is __?__ in one.
4. An acr*onym* is a __?__ made from initial letters.
5. A *ped*al is something operated by one's __?__.
6. *Manu*al work is done with one's __?__s.
7. An *equi*ne manner is like that of a __?__.
8. *Spir*it is literally __?__.
9. *Ment*ality has to do with one's __?__.
10. Sub*aque*ous life exists under __?__.
11. To in*scribe* a book is to __?__ something in it.
12. A *chrono*meter measures __?__.
13. An *astro*naut is a sailor among the __?__s.
14. Amphi*bious* creatures can __?__ both on land and in the water.
15. A *eu*logy is a speaking __?__ of someone.

Unit 16

Write the definition that goes in each blank.

1. A de*fini*tion of a word sets a __?__ to its meaning.
2. *Grati*tude shows that one is __?__d.
3. A mono*logue* consists of one person __?__.
4. To e*rupt* is to __?__ out.
5. An op*pon*ent will __?__ himself against you.
6. To bi*sect* an angle is to __?__ it into two parts.
7. *Therm*ite generates intense __?__.
8. Because the state __?__ it, the school is *mand*atory.
9. A road *junct*ion is a place where two highways __?__.
10. When magnetized nails co*here*, they __?__ together.
11. When an army is im*mob*ilized, it cannot __?__.
12. A *mut*ation in biology is an unexpected __?__ in the offspring.
13. A *plen*ary session is a __?__ session with everyone present.
14. Anti*pathy* is strong __?__ against something.
15. Fratri*cide* is the __?__ing of a brother.

Unit 17

Write the base word from this unit which belongs in each blank.

1. The __?__ (short play) was about a __?__ (act or deed) that had a tragic __?__ (outcome).
2. Her __?__ (part she played) was that of an __?__ (child) *terrible.*
3. The __?__ (military group) executed a skillful __?__ (stroke or blow).
4. The two girls sat in a room of Marie's __?__ (country home) and discussed the forthcoming __?__ (outdoor party).
5. The sergeant's __?__ (store of material) lasted until __?__ (morning call to get up).
6. "La __?__" (war) left its __?__ (card) *de visite* in the form of a chest wound.
7. They sat __?__-*à*-__?__ (head to head) and said "__?__" ("Good day") to each person who passed.

Unit 18

Write the base word from this unit which belongs in each blank.

1. The __?__ (select persons) of thirty years ago are now __?__ (out-moded).
2. "__?__ (good) *ami!*" was Andre's greeting __?__ (without) *peur* (fear).
3. "__?__ (well) *entendue!*", was the __?__ (young) *fille's* greeting.
4. The __?__ (first or prime minister) has a __?__ (small, tiny) wife.
5. Suzanne has __?__ (beautiful) eyes but __?__ (awkward) manners.
6. Madame Rideau, __?__ (born) Alice Jones, is one of the __?__x (newly) *riches* (rich).
7. The __?__ (outside) *de ouevres* will be served __?__ *de suite* (at once) and the __?__ (main course) will follow soon.

Unit 19

Write the base word from this unit which belongs in each blank.

1. __?__ (brisk, lively) music is youthful, __?__ (slow and graceful) suggests adults.
2. The __?__ (increasing volume) goes from __?__ (very, very softly) to *fortissimo*.
3. Part of the __?__ (short piece between acts) is played __?__ (with plucked strings).
4. The __?__ (cave) re-echoed with the man's __?__ (violent, prolonged outburst) against cowards.
5. The __?__ (text of the opera) does not mention a __?__ (slender dagger).
6. Play the dance __?__ (rapidly) and the autumn scene __?__ (slow and stately manner).
7. The __?__ (director) displays __?__ (zest) and his tempo is __?__ (moderately slow).

Unit 20

Write the base word from this unit that goes in each blank.

1. A __?__ (bull fighter) visited the __?__ (enclosure for live-stock).
2. Alice visited the __?__ (small tableland) during __?__ (festival).
3. The __?__ (Spanish gentleman) faced the __?__ (desperate law breaker) bravely.
4. The __?__ (short, loose jacket) was left in the __?__ (court-yard).
5. The boy on the __?__ (varicolored pony) entered the __?__ (cattle-roping show) with great __?__ (show of courage).
6. The bandit said "__?__" ("Farewell") as he left for the __?__ (prison).
7. The Spanish soldiers did not let a __?__ (rest period at mid-day) delay their __?__ (zealous action) against the invaders.

Unit 21

Write the base word from this unit that goes in each blank.

1. Ivan's family made the long __?__ (journey) across the __?__ (icy Arctic plain).
2. The __?__ (heroic tale) of the earthbound __?__ (angel) is a Christmas story.
3. The Poles tried in vain to __?__ (defeat) the German __?__ (lightning war) in 1939.
4. Jack almost went __?__ (violent) trying to explain the principal's __?__ (official decree).
5. The __?__ (unmarried girl) perished in a __?__ (whirlpool).
6. Sally brewed __?__ (substitute) coffee in a __?__ (urn for making tea).
7. A __?__ (country youth) was slain by a __?__ (bear).
8. __?__ (sanctioned) food is a must in strict Jewish observance.
9. That phrase has become a __?__ (password) for the society.

Unit 22

Write the base word from this unit which goes in each blank.

1. The __?__ (native ruler) was eating a __?__ (orangelike fruit).
2. With a shrill __?__ (battle cry) the Japanese shot the __?__ (Hindu mystic).
3. The __?__ (Indian chief) held a __?__ (talkfest) in his __?__ (tent).
4. The __?__ (procession) brought products for the __?__ (fair).
5. A __?__ (very low bow) is less abject and takes less exertion than a __?__ (ground-touching bow).
6. Does Alaska have a __?__ (much-visited center) for __?__s (light, canoe-like boat).
7. War is a __?__ (object of self-destroying devotion).
8. __?__ (Japanese wrestling tricks) is a form of self-protection.

Unit 23

Write the base word from this unit which fits best in each blank.

1. The __?__s (changes from disease) of the boy's lungs caused __?__s (bleeding).
2. The man's injuries include __?__s (surface injuries) and __?__ (severe cuts).
3. Doctors tried to __?__ (identify) the illness and find out whether it could __?__ (render impure) the water supply.
4. In a brain operation the patient will __?__ (give up his life) if the __?__ (surgeon's cut) is a fraction of an inch too deep.
5. Remove the __?__ (surgical stitches) when the blood has __?__d (thickened).
6. The doctor cannot __?__ (sear) a __?__ (bruise type of injury).
7. __?__ (destroy germs with a vapor) the room by boiling a __?__ (solution) of some disinfectant after you __?__ (cut off) the leg.

Part III

Unit 24

Write the words below, filling in the missing letter(s).

1. For__gn films.
2. A rare priv__l__ge.
3. We usu__ly go.
4. Last oc__ur__nce.
5. W__rd (queer) noises.
6. Printed station__ry.
7. Prompt acknowl____ment.
8. A gram__r test.
9. Many enem__s.
10. A spelling princip__.

11. A dated rec__pt.
12. Paral__l lives.
13. My n____bor next door.
14. Vocal solo__ (plural).
15. Picnic__ng in May.
16. A grade of nin__ty.
17. To mis__pel__ a word.
18. Lost cons__ousness.
19. A dis__pointing score.
20. Danc r__thms.

Unit 25

Write the base word from this unit which goes in each blank.

1. __?__s (shiftless persons) sometimes carry __?__s (cudgels).
2. Why build a __?__ (splendid tomb) for a __?__ (strict drill master)?
3. All the animals seemed to __?__ (refuse to patronize) the __?__ (hunters).
4. Are __?__ (legislators) fond of __?__ (nonsense poems)?
5. The lumber __?__ (king, ruler) likes __?__s (transposing sounds by mistake).
6. The __?__ (beheading machine) seemed to __?__ (put under its charms) the thousands who watched it operate.
7. The villagers want to __?__ (execute without trial) the man wearing a __?__ (hat covering which protects the neck) who __?__ed (wandered aimlessly) across their flower gardens.

LIST OF WORDS

This list contains only the base words, prefixes, and roots in the regular units. The number following each entry gives the page on which the word may be found.

If all of the supplementary words in the regular units and all of the words presented or covered in the word-building and spelling-emphasis units were included, this section would contain several thousand items, and its bulk would be out of proportion to the rest of the book.